Materials excerpted from Windows® 7 Configuration

Microsoft®
Official Academic Course

Microsoft® Certified Technology Specialist Exam 70-680

Craig Zacker

WILEY *Custom*

LEARNING SOLUTIONS

To order books or for customer service, please call 1(800)-CALL-WILEY (225-5945).

Printed in the United States of America.

ISBN 978-1-118-18516-2
Printed and bound by Bind Rite.

10 9 8 7 6 5 4 3 2

The content of this text has been taken from

Microsoft® Official Academic Course
Windows® 7 Configuration
Microsoft Certified Technology Specialist Exam 70-680

Since this custom text is based on excerpts of the full Microsoft® Official Academic Course textbook for 70-680, it is not intended to cover the entire objective domain for the Microsoft® certification exam. In that way, this custom text is not meant to be a preparatory text for the Microsoft® 70-680 certification exam.

Contents

Microsoft® Official Academic Course

Windows 7 Configuration,
Exam 70-680

WILEY

Credits

EXECUTIVE EDITOR	John Kane
DIRECTOR OF SALES	Mitchell Beaton
EXECUTIVE MARKETING MANAGER	Chris Ruel
MICROSOFT SENIOR PRODUCT MANAGER	Merrick Van Dongen of Microsoft Learning
EDITORIAL PROGRAM ASSISTANT	Jennifer Lartz
PRODUCTION MANAGER	Micheline Frederick
PRODUCTION EDITOR	Kerry Weinstein
CREATIVE DIRECTOR	Harry Nolan
COVER DESIGNER	Jim O'Shea
TECHNOLOGY AND MEDIA	Tom Kulesa/Wendy Ashenberg

This book was set in Garamond by Aptara, Inc. and printed and bound by Bind Rite Graphics.
The cover was printed by Phoenix Color.

Microsoft, ActiveX, Excel, InfoPath, Microsoft Press, MSDN, OneNote, Outlook, PivotChart, PivotTable, PowerPoint, SharePoint, SQL Server, Visio, Windows, Windows Mobile, Windows Server, Windows Vista, and Windows 7 are either registered trademarks or trademarks of Microsoft Corporation in the United States and/or other countries. Other product and company names mentioned herein may be the trademarks of their respective owners.

The example companies, organizations, products, domain names, e-mail addresses, logos, people, places, and events depicted herein are fictitious. No association with any real company, organization, product, domain name, e-mail address, logo, person, place, or event is intended or should be inferred.

The book expresses the author's views and opinions. The information contained in this book is provided without any express, statutory, or implied warranties. Neither the authors, John Wiley & Sons, Inc., Microsoft Corporation, nor their resellers or distributors will be held liable for any damages caused or alleged to be caused either directly or indirectly by this book.

Evaluation copies are provided to qualified academics and professionals for review purposes only, for use in their courses during the next academic year. These copies are licensed and may not be sold or transferred to a third party. Upon completion of the review period, please return the evaluation copy to Wiley. Return instructions and a free of charge return shipping label are available at www.wiley.com/go/returnlabel. Outside of the United States, please contact your local representative.

ISBN 978-0-470-87509-4

Printed in the United States of America

10 9 8 7 6 5 4 3 2 1

Foreword from the Publisher

Wiley's publishing vision for the Microsoft Official Academic Course series is to provide students and instructors with the skills and knowledge they need to use Microsoft technology effectively in all aspects of their personal and professional lives. Quality instruction is required to help both educators and students get the most from Microsoft's software tools and to become more productive. Thus our mission is to make our instructional programs trusted educational companions for life.

To accomplish this mission, Wiley and Microsoft have partnered to develop the highest quality educational programs for Information Workers, IT Professionals, and Developers. Materials created by this partnership carry the brand name "Microsoft Official Academic Course," assuring instructors and students alike that the content of these textbooks is fully endorsed by Microsoft, and that they provide the highest quality information and instruction on Microsoft products. The Microsoft Official Academic Course textbooks are "Official" in still one more way—they are the officially sanctioned courseware for Microsoft IT Academy members.

The Microsoft Official Academic Course series focuses on *workforce development*. These programs are aimed at those students seeking to enter the workforce, change jobs, or embark on new careers as information workers, IT professionals, and developers. Microsoft Official Academic Course programs address their needs by emphasizing authentic workplace scenarios with an abundance of projects, exercises, cases, and assessments.

The Microsoft Official Academic Courses are mapped to Microsoft's extensive research and job-task analysis, the same research and analysis used to create the Microsoft Certified Technology Specialist (MCTS) exam. The textbooks focus on real skills for real jobs. As students work through the projects and exercises in the textbooks they enhance their level of knowledge and their ability to apply the latest Microsoft technology to everyday tasks. These students also gain resume-building credentials that can assist them in finding a job, keeping their current job, or in furthering their education.

The concept of lifelong learning is today an utmost necessity. Job roles, and even whole job categories, are changing so quickly that none of us can stay competitive and productive without continuously updating our skills and capabilities. The Microsoft Official Academic Course offerings, and their focus on Microsoft certification exam preparation, provide a means for people to acquire and effectively update their skills and knowledge. Wiley supports students in this endeavor through the development and distribution of these courses as Microsoft's official academic publisher.

Today educational publishing requires attention to providing quality print and robust electronic content. By integrating Microsoft Official Academic Course products and Microsoft certifications, we are better able to deliver efficient learning solutions for students and teachers alike.

Bonnie Lieberman

General Manager and Senior Vice President

Preface

Welcome to the Microsoft Official Academic Course (MOAC) program for Windows 7 Configuration. MOAC represents the collaboration between Microsoft Learning and John Wiley & Sons, Inc. publishing company. Microsoft and Wiley teamed up to produce a series of textbooks that deliver compelling and innovative teaching solutions to instructors and superior learning experiences for students. Infused and informed by in-depth knowledge from the creators of Windows 7 and crafted by a publisher known worldwide for the pedagogical quality of its products, these textbooks maximize skills transfer in minimum time. Students are challenged to reach their potential by using their new technical skills as highly productive members of the workforce.

Because this knowledgebase comes directly from Microsoft, architect of Windows 7 and creator of the Microsoft Certified Technology Specialist exams (www.microsoft.com/learning/mcp/mcts), you are sure to receive the topical coverage that is most relevant to students' personal and professional success. Microsoft's direct participation not only assures you that MOAC textbook content is accurate and current; it also means that students will receive the best instruction possible to enable their success on certification exams and in the workplace.

■ The Microsoft Official Academic Course Program

The *Microsoft Official Academic Course* series is a complete program for instructors and institutions to prepare and deliver great courses on Microsoft software technologies. With MOAC, we recognize that, because of the rapid pace of change in the technology and curriculum developed by Microsoft, there is an ongoing set of needs beyond classroom instruction tools for an instructor to be ready to teach the course. The MOAC program endeavors to provide solutions for all these needs in a systematic manner in order to ensure a successful and rewarding course experience for both instructor and student—technical and curriculum training for instructor readiness with new software releases; the software itself for student use at home for building hands-on skills, assessment, and validation of skill development; and a great set of tools for delivering instruction in the classroom and lab. All are important to the smooth delivery of an interesting course on Microsoft software, and all are provided with the MOAC program. We think about the model below as a gauge for ensuring that we completely support you in your goal of teaching a great course. As you evaluate your instructional materials options, you may wish to use the model for comparison purposes with available products.

www.wiley.com/college/microsoft *or*
call the MOAC Toll-Free Number: 1+(888) 764-7001 (U.S. & Canada only)

■ Pedagogical Features

The MOAC textbook for Windows 7 Configuration is designed to cover all the learning objectives for that MCTS exam, which is referred to as its "objective domain." The Microsoft Certified Technology Specialist (MCTS) exam objectives are highlighted throughout the textbook. Many pedagogical features have been developed specifically for *Microsoft Official Academic Course* programs.

Presenting the extensive procedural information and technical concepts woven throughout the textbook raises challenges for the student and instructor alike. The Illustrated Book Tour that follows provides a guide to the rich features contributing to *Microsoft Official Academic Course* program's pedagogical plan. Following is a list of key features in each lesson designed to prepare students for success on the certification exams and in the workplace:

- Each lesson begins with an **Objective Domain Matrix**. More than a standard list of learning objectives, the Objective Domain Matrix correlates each software skill covered in the lesson to the specific MCTS exam objective domain.

- Concise and frequent Step-by-Step instructions teach students new features and provide an opportunity for hands-on practice. Numbered steps give detailed step-by-step instructions to help students learn software skills. The steps also show results and screen images to match what students should see on their computer screens.

- **Illustrations:** Screen images provide visual feedback as students work through the exercises. The images reinforce key concepts, provide visual clues about the steps, and allow students to check their progress.

- **Key Terms:** Important technical vocabulary is listed at the beginning of the lesson. When these terms are first used later in the lesson, they appear in bold italic type and are defined.

- Engaging point-of-use **Reader aids**, located throughout the lessons, tell students why this topic is relevant (*The Bottom Line*), provide students with helpful hints (*Take Note*), or show alternate ways to accomplish tasks (*Another Way*). Reader aids also provide additional relevant or background information that adds value to the lesson.

- **Certification Ready?** features throughout the text signal students where a specific certification objective is covered. They provide students with a chance to check their understanding of that particular MCTS exam objective and, if necessary, review the section of the lesson where it is covered.

- **Knowledge Assessments** provide progressively more challenging lesson-ending activities, including practice exercises and case scenarios.

- A **Lab Manual** accompanies this textbook package. The Lab Manual contains hands-on lab work corresponding to each of the lessons within the textbook. Numbered steps give detailed, step-by-step instructions to help students learn workplace skills associated with Windows 7. The labs are constructed using real-world scenarios to mimic the tasks students will see in the workplace.

■ Lesson Features

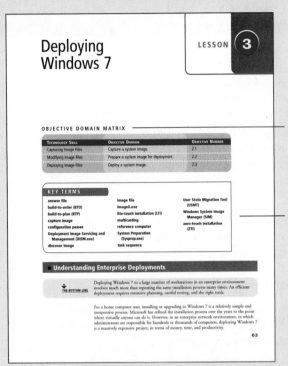

Objective Domain Matrix

Key Terms

Warning Reader Aid

Bottom Line Reader Aid

Certification Ready? Alerts

Take Note Reader Aid

More Information Reader Aid

Easy-to-Read Tables

Step-by-Step Exercises

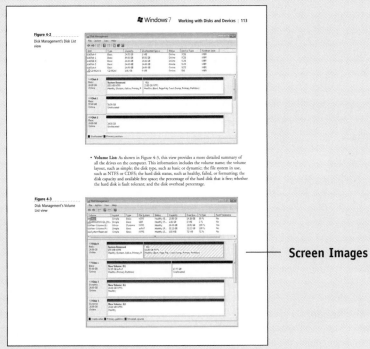

Screen Images

www.wiley.com/college/microsoft *or*
call the MOAC Toll-Free Number: 1+(888) 764-7001 (U.S. & Canada only)

Another Way Reader Aid

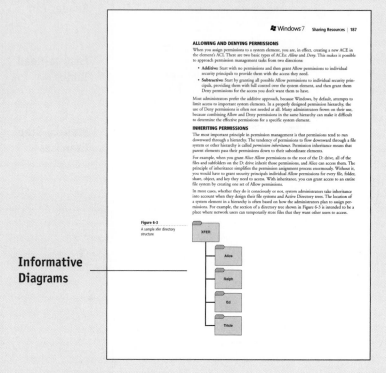

Informative Diagrams

X-Ref Reader Aid

Skill Summary

Knowledge Assessment

Case Scenarios

🪟 Windows 7   Deploying Windows 7 | 103

configurability and scale. SCCM enables you to configure every aspect of the deployment in great detail, before the deployment actually begins. SCCM is also designed to distribute software to networks of virtually any size. You can also create multiple distribution points all over the network to distribute a deployment's bandwidth requirements.

SCCM can discover computers on a network that are already running a Windows operating system, but to deploy new, bare-metal computers, you must first add the computers to the SCCM database. This is what makes the zero-touch installation possible, because the workstation can immediately connect to the SCCM/MDT server and execute the task sequence that deploys the workstation configuration.

SKILL SUMMARY

IN THIS LESSON YOU LEARNED:

- The objectives of a large-scale Windows 7 deployment include the creation of standardized computing environments and minimized user interaction at the workstation.
- The basic steps of a workstation deployment are: build a deployment share, perform a reference computer installation, capture an image of the reference computer, boot the target computers, and apply the Windows 7 reference computer image.
- The Windows 7 Automated Installation Kit (AIK) is designed to support OEMs, who typically deploy Windows 7 workstations in one of two ways: a build-to-plan (BTP) installation, which captures a single image file and deploys it to each computer with no changes, or a build-to-order (BTO) installation, which captures a baseline image and deploys it to each computer, and then starts the computer in audit mode and performs a scripted procedure that customizes the configuration.
- MDT 2010 defines and supports four different deployment scenarios: New computer, Upgrade computer, Replace computer, and Refresh computer.
- The typical method for creating a customized image file for deployment to Windows 7 workstations is to install and configure Windows 7 on a reference computer and then capture an image of the reference computer's hard disk. This process can be manual or automatic, relatively simple or extremely complex.
- Using the Windows SIM utility, you can create answer files that automate the Windows 7 installation process.
- A capture image is a bootable image that you can deploy using WDS, and which includes a wizard-based client that runs on the reference computer and enables you to capture an image and upload it back to the WDS server.
- A task sequence is to MDT 2010 what an answer file is to Windows 7 AIK, a script that guides the workstation deployment process.
- With the DISM.exe tool, you can add device drivers, language packs, and packaged updates to an offline image file.
- A thick image is an image file that contains all of the elements of a workstation configuration, including applications, drivers, updates, and all configuration settings. Thin images are more generic than thick images, and contain fewer of the configuration-specific elements, such as applications and language packs. A hybrid image installs all of the applications, settings, and software components a workstation needs, but it does not include all of the applications and other components in the actual image file. Instead, it accesses some or all of them from a shared folder on the network.
- To perform a zero-touch installation deployment, you must have System Center Configuration Manager 2007 installed on your network. SCCM 2007 is comprehensive network management product that, among many other things, can distribute software to the computers on your network.

---

104 | Lesson 3

■ Knowledge Assessment

Fill in the Blank

Complete the following sentences by writing the correct word or words in the blanks provided.

1. An image file that contains an entire workstation configuration, including all applications, packages, and configuration settings, is called a _____ image.

2. The two programs that make up the User State Migration Tool are called _____ and _____.

3. A _____ installation is one in which the installers capture a single image file and deploy it to each computer with no changes.

4. Windows Deployment Services can reduce network bandwidth requirements while deploying install images by using _____.

5. Before you can modify an offline image file using DISM.exe, you must _____ the image.

6. To partition a disk using an answer file, you must add settings to the _____ configuration pass.

7. The Windows 7 AIK tool that you use to create answer files is called _____.

8. To boot from an image transmitted over the network by a WDS server, a workstation must have a network adapter that supports _____.

9. The deployment scenario in which you save a workstation's user state data, wipe its disk, install Windows 7, and then restore the user state data is called the _____ scenario.

10. A _____ image enables a workstation to boot from a disk and connect to a WDS server.

True / False

Circle T if the statement is true or F if the statement is false.

T | F   1. To perform a Windows 7 deployment using ZTI, you must have a SQL Server on your network.

T | F   2. To create a capture image, you use the Deployment Workbench console.

T | F   3. The Windows 7 AIK script files used to perform unattended installations are called task sequences.

T | F   4. You can use the boot images created by Deployment Workbench to start workstations using either boot disks or WDS.

T | F   5. The computer that you use to capture an image of a workstation configuration is called the target computer.

T | F   6. An LTI deployment provides greater flexibility than a ZTI deployment.

T | F   7. ImageX.exe is a command-line tool that you can use to capture and deploy image files.

T | F   8. To use the upgrade computer scenario, a workstation must be running Windows XP SP2 or later.

T | F   9. Before you can capture an image of a Windows 7 workstation, you must run the Sysprep.exe program.

T | F 10. Sector-based image files are spannable, editable, and bootable.

🪟 Windows 7   Deploying Windows 7 | 105

Review Questions

1. Describe the difference between an LTI and a ZTI deployment in terms of the activity at the target computer during the Windows 7 installation.

2. List the five basic steps in an enterprise Windows 7 workstation deployment.

■ Case Scenarios

Scenario 3-1: Capturing an Image

After performing a manual installation of a reference computer, installing several applications, and configuring a multitude of settings, Howard runs Sysprep.exe with the /generalize parameter, opens a command prompt window, and attempts to capture an image of the computer using ImageX.exe. When he types the ImageX.exe command and presses enter, an error message appears, stating "The process cannot access the file because it is being used by another process." What has gone wrong, and what does Howard have to do to capture an image of the reference computer?

Scenario 3-2: Multicasting Images

Serge is responsible for deploying 100 new workstations on his company network, and he wants to use the multicasting capabilities of Windows Deployment Services to minimize the amount of bandwidth required. He has already built a reference computer and captured an image of it using Microsoft Deployment Toolkit 2010. After adding the captured image and the boot image created by MDT to his WDS server, he configures the WDS multicasting parameters and performs a test by initiating a deployment on five new target workstations at the same time, while capturing network traffic samples with a protocol analyzer. Examining the traffic analysis afterward, Serge realizes that no multicasting has occurred. What is the problem, and how can he resolve it.

Conventions and Features Used in This Book

This book uses particular fonts, symbols, and heading conventions to highlight important information or to call your attention to special steps. For more information about the features in each lesson, refer to the Illustrated Book Tour section.

CONVENTION	MEANING
↓ THE BOTTOM LINE	This feature provides a brief summary of the material to be covered in the section that follows.
CERTIFICATION READY?	This feature signals the point in the text where a specific certification objective is covered. It provides you with a chance to check your understanding of that particular MCTS objective and, if necessary, review the section of the lesson where it is covered.
TAKE NOTE*	Reader aids appear in shaded boxes found in your text. *Take Note* provides helpful hints related to particular tasks or topics.
◆ ANOTHER WAY	*Another Way* provides an alternative procedure for accomplishing a particular task.
X REF	These notes provide pointers to information discussed elsewhere in the textbook or describe interesting features of Windows 7 that are not directly addressed in the current topic or exercise.
A ***shared printer*** can be used by many individuals on a network.	Key terms appear in bold italic on first appearance.

Instructor Support Program

The *Microsoft Official Academic Course* programs are accompanied by a rich array of resources that incorporate the extensive textbook visuals to form a pedagogically cohesive package. These resources provide all the materials instructors need to deploy and deliver their courses:

- Perhaps the most valuable resource for teaching this course is the software used in the course lab work. The **MSDN Academic Alliance (MSDN AA)** is designed to provide the easiest and most inexpensive developer tools, products, and technologies available to faculty and students in labs, classrooms, and on student PCs. A free 3-year membership to the MSDN AA is available to qualified MOAC adopters.

  Note: Windows 7 can be downloaded from MSDN AA for use by students in this course.

  Resources available online for download include:

- The **Instructor's Guide** contains solutions to all the textbook exercises as well as chapter summaries and lecture notes. The Instructor's Guide and Syllabi for various term lengths are available from the Book Companion site (www.wiley.com/college/microsoft).

- The **Test Bank** contains hundreds of questions organized by lesson in multiple-choice, true-false, short answer, and essay formats and is available to download from the Instructor's Book Companion site (www.wiley.com/college/microsoft). A complete answer key is provided.

- **PowerPoint Presentations and Images.** A complete set of PowerPoint presentations is available on the Instructor's Book Companion site (www.wiley.com/college/microsoft) to enhance classroom presentations. Tailored to the text's topical coverage and Skills Matrix, these presentations are designed to convey key Windows 7 concepts addressed in the text.

  All figures from the text are on the Instructor's Book Companion site (www.wiley.com/college/microsoft). You can incorporate them into your PowerPoint presentations or create your own overhead transparencies and handouts.

  By using these visuals in class discussions, you can help focus students' attention on key elements of the products being used and help them understand how to use them effectively in the workplace.

- When it comes to improving the classroom experience, there is no better source of ideas and inspiration than your fellow colleagues. The **Wiley Faculty Network** connects teachers with technology, facilitates the exchange of best practices, and helps to enhance instructional efficiency and effectiveness. Faculty Network activities include technology training and tutorials, virtual seminars, peer-to-peer exchanges of experiences and ideas, personal consulting, and sharing of resources. For details visit www.WhereFacultyConnect.com.

WileyPLUS

WileyPLUS is an innovative, research-based, online environment for effective teaching and learning.

What do Students Receive with *WileyPLUS*?

A Research-based Design. *WileyPLUS* provides an online environment that integrates relevant resources, including the entire digital textbook, in an easy-to-navigate framework that helps students study more effectively.

- *WileyPLUS* adds structure by organizing textbook content into smaller, more manageable "chunks".
- Related media, examples, and sample practice items reinforce the learning objectives.
- Innovative features such as calendars, visual progress tracking, and self-evaluation tools improve time management and strengthen areas of weakness.

One-on-one Engagement. With *WileyPLUS* for MOAC 70-680: Windows 7 Configuration, students receive 24/7 access to resources that promote positive learning outcomes. Students engage with related examples (in various media) and sample practice items specific to each lesson.

Measurable Outcomes. Throughout each study session, students can assess their progress and gain immediate feedback. *WileyPLUS* provides precise reporting of strengths and weaknesses, as well as individualized quizzes, so that students are confident they are spending their time on the right things. With *WileyPLUS*, students always know the exact outcome of their efforts.

What do Instructors Receive with *WileyPLUS*?

WileyPLUS provides reliable, customizable resources that reinforce course goals inside and outside of the classroom as well as visibility into individual student progress. Pre-created materials and activities help instructors optimize their time.

Customizable Course Plan: *WileyPLUS* comes with a pre-created Course Plan designed by a subject matter expert uniquely for this course. Simple drag-and-drop tools make it easy to assign the course plan as is or modify it to reflect your course syllabus.

Pre-created Activity Types Include:

- Questions
- Readings and resources
- Print Tests
- Projects

Course Materials and Assessment Content:

- Lecture Notes PowerPoint Slides
- Image Gallery
- Instructor's Guide
- Gradable Reading Assignment Questions (embedded with online text)
- Testbank

Gradebook: *WileyPLUS* provides instant access to reports on trends in class performance, student use of course materials, and progress toward learning objectives, helping inform decisions and drive classroom discussions.

WileyPLUS. **Learn More. www.wileyplus.com.**

Powered by proven technology and built on a foundation of cognitive research, *WileyPLUS* has enriched the education of millions of students in over 20 countries around the world.

www.wiley.com/college/microsoft or
call the MOAC Toll-Free Number: 1+(888) 764-7001 (U.S. & Canada only)

MSDN ACADEMIC ALLIANCE—FREE 3-YEAR MEMBERSHIP AVAILABLE TO QUALIFIED ADOPTERS!

The Microsoft Developer Network Academic Alliance (MSDN AA) is designed to provide the easiest and most inexpensive way for universities to make the latest Microsoft developer tools, products, and technologies available in labs, classrooms, and on student PCs. MSDN AA is an annual membership program for departments teaching Science, Technology, Engineering, and Mathematics (STEM) courses. The membership provides a complete solution to keep academic labs, faculty, and students on the leading edge of technology.

Software available in the MSDN AA program is provided at no charge to adopting departments through the Wiley and Microsoft publishing partnership.

As a bonus to this free offer, faculty will be introduced to Microsoft's Faculty Connection and Academic Resource Center. It takes time and preparation to keep students engaged while giving them a fundamental understanding of theory, and the Microsoft Faculty Connection is designed to help STEM professors with this preparation by providing articles, curriculum, and tools that professors can use to engage and inspire today's technology students.

Contact your Wiley rep for details.

For more information about the MSDN Academic Alliance program, go to:

msdn.microsoft.com/academic/

Note: Windows 7 can be downloaded from MSDN AA for use by students in this course.

Important Web Addresses and Phone Numbers

To locate the Wiley Higher Education Rep in your area, go to the following Web address and click on the "*Who's My Rep?*" link at the top of the page.

www.wiley.com/college

Or call the MOAC toll-free number: 1 + (888) 764-7001 (U.S. & Canada only).

To learn more about becoming a Microsoft Certified Professional and exam availability, visit www.microsoft.com/learning/mcp.

Student Support Program

Book Companion Web Site (www.wiley.com/college/microsoft)

The students' book companion site for the MOAC series includes any resources, exercise files, and Web links that will be used in conjunction with this course.

Wiley Desktop Editions

Wiley MOAC Desktop Editions are innovative, electronic versions of printed textbooks. Students buy the desktop version for 50% off the U.S. price of the printed text and get the added value of permanence and portability. Wiley Desktop Editions provide students with numerous additional benefits that are not available with other e-text solutions.

Wiley Desktop Editions are NOT subscriptions; students download the Wiley Desktop Edition to their computer desktops. Students own the content they buy to keep for as long as they want. Once a Wiley Desktop Edition is downloaded to the computer desktop, students have instant access to all of the content without being online. Students can also print the sections they prefer to read in hard copy. Students also have access to fully integrated resources within their Wiley Desktop Edition. From highlighting their e-text to taking and sharing notes, students can easily personalize their Wiley Desktop Edition as they are reading or following along in class.

Microsoft Visual Studio Software

As an adopter of a MOAC textbook, your school's department is eligible for a free three-year membership to the MSDN Academic Alliance (MSDN AA). Through MSDN AA, full versions of Windows 7 are available for your use with this course. See your Wiley rep for details.

Preparing to Take the Microsoft Certified Technology Specialist (MCTS) Exam

Microsoft Certified Technology Specialist

The new Microsoft Certified Technology Specialist (MCTS) credential highlights your skills using a specific Microsoft technology. You can demonstrate your abilities as an IT professional or developer with in-depth knowledge of the Microsoft technology that you use today or are planning to deploy.

The MCTS certifications enable professionals to target specific technologies and to distinguish themselves by demonstrating in-depth knowledge and expertise in their specialized technologies. Microsoft Certified Technology Specialists are consistently capable of implementing, building, troubleshooting, and debugging a particular Microsoft technology.

You can learn more about the MCTS program at www.microsoft.com/learning/mcp/mcts.

Preparing to Take an Exam

Unless you are a very experienced user, you will need to use a test preparation course to prepare to complete the test correctly and within the time allowed. The *Microsoft Official Academic Course* series is designed to prepare you with a strong knowledge of all exam topics, and with some additional review and practice on your own, you should feel confident in your ability to pass the appropriate exam.

After you decide which exam to take, review the list of objectives for the exam. You can easily identify tasks that are included in the objective list by locating the Lesson Skill Matrix at the start of each lesson and the Certification Ready sidebars in the margin of the lessons in this book.

To take an exam, visit www.microsoft.com/learning/mcp to locate your nearest testing center. Then call the testing center directly to schedule your test. The amount of advance notice you should provide will vary for different testing centers, and it typically depends on the number of computers available at the testing center, the number of other testers who have already been scheduled for the day on which you want to take the test, and the number of times per week that the testing center offers testing. In general, you should call to schedule your test at least two weeks prior to the date on which you want to take the test.

When you arrive at the testing center, you might be asked for proof of identity. A driver's license or passport is an acceptable form of identification. If you do not have either of these items of documentation, call your testing center and ask what alternative forms of identification will be accepted. If you are retaking a test, bring your identification number, which will have been given to you when you previously took the test. If you have not prepaid or if your organization has not already arranged to make payment for you, you will need to pay the test-taking fee when you arrive.

Acknowledgments

MOAC Instructor Advisory Board

We thank our Instructor Advisory Board, an elite group of educators who has assisted us every step of the way in building these products. Advisory Board members have acted as our sounding board on key pedagogical and design decisions leading to the development of these compelling and innovative textbooks for future Information Workers. Their dedication to technology education is truly appreciated.

Charles DeSassure, Tarrant County College

Charles DeSassure is Department Chair and Instructor of Computer Science & Information Technology at Tarrant County College Southeast Campus, Arlington, Texas. He has had experience as a MIS manager, system analyst, field technology analyst, LAN administrator, microcomputer specialist, and public school teacher in South Carolina. DeSassure has worked in higher education for more than ten years and received the Excellence Award in Teaching from the National Institute for Staff and Organizational Development (NISOD). He currently serves on the Educational Testing Service (ETS) iSkills National Advisory Committee and chaired the Tarrant County College District Student Assessment Committee. He has written proposals and makes presentations at major educational conferences nationwide. DeSassure has served as a textbook reviewer for John Wiley & Sons and Prentice Hall. He teaches courses in information security, networking, distance learning, and computer literacy. DeSassure holds a master's degree in Computer Resources & Information Management from Webster University.

Kim Ehlert, Waukesha County Technical College

Kim Ehlert is the Microsoft Program Coordinator and a Network Specialist instructor at Waukesha County Technical College, teaching the full range of MCSE and networking courses for the past nine years. Prior to joining WCTC, Kim was a professor at the Milwaukee School of Engineering for five years where she oversaw the Novell Academic Education and the Microsoft IT Academy programs. She has a wide variety of industry experience including network design and management for Johnson Controls, local city fire departments, police departments, large church congregations, health departments, and accounting firms. Kim holds many industry certifications including MCDST, MCSE, Security+, Network+, Server+, MCT, and CNE.

Kim has a bachelor's degree in Information Systems and a master's degree in Business Administration from the University of Wisconsin Milwaukee. When she is not busy teaching, she enjoys spending time with her husband Gregg and their two children—Alex and Courtney.

Penny Gudgeon, Corinthian Colleges, Inc.

Penny Gudgeon is the Program Manager for IT curriculum at Corinthian Colleges, Inc. Previously, she was responsible for computer programming and web curriculum for twenty-seven campuses in Corinthian's Canadian division, CDI College of Business, Technology and Health Care. Penny joined CDI College in 1997 as a computer programming instructor at one of the campuses outside of Toronto. Prior to joining CDI College, Penny taught productivity software at another Canadian college, the Academy of Learning, for four years. Penny has experience in helping students achieve their goals through various learning models from instructor-led to self-directed to online.

Before embarking on a career in education, Penny worked in the fields of advertising, marketing/sales, mechanical and electronic engineering technology, and computer programming. When not working from her home office or indulging her passion for lifelong learning, Penny likes to read mysteries, garden, and relax at home in Hamilton, Ontario, with her Shih-Tzu, Gracie.

Margaret Leary, Northern Virginia Community College

Margaret Leary is Professor of IST at Northern Virginia Community College, teaching Networking and Network Security Courses for the past ten years. She is the Co-Principal Investigator on the CyberWATCH initiative, an NSF-funded regional consortium of higher education institutions and businesses working together to increase the number of network security personnel in the workforce. She also serves as a Senior Security Policy Manager and Research Analyst at Nortel Government Solutions and holds a CISSP certification.

Margaret holds a B.S.B.A. and MBA/Technology Management from the University of Phoenix and is pursuing her Ph.D. in Organization and Management with an IT Specialization at Capella University. Her dissertation is titled "Quantifying the Discoverability of Identity Attributes in Internet-Based Public Records: Impact on Identity Theft and Knowledge-Based Authentication." She has several other published articles in various government and industry magazines, notably on identity management and network security.

Wen Liu, ITT Educational Services, Inc.

Wen Liu is Director of Corporate Curriculum Development at ITT Educational Services, Inc. He joined the ITT corporate headquarters in 1998 as a Senior Network Analyst to plan and deploy the corporate WAN infrastructure. A year later he assumed the position of Corporate Curriculum Manager supervising the curriculum development of all IT programs. After he was promoted to his current position three years ago, he continued to manage the curriculum research and development for all the programs offered in the School of Information Technology in addition to supervising the curriculum development in other areas (such as Schools of Drafting and Design and Schools of Electronics Technology). Prior to his employment with ITT Educational Services, Liu was a Telecommunications Analyst at the state government of Indiana working on the state backbone project that provided Internet and telecommunications services to the public users such as K-12 and higher education institutions, government agencies, libraries, and health-care facilities.

Wen Liu has an M.A. in Student Personnel Administration in Higher Education and an M.S. in Information and Communications Sciences from Ball State University, Indiana. He was formerly the director of special projects on the board of directors of the Indiana Telecommunications User Association, and used to serve on Course Technology's IT Advisory Board. He is currently a member of the IEEE and its Computer Society.

Jared Spencer, Westwood College Online

Jared Spencer has been the Lead Faculty for Networking at Westwood College Online since 2006. He began teaching in 2001 and has taught both on-ground and online for a variety of institutions, including Robert Morris University and Point Park University. In addition to his academic background, he has more than fifteen years of industry experience working for companies including the Thomson Corporation and IBM.

Jared has a master's degree in Internet Information Systems and is currently ABD and pursuing his doctorate in Information Systems at Nova Southeastern University. He has authored several papers that have been presented at conferences and appeared in publications such as the Journal of Internet Commerce and the Journal of Information Privacy and Security (JIPC). He holds a number of industry certifications, including AIX (UNIX), A+, Network+, Security+, MCSA on Windows 2000, and MCSA on Windows 2003 Server.

We thank Katherine James at Seneca College, Patrick Smith at Marshall Community and Technical College, Saraswathi Singh at National College, Ray Esparza at Glendale Community College, Gary Rollinson at Cabrillo College, Terry Williams at CDI College–Edmonton South Campus, Don Bowers at College of Western Idaho, Jason Eckert at triOS College, Ron Handlon at Remington College–Tampa, Derrell Harris at Okefenokee Technical College, and Jeff Riley for their diligent review and for providing invaluable feedback in the service of quality instructional materials.

Focus Group and Survey Participants

Finally, we thank the hundreds of instructors who participated in our focus groups and surveys to ensure that the Microsoft Official Academic Courses best met the needs of our customers.

Jean Aguilar, Mt. Hood Community College

Konrad Akens, Zane State College

Michael Albers, University of Memphis

Diana Anderson, Big Sandy Community & Technical College

Phyllis Anderson, Delaware County Community College

Judith Andrews, Feather River College

Damon Antos, American River College

Bridget Archer, Oakton Community College

Linda Arnold, Harrisburg Area Community College–Lebanon Campus

Neha Arya, Fullerton College

Mohammad Bajwa, Katharine Gibbs School–New York

Virginia Baker, University of Alaska Fairbanks

Carla Bannick, Pima Community College

Rita Barkley, Northeast Alabama Community College

Elsa Barr, Central Community College–Hastings

Ronald W. Barry, Ventura County Community College District

Elizabeth Bastedo, Central Carolina Technical College

Karen Baston, Waubonsee Community College

Karen Bean, Blinn College

Scott Beckstrand, Community College of Southern Nevada

Paulette Bell, Santa Rosa Junior College

Liz Bennett, Southeast Technical Institute

Nancy Bermea, Olympic College

Lucy Betz, Milwaukee Area Technical College

Meral Binbasioglu, Hofstra University

Catherine Binder, Strayer University & Katharine Gibbs School–Philadelphia

Terrel Blair, El Centro College

Ruth Blalock, Alamance Community College

Beverly Bohner, Reading Area Community College

Henry Bojack, Farmingdale State University

Matthew Bowie, Luna Community College

Julie Boyles, Portland Community College

Karen Brandt, College of the Albemarle

Stephen Brown, College of San Mateo

Jared Bruckner, Southern Adventist University

Pam Brune, Chattanooga State Technical Community College

Sue Buchholz, Georgia Perimeter College

Roberta Buczyna, Edison College

Angela Butler, Mississippi Gulf Coast Community College

Rebecca Byrd, Augusta Technical College

Kristen Callahan, Mercer County Community College

Judy Cameron, Spokane Community College

Dianne Campbell, Athens Technical College

Gena Casas, Florida Community College at Jacksonville

Jesus Castrejon, Latin Technologies

Gail Chambers, Southwest Tennessee Community College

Jacques Chansavang, Indiana University–Purdue University Fort Wayne

Nancy Chapko, Milwaukee Area Technical College

Rebecca Chavez, Yavapai College

Sanjiv Chopra, Thomas Nelson Community College

Greg Clements, Midland Lutheran College

Dayna Coker, Southwestern Oklahoma State University–Sayre Campus

Tamra Collins, Otero Junior College

Janet Conrey, Gavilan Community College

Carol Cornforth, West Virginia Northern Community College

Gary Cotton, American River College

Edie Cox, Chattahoochee Technical College

Rollie Cox, Madison Area Technical College

David Crawford, Northwestern Michigan College

J.K. Crowley, Victor Valley College

Rosalyn Culver, Washtenaw Community College

Sharon Custer, Huntington University

Sandra Daniels, New River Community College

Anila Das, Cedar Valley College

Brad Davis, Santa Rosa Junior College

Susan Davis, Green River Community College

Mark Dawdy, Lincoln Land Community College

Jennifer Day, Sinclair Community College

Carol Deane, Eastern Idaho Technical College

Julie DeBuhr, Lewis-Clark State College

Janis DeHaven, Central Community College

Drew Dekreon, University of Alaska–Anchorage

Joy DePover, Central Lakes College

Salli DiBartolo, Brevard Community College

Melissa Diegnau, Riverland Community College

Al Dillard, Lansdale School of Business

Marjorie Duffy, Cosumnes River College

Sarah Dunn, Southwest Tennessee Community College

Shahla Durany, Tarrant County College–South Campus

Kay Durden, University of Tennessee at Martin

Dineen Ebert, St. Louis Community College–Meramec

Donna Ehrhart, State University of New York–Brockport

Larry Elias, Montgomery County Community College

Glenda Elser, New Mexico State University at Alamogordo

Angela Evangelinos, Monroe County Community College

Angie Evans, Ivy Tech Community College of Indiana

Linda Farrington, Indian Hills Community College

Dana Fladhammer, Phoenix College

Richard Flores, Citrus College

Connie Fox, Community and Technical College at Institute of Technology West Virginia University

Wanda Freeman, Okefenokee Technical College

Brenda Freeman, Augusta Technical College

Susan Fry, Boise State University

Roger Fulk, Wright State University–Lake Campus

Sue Furnas, Collin County Community College District

Sandy Gabel, Vernon College

Laura Galvan, Fayetteville Technical Community College

Candace Garrod, Red Rocks Community College

Sherrie Geitgey, Northwest State Community College

Chris Gerig, Chattahoochee Technical College

Barb Gillespie, Cuyamaca College

Jessica Gilmore, Highline Community College

Pamela Gilmore, Reedley College

Debbie Glinert, Queensborough Community College

Steven Goldman, Polk Community College

Bettie Goodman, C.S. Mott Community College

Mike Grabill, Katharine Gibbs School–Philadelphia

Francis Green, Penn State University

Walter Griffin, Blinn College

Fillmore Guinn, Odessa College

Helen Haasch, Milwaukee Area Technical College

John Habal, Ventura College

Joy Haerens, Chaffey College

Norman Hahn, Thomas Nelson Community College

Kathy Hall, Alamance Community College

Teri Harbacheck, Boise State University

Linda Harper, Richland Community College

Maureen Harper, Indian Hills Community College

Steve Harris, Katharine Gibbs School–New York

Robyn Hart, Fresno City College

Darien Hartman, Boise State University

Gina Hatcher, Tacoma Community College

Winona T. Hatcher, Aiken Technical College

BJ Hathaway, Northeast Wisconsin Tech College

Cynthia Hauki, West Hills College–Coalinga

Mary L. Haynes, Wayne County Community College

Marcie Hawkins, Zane State College

Steve Hebrock, Ohio State University Agricultural Technical Institute

Sue Heistand, Iowa Central Community College

Heith Hennel, Valencia Community College

Donna Hendricks, South Arkansas Community College

Judy Hendrix, Dyersburg State Community College

Gloria Hensel, Matanuska-Susitna College University of Alaska Anchorage

Gwendolyn Hester, Richland College

Tammarra Holmes, Laramie County Community College

Dee Hobson, Richland College

Keith Hoell, Katharine Gibbs School–New York

Pashia Hogan, Northeast State Technical Community College

Susan Hoggard, Tulsa Community College

Kathleen Holliman, Wallace Community College Selma

Chastity Honchul, Brown Mackie College/Wright State University

Christie Hovey, Lincoln Land Community College

Peggy Hughes, Allegany College of Maryland

Sandra Hume, Chippewa Valley Technical College

John Hutson, Aims Community College

Celia Ing, Sacramento City College

Joan Ivey, Lanier Technical College

Barbara Jaffari, College of the Redwoods

Penny Jakes, University of Montana College of Technology

Eduardo Jaramillo, Peninsula College

Barbara Jauken, Southeast Community College

Susan Jennings, Stephen F. Austin State University

Leslie Jernberg, Eastern Idaho Technical College

Linda Johns, Georgia Perimeter College

Brent Johnson, Okefenokee Technical College

Mary Johnson, Mt. San Antonio College

Shirley Johnson, Trinidad State Junior College–Valley Campus

Sandra M. Jolley, Tarrant County College

Teresa Jolly, South Georgia Technical College

Dr. Deborah Jones, South Georgia Technical College

Margie Jones, Central Virginia Community College

Randall Jones, Marshall Community and Technical College

Diane Karlsbraaten, Lake Region State College

Teresa Keller, Ivy Tech Community College of Indiana

Charles Kemnitz, Pennsylvania College of Technology

Sandra Kinghorn, Ventura College

Bill Klein, Katharine Gibbs School–Philadelphia

Bea Knaapen, Fresno City College

Kit Kofoed, Western Wyoming Community College

Maria Kolatis, County College of Morris

Barry Kolb, Ocean County College

Karen Kuralt, University of Arkansas at Little Rock

Belva-Carole Lamb, Rogue Community College

Betty Lambert, Des Moines Area Community College

Anita Lande, Cabrillo College

Junnae Landry, Pratt Community College

Karen Lankisch, UC Clermont

David Lanzilla, Central Florida Community College

Nora Laredo, Cerritos Community College

Jennifer Larrabee, Chippewa Valley Technical College

Debra Larson, Idaho State University

Barb Lave, Portland Community College

Audrey Lawrence, Tidewater Community College

Deborah Layton, Eastern Oklahoma State College

Larry LeBlanc, Owen Graduate School–Vanderbilt University

Philip Lee, Nashville State Community College

Michael Lehrfeld, Brevard Community College

Vasant Limaye, Southwest Collegiate Institute for the Deaf – Howard College

Anne C. Lewis, Edgecombe Community College

Stephen Linkin, Houston Community College

Peggy Linston, Athens Technical College

Hugh Lofton, Moultrie Technical College

Donna Lohn, Lakeland Community College

Jackie Lou, Lake Tahoe Community College

Donna Love, Gaston College

Curt Lynch, Ozarks Technical Community College

Sheilah Lynn, Florida Community College–Jacksonville

Pat R. Lyon, Tomball College

Bill Madden, Bergen Community College

Heather Madden, Delaware Technical & Community College

Donna Madsen, Kirkwood Community College

Jane Maringer-Cantu, Gavilan College

Suzanne Marks, Bellevue Community College

Carol Martin, Louisiana State University–Alexandria

Cheryl Martucci, Diablo Valley College

Roberta Marvel, Eastern Wyoming College

Tom Mason, Brookdale Community College

Mindy Mass, Santa Barbara City College

Dixie Massaro, Irvine Valley College

Rebekah May, Ashland Community & Technical College

Emma Mays-Reynolds, Dyersburg State Community College

Timothy Mayes, Metropolitan State College of Denver

Reggie McCarthy, Central Lakes College

Matt McCaskill, Brevard Community College

Kevin McFarlane, Front Range Community College

Donna McGill, Yuba Community College

Terri McKeever, Ozarks Technical Community College

Patricia McMahon, South Suburban College

Sally McMillin, Katharine Gibbs School–Philadelphia

Charles McNerney, Bergen Community College

Lisa Mears, Palm Beach Community College

Imran Mehmood, ITT Technical Institute–King of Prussia Campus

Virginia Melvin, Southwest Tennessee Community College

Jeanne Mercer, Texas State Technical College

Denise Merrell, Jefferson Community & Technical College

Catherine Merrikin, Pearl River Community College

Diane D. Mickey, Northern Virginia Community College

Darrelyn Miller, Grays Harbor College

Sue Mitchell, Calhoun Community College

Jacquie Moldenhauer, Front Range Community College

Linda Motonaga, Los Angeles City College

Sam Mryyan, Allen County Community College

Cindy Murphy, Southeastern Community College

Ryan Murphy, Sinclair Community College

Sharon E. Nastav, Johnson County Community College

Christine Naylor, Kent State University Ashtabula

Haji Nazarian, Seattle Central Community College

Nancy Noe, Linn-Benton Community College

Jennie Noriega, San Joaquin Delta College

Linda Nutter, Peninsula College

Thomas Omerza, Middle Bucks Institute of Technology

Edith Orozco, St. Philip's College

Dona Orr, Boise State University

Joanne Osgood, Chaffey College

Janice Owens, Kishwaukee College

Tatyana Pashnyak, Bainbridge College

John Partacz, College of DuPage

Tim Paul, Montana State University–Great Falls

Joseph Perez, South Texas College

Mike Peterson, Chemeketa Community College

Dr. Karen R. Petitto, West Virginia Wesleyan College

Terry Pierce, Onandaga Community College

Ashlee Pieris, Raritan Valley Community College

Jamie Pinchot, Thiel College

Michelle Poertner, Northwestern Michigan College

Betty Posta, University of Toledo

Deborah Powell, West Central Technical College

Mark Pranger, Rogers State University

www.wiley.com/college/microsoft *or*
call the MOAC Toll-Free Number: 1+(888) 764-7001 (U.S. & Canada only)

Carolyn Rainey, Southeast Missouri State University

Linda Raskovich, Hibbing Community College

Leslie Ratliff, Griffin Technical College

Mar-Sue Ratzke, Rio Hondo Community College

Roxy Reissen, Southeastern Community College

Silvio Reyes, Technical Career Institutes

Patricia Rishavy, Anoka Technical College

Jean Robbins, Southeast Technical Institute

Carol Roberts, Eastern Maine Community College and University of Maine

Teresa Roberts, Wilson Technical Community College

Vicki Robertson, Southwest Tennessee Community College

Betty Rogge, Ohio State Agricultural Technical Institute

Lynne Rusley, Missouri Southern State University

Claude Russo, Brevard Community College

Ginger Sabine, Northwestern Technical College

Steven Sachs, Los Angeles Valley College

Joanne Salas, Olympic College

Lloyd Sandmann, Pima Community College–Desert Vista Campus

Beverly Santillo, Georgia Perimeter College

Theresa Savarese, San Diego City College

Sharolyn Sayers, Milwaukee Area Technical College

Judith Scheeren, Westmoreland County Community College

Adolph Scheiwe, Joliet Junior College

Marilyn Schmid, Asheville-Buncombe Technical Community College

Janet Sebesy, Cuyahoga Community College

Phyllis T. Shafer, Brookdale Community College

Ralph Shafer, Truckee Meadows Community College

Anne Marie Shanley, County College of Morris

Shelia Shelton, Surry Community College

Merilyn Shepherd, Danville Area Community College

Susan Sinele, Aims Community College

Beth Sindt, Hawkeye Community College

Andrew Smith, Marian College

Brenda Smith, Southwest Tennessee Community College

Lynne Smith, State University of New York–Delhi

Rob Smith, Katharine Gibbs School–Philadelphia

Tonya Smith, Arkansas State University–Mountain Home

Del Spencer–Trinity Valley Community College

Jeri Spinner, Idaho State University

Eric Stadnik, Santa Rosa Junior College

Karen Stanton, Los Medanos College

Meg Stoner, Santa Rosa Junior College

Beverly Stowers, Ivy Tech Community College of Indiana

Marcia Stranix, Yuba College

Kim Styles, Tri-County Technical College

Sylvia Summers, Tacoma Community College

Beverly Swann, Delaware Technical & Community College

Ann Taff, Tulsa Community College

Mike Theiss, University of Wisconsin–Marathon Campus

Romy Thiele, Cañada College

Sharron Thompson, Portland Community College

Ingrid Thompson-Sellers, Georgia Perimeter College

Barbara Tietsort, University of Cincinnati–Raymond Walters College

Janine Tiffany, Reading Area Community College

Denise Tillery, University of Nevada Las Vegas

Susan Trebelhorn, Normandale Community College

Noel Trout, Santiago Canyon College

Cheryl Turgeon, Asnuntuck Community College

Steve Turner, Ventura College

Sylvia Unwin, Bellevue Community College

Lilly Vigil, Colorado Mountain College

Sabrina Vincent, College of the Mainland

Mary Vitrano, Palm Beach Community College

Brad Vogt, Northeast Community College

Cozell Wagner, Southeastern Community College

Carolyn Walker, Tri-County Technical College

Sherry Walker, Tulsa Community College

Qi Wang, Tacoma Community College

Betty Wanielista, Valencia Community College

Marge Warber, Lanier Technical College–Forsyth Campus

Marjorie Webster, Bergen Community College

Linda Wenn, Central Community College

Mark Westlund, Olympic College

Carolyn Whited, Roane State Community College

Winona Whited, Richland College

Jerry Wilkerson, Scott Community College

Joel Willenbring, Fullerton College

Barbara Williams, WITC Superior

Charlotte Williams, Jones County Junior College

Bonnie Willy, Ivy Tech Community College of Indiana

Diane Wilson, J. Sargeant Reynolds Community College

James Wolfe, Metropolitan Community College

Marjory Wooten, Lanier Technical College

Mark Yanko, Hocking College

Alexis Yusov, Pace University

Naeem Zaman, San Joaquin Delta College

Kathleen Zimmerman, Des Moines Area Community College

We also thank Lutz Ziob, Merrick Van Dongen, Jim LeValley, Bruce Curling, Joe Wilson, Rob Linsky, Jim Clark, Scott Serna, Ben Watson, and David Bramble at Microsoft for their encouragement and support in making the Microsoft Official Academic Course programs the finest instructional materials for mastering the newest Microsoft technologies for both students and instructors.

Brief Contents

Contents

Lesson 12: Using Mobile Computers   446

Introducing Windows 7

OBJECTIVE DOMAIN MATRIX

TECHNOLOGY SKILL	OBJECTIVE DOMAIN	OBJECTIVE NUMBER
Understanding Windows 7 System Requirements	Perform a clean installation.	1.1
Running Windows 7 Upgrade Advisor	Upgrade to Windows 7 from previous versions of Windows.	1.2

KEY TERMS

Action Center	federated search	ReadyBoost
Aero Peek	jump list	Resource Monitor
Aero Shake	language-agnostic	starter GPOs
Aero Snap	Libraries	VPN Reconnect
BranchCache	MinWin	Wake on Wireless LAN
DirectAccess	Problem Steps Recorder	Windows PowerShell 2.0

■ Understanding Course Requirements

THE BOTTOM LINE | Windows Vista was the first major revision of the Microsoft Windows desktop operating system since the initial release of Windows XP in 2001. Windows 7 is a refinement of Windows Vista that retains the same basic architecture but improves performance and adds many new features.

For new users, Windows 7 provides a sleek new interface that many will find intuitive and easy to use. For experienced Windows XP users, an upgrade to Windows 7 will require a period of adjustment as they learn new procedures to perform familiar tasks.

For IT support personnel accustomed to working with Windows Vista, Windows 7 will be a minor adjustment. For Windows XP technicians, Windows 7 represents not only a new interface and all of the support issues that accompany it, but also an entirely new operating system (OS) architecture. In other words, not only do XP users have to learn to drive a new type of vehicle, but XP mechanics have to learn to repair a new type of engine as well.

In this course, you learn to install, configure, and manage Windows 7, all tasks that differ significantly from their Windows XP counterparts. You study the Windows 7 installation process for individual computers, as well as the deployment of Windows 7 on an enterprise network. You also learn to configure many of Windows 7's hardware, security, and networking controls; install and deploy applications; and manage configuration settings for a large fleet of Windows 7 desktops.

The book you are currently reading is the course textbook, which contains background and explanatory material on Windows 7, along with a number of exercises and scenarios to test how much you have learned. Your other book is a lab manual, which guides you through a series of hands-on exercises corresponding to the material in the textbook.

If you diligently work your way through the textbook and the lab manual, and complete all of the assignments given to you by your instructor, you will come out of this course ready to provide technical support for Windows 7 users and computers.

■ What's New in Windows 7?

Compared to Windows Vista, and even more so to Windows XP, Windows 7 has a great many improvements. The user interface has been modified, and Windows 7 also includes a number of new and enhanced features and applications.

As a Windows 7 technical specialist, you might have experience with Windows Vista, or you might be coming right from Windows XP. For XP users, Windows 7 requires more of an adjustment, but even those familiar with Windows Vista will find a lot that is new in Windows 7. The following sections examine the interface enhancements, the new features, and the security modifications in Windows 7.

Using the Windows 7 Interface

The first changes that are apparent to the user or the technical specialist in Windows 7 are the modifications to the user interface.

Although the basic components of the interface are the same as those in Windows Vista, Windows 7 introduces some refinements. However, many of the interface modifications in Windows 7 are simply changes to default settings. In many cases, you can reconfigure the interface elements to appear as they did in Vista, or even as they did in earlier Windows versions.

WORKING THE DESKTOP

In Windows 7, the taskbar is taller than in Windows Vista and Windows XP because its default setting displays running applications as large icons without the application name, as shown in Figure 1-1. The Quick Launch toolbar is gone; instead, you can now right click an application in the Start menu and select Pin To Taskbar from the context menu. This creates a permanent icon on the taskbar for the application you selected, whether it is running or not.

When you mouse over the taskbar icon for a running application while Aero is enabled, Windows 7 displays a live taskbar preview, that is, live thumbnail images of all the documents you have open in that application. Mousing over one of the thumbnails displays a full-screen preview, and clicking a thumbnail opens the document.

Figure 1-1

The default Windows 7 desktop

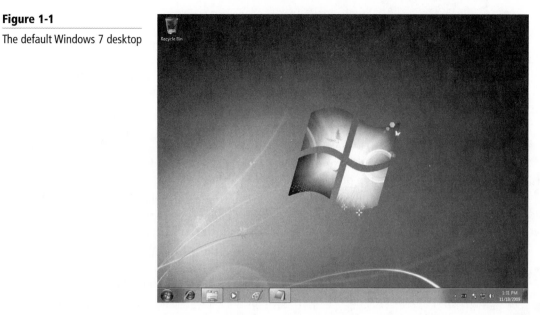

Icons on the taskbar, and in the Start menu, also now have ***jump lists***, context menus that display the application's most frequently used functions. For example, right clicking the Internet Explorer icon displays the sites you have visited most often, as well as other useful functions, as shown in Figure 1-2.

Figure 1-2

A Windows 7 jump list

The notification area—known as the tray in Windows XP—is noticeably smaller as well. This is because Windows 7 displays only the Network and Action Center icons by default, as well as a few hardware-specific icons, such as a battery icon on mobile computers.

The Sidebar application from Windows Vista is also gone. However, the gadgets are still available when you right click the desktop and select Gadgets from the context menu, as shown in Figure 1-3. You can also now place gadgets anywhere on the Windows 7 desktop.

Figure 1-3

The Windows 7 gadget gallery

MANIPULATING WINDOWS

The fundamental paradigm that gives Windows its name is, of course, unchanged in Windows 7. You still open multiple windows on the desktop containing different applications, which you can manipulate as needed. However, Windows 7 adds some new methods for moving and resizing the windows on the desktop, including the following:

- **Aero Snap:** When you drag a window to the top of the screen, Windows 7 automatically maximizes it. When you drag a window to the left or right side of the screen, Windows 7 configures the window to exactly half of the screen size. When you drag a corner of a window to the top or bottom of the screen, Windows 7 extends the window vertically from the top of the screen to the bottom.
- **Aero Shake:** When you click the title bar of a window and shake it back and forth with the mouse, Windows 7 minimizes all of the windows except the one you shook. Shaking the active window again restores the other windows to their previous states.
- **Aero Peek:** Mousing over the right end of the taskbar with Aero enabled causes Windows 7 to render all of the windows on the desktop transparent, enabling you to see any gadgets on the desktop underneath. Clicking the right end of the taskbar minimizes all of the windows on the desktop.
- **Aero task switching:** When Aero is enabled, pressing Alt+Tab displays thumbnails of the open applications instead of the standard icons.

TAKE NOTE *

Despite their names, the Aero Snap and Aero Shake features work whether Aero is enabled on the computer or not. However, to render the windows transparent using Aero Peek or display thumbnails of open applications, Windows 7 must have Aero enabled.

USING KEYSTROKE SHORTCUTS

Windows power users are accustomed to using keyboard shortcuts to manipulate the desktop, and the Windows key is particularly useful in that respect. Windows 7 adds some new Windows key shortcuts and also modifies the functions of some of the existing ones as follows:

- Windows + Space: Causes the system to enter "peek at desktop" mode, as long as you hold the keys down.
- Windows + Up Arrow: Maximizes the active window.
- Windows + Down Arrow: Restores the active window to its default size.
- Windows + Left Arrow: Snaps the active window to the left side of the screen.
- Windows + Right Arrow: Snaps the active window to the right side of the screen.
- Windows + Shift + Left Arrow: When using dual monitors, moves the active window to the left screen.
- Windows + Shift + Right Arrow: When using dual monitors, moves the active window to the right screen.
- Windows + Home: Toggles between minimizing and restoring all windows but the active one.
- Windows + +: Launches Magnifier and zooms in on the current cursor location.
- Windows + –: Zooms out when the screen is magnified.
- Windows + G: Brings the gadgets on the desktop to the front of the display.
- Windows + P: Cycles among the available presentation modes, such as single, clone, and extend.
- Windows + T: Cycles among the icons on the taskbar from right to left.
- Windows + Shift + T: Cycles among the icons on the taskbar from left to right.
- Windows + 1: Starts the first program on the taskbar.
- Windows + 2: Starts the second program on the taskbar.
- Windows + 3: Starts the third program on the taskbar.
- Windows + 4: Starts the fourth program on the taskbar.
- Windows + 5: Starts the fifth program on the taskbar.

Understanding Windows Feature Refinements

> Windows Vista introduced many new features, and most of those features are still found in Windows 7. However, many of those features have been refined or enhanced.

Many of the feature refinements in Windows 7 are relatively subtle; technical specialists looking for big changes might overlook the small things. However, it is often the small things that cause problems for end users, and it is a good idea for technicians to familiarize themselves with the new aspects of the features discussed in the following sections.

USING EXPLORER LIBRARIES

The redesigned Windows Explorer interface from Windows Vista is retained in Windows 7, with a few refinements. When you open a Windows Explorer window in Windows 7, the most immediately identifiable new feature in the default view is the Libraries folder, as shown in Figure 1-4. *Libraries* enable users to aggregate files on multiple computers into a single folder that makes them appear as though they are all on a local drive.

Figure 1-4

A Windows Explorer window

By default, Windows Explorer has four libraries, called Documents, Music, Pictures, and Video. Users can create as many additional libraries as they need. Each library consists of one or more locations, and each location is a folder on the local or a network computer. For example, the Documents library has two locations: the user's My Documents folder and the Public Documents folder. When you look at the Documents library, you see the files in both locations.

If you add more locations to the library, using the Properties sheet shown in Figure 1-5, the files in those locations appear in the library as well. In every library, one of the locations is designated as the save location, and this is where files go that the user saves to the library.

In addition to Windows Explorer windows, libraries also appear in Open and Save As combo boxes, and on the right side of the Start menu, where they replace the individual Documents, Pictures, and Music user profile folders.

Figure 1-5

A library's Properties sheet

USING WINDOWS SEARCH

Windows Vista introduced a drastic overhaul in Window's search capabilities by eliminating the Search Assistant and replacing it with a discreet little Search box, which you can find on the Start menu, on Explorer windows, in Windows Media Player, and in other places throughout the operating system. This box is the interface to the new Windows Search Engine (WSE), which enables users to perform context-sensitive, metadata-based, as-you-type searches from almost anywhere.

In Windows 7, the search interface now includes an Add a Search Filter option, and search results are more detailed, with the search term highlighted, as shown in Figure 1-6.

Figure 1-6

The Windows Search interface

Windows 7 also enhances the behavior of the Start menu search. When you type a string in the Search box on the Start menu, the groups that the system searches are changed, as shown in Table 1-1.

Table 1-1

Start menu search groups in Windows 7 and Windows Vista

WINDOWS 7	WINDOWS VISTA
Programs	Programs
Control Panel	Favorites and History
Libraries	Communications
Indexed locations	Files

You can now locate Control Panel settings right from the Start menu and search entire libraries as well, as shown in Figure 1-7.

Figure 1-7

Windows 7 Start menu search results

Windows 7 also includes the ability to perform searches in shared folders on the network. To do this, the remote computer must be running the Windows Search service, and the shared folders must be indexed. Searching a remote share uses the Windows Search engine and the index on the remote computer, but Windows 7 displays only the results that the permissions on the remote system make accessible to it.

> **TAKE NOTE** *
>
> Windows 7 runs the Windows Search 4.0 service by default, but on servers running Windows Server 2008 R2 or Windows Server 2008, you must install the service manually using Server Manager by adding the File Services role and selecting the Windows Search role service. For older versions of Windows, it is recommended that you upgrade the service to Windows Search 4.0.

USING FEDERATED SEARCH

In addition to the refinements already described, Windows Search supports a new feature called federated search. ***Federated search*** enables users to perform searches on Windows SharePoint sites, intranets, and specific Internet sites, right from the Windows Explorer interface.

To use federated search, you must download or create search connectors, which are XML files for specific sites. When you install a search connector in Windows 7, a shortcut for the site appears under Favorites in the Windows Explorer window. Selecting the favorite and typing a string in the Search box performs a search on the site and displays the results in Explorer, as shown in Figure 1-8.

Figure 1-8

Windows 7 Federated Search results

OFFLINE FILES

Offline files is a feature that enables users to automatically store copies of network files on a local drive, so that they can access the files even when the network is not available. In Windows 7, administrators can configure offline files to exclude specific file types from synchronization. For example, by setting the Exclude Files from Being Cached policy, as shown in Figure 1-9, with the extensions of video file formats, administrators can prevent users from overloading the network and their local drives with large video files.

Figure 1-9

The Exclude Files from Being Cached policy

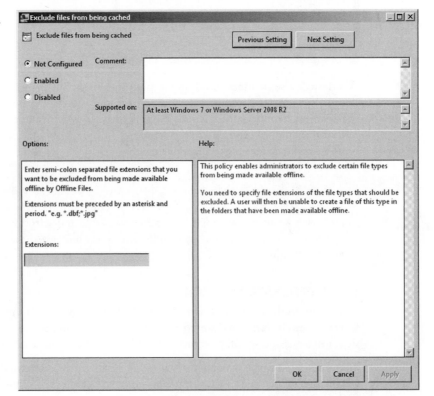

The most complicated aspect of offline files is the synchronization of the local copies with the originals on the network. When a user working offline modifies a file, the system must synchronize the file with the server copy once the workstation regains access to the network. In the previous version of Windows, synchronizations occurred when the user logged on or logged off. In Windows 7, synchronizations can now occur automatically, in the background, making the process invisible to users.

VPN RECONNECT

Mobile users have employed virtual private network (VPN) connections over the Internet to access resources on their enterprise networks for years, but it is only relatively recently that mobile connectivity has been largely wireless. Wireless Internet connections can often be intermittent, and one of the big problems this causes for remote network users is the loss of the VPN connection and the subsequent need to log on and authenticate all over again. This re-authentication process can often take several minutes, thereby reducing user productivity and increasing user frustration. Windows 7 now includes a feature called *VPN Reconnect* that enables a remote computer to automatically re-establish a connection to a VPN server running Windows Server 2008 R2.

GROUP POLICY

Group Policy has been a part of Windows since the introduction of Active Directory in Windows 2000. Administrators use Group Policy to automate the deployment of configuration settings to computers on the network. Each new Windows version, including Windows 7, has enhanced Group Policy by adding new settings and other features.

In Windows 7, the Group Policy preferences that were a downloadable feature in Windows Vista are included by default. Preferences are Group Policy settings that can configure Windows elements such as drive mappings and desktop shortcuts without locking them so that users can't modify them. Windows 7 also supports new preference settings that enable administrators to exercise greater control over power management and task scheduling.

Group Policy objects (GPOs) are the containers in which administrators select and configure Group Policy settings. On a complex Windows network, administrators might have to create and manage dozens of GPOs for various purposes. Windows 7 makes this process a bit easier by including a collection of starter GPOs. *Starter GPOs* are administrative templates with preconfigured settings that administrators can use as a baseline for creating new GPOs. It is also possible to create new starter GPOs to construct your own templates.

READYBOOST

ReadyBoost is a feature first introduced in Windows Vista that enables a computer to utilize an external storage device, such as a universal serial bus (USB) flash drive or secure digital (SD) memory card, as a cache for data that would ordinarily be swapped to a (slower) hard disk. The Windows 7 version of ReadyBoost enhances the system's caching capability by supporting larger caches on as many as eight external devices simultaneously.

Introducing New Windows 7 Features

In addition to its modified interface and refinements of existing features, Windows 7 also includes a number of new features and applications.

Many of the new features in Windows 7 enhance the operating system's ability to communicate with other computers on the network safely and efficiently. The following sections discuss some of the most prominent of these new features.

ACTION CENTER

The Windows 7 *Action Center*, shown in Figure 1-10, is a replacement for the Security Center found in Windows Vista. The name change is due to the fact that, in addition to

X REF
For more information on virtual private networking, see Lesson 5, "Connecting to a Network."

X REF
For more information on ReadyBoost, see Lesson 8, "Managing and Monitoring Windows 7 Performance."

Figure 1-10

The Windows 7 Action Center

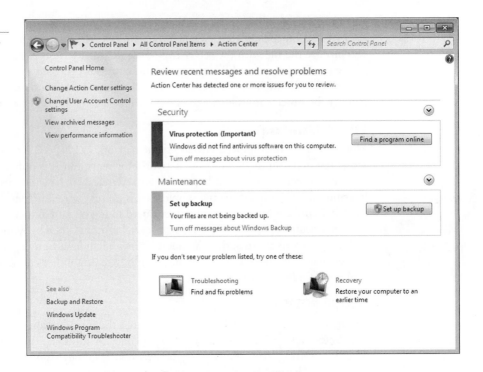

security notifications, Action Center also displays alerts generated by other Windows 7 applications and services, including backups and problem reports.

BRANCHCACHE

For more information on how BranchCache works and how to configure it, see Lesson 8, "Managing and Monitoring Windows 7 Performance."

BranchCache is a new feature in Windows 7 and Windows Server 2008 R2 that is designed to reduce the wide area network (WAN) bandwidth utilized by branch office file sharing and provide branch office users with faster and more reliable access to the offsite files they need. Like all caching software, BranchCache is essentially a buffer that stores data accessed from a relatively slow medium on a faster medium. In this case, a computer on a branch network stores copies of the files that users access on remote servers, so that when other users need those files, they can access them locally.

DIRECTACCESS

Even with the VPN Reconnect feature described earlier in this lesson, establishing remote VPN connections can be time consuming and can require a greater understanding of networking concepts than many users possess. *DirectAccess* is a new remote connection technology that is completely invisible to the end user. Whenever the remote computer has access to the Internet, it automatically establishes a connection with a DirectAccess server on the enterprise network. DirectAccess has other advantages as well, such as the ability to connect through firewalls that would block VPN connections; however, for administrators, it is more difficult to set up than a VPN and requires servers running Windows Server 2008 R2.

For more information on DirectAccess, see Lesson 5, "Connecting to a Network."

WINDOWS POWERSHELL 2.0

Microsoft is clearly positioning Windows PowerShell as the dominant scripting and command line language for all of its operating systems, replacing VB Script and the other languages supported by Windows Script Host. Windows 7 and Windows Server 2008 R2 both have *Windows PowerShell 2.0* installed by default, rather than requiring a separate download, as with previous Windows versions.

Windows 7 includes both a PowerShell command prompt and a graphical interface, the Windows PowerShell Integrated Scripting environment (ISE), as shown in Figure 1-11. Using its native commands and add-on modules, administrators can utilize Windows PowerShell to perform almost any task from a command prompt. PowerShell also functions as a rich scripting language, enabling administrators to automate tasks and create logon and startup scripts.

Figure 1-11

Windows PowerShell ISE

PROBLEM STEPS RECORDER

When computer users encounter a problem and call for help, one of the troublesome issues for the technical specialist is getting adequate information about what happened. The *Problem Steps Recorder*, shown in Figure 1-12, is a new Windows 7 tool that enables users and administrators to document the process that generated an error.

Figure 1-12

The Windows 7 Problem Steps Recorder

When you click Start Record in the Problem Steps Recorder, the program tracks your mouse movements and compiles a log of all the actions leading up to the error. You can add comments as you go, and when you click Stop Record, the program saves the log, with captured graphics of the screens you were working on, as shown in Figure 1-13. Users can provide this log to the help desk, and lower-level technicians can pass the information along to technical specialists when escalating an issue.

Figure 1-13

A log generated by the Problem Steps Recorder

X REF

For more information about Resource Monitor, see Lesson 8, "Managing and Monitoring Windows 7 Performance."

RESOURCE MONITOR

Resource Monitor is a new performance monitoring and troubleshooting tool that displays information about the CPU, disk, network, and memory resources used by Windows 7 on a single screen, as shown in Figure 1-14. Resource Monitor lists the processes that are consuming resources and enables you to suspend, resume, and end processes as needed.

Figure 1-14

Windows 7 Resource Monitor

WAKE ON WIRELESS LAN

Previous versions of Windows support Wake on LAN (WoL), a type of network packet filter that enables a computer in sleep mode to wake up on receipt of a specific message (called a magic packet). WoL is an Ethernet standard that is limited to wired networks. Windows 7 adds support for *Wake on Wireless LAN* (WoWLAN), an equivalent standard for wireless networks.

■ Introducing Windows 7 Editions

THE BOTTOM LINE

Windows 7 is available in six editions. Understanding the features and capabilities of each edition is crucial for technical specialists who must recommend a specific product for their users.

Microsoft originally released Windows XP in two versions, Windows XP Home and Windows XP Professional, and eventually produced a number of hardware-specific editions, including Windows XP Media Center Edition and Windows XP Tablet PC Edition. The primary difference between the Home and Professional versions is the ability of the operating system to connect to a Windows network domain.

➕ MORE INFORMATION

The history of Microsoft Windows on desktop computers follows two parallel courses. Originally, Windows was a shell program that ran on top of the 16-bit MS-DOS operating system. Eventually, Microsoft combined MS-DOS and Windows into a single operating system product and developed it through several versions, including Windows 95, Windows 98, and Windows Me, which was the final product to use the MS-DOS kernel. At the same time, Microsoft was working on a completely new, 32-bit operating system that overcame most of the memory- and hardware-handling difficulties that were inherent in MS-DOS. Originally released as Windows NT 3.1 in 1993, the same basic NT kernel also formed the core of the Windows NT 4.0 and Windows 2000 operating system products. Intended primarily for servers at first, the NT kernel gradually gained popularity on the desktop, especially in business environments. With the release of Windows XP in 2001, Microsoft stopped using the MS-DOS kernel entirely; the NT kernel is now the basis of all new Windows operating systems, including Windows 7 and Windows Server 2008 R2. With Windows Vista, and now Windows 7, Microsoft has expanded its scope, making the operating system available in six versions.

The six versions of Windows 7 are as follows:

- **Windows 7 Starter:** Microsoft intends the Starter edition of Windows 7 to be a low-cost operating system alternative for original equipment manufacturers (OEMs) to use in netbook and low-end laptop products. Windows 7 Starter will be available worldwide, unlike Windows Vista Starter, but only on new computers sold through OEMs, and not through normal retail channels. The Starter edition has substantial limitations, such as no 64-bit version, no Windows Aero features, and limited processor support.

TAKE NOTE ✱

Aside from being available only in emerging markets, Windows Vista Starter edition was limited to running only three applications at a time. However, Microsoft has decided to remove this limitation from Windows 7 Starter edition.

- **Windows 7 Home Basic:** Microsoft intends Home Basic for emerging markets only, which means that it will not be an option available to most users and businesses. Home Basic lacks most Aero support, has limited networking capabilities, and does not include the Windows Media Center application.

TAKE NOTE ✱

In Windows 7, Microsoft has reversed the roles of the Starter and Home Basic editions. In Windows Vista, the Starter edition was distributed only in emerging markets and Home Basic was distributed through OEMs. In Windows 7, exactly the opposite is true.

- **Windows 7 Home Premium:** Home Premium is intended to be the primary retail and OEM version of Windows 7 for home users. This version includes full Aero support and multimedia capabilities, but it lacks business features, such as the ability to join an Active Directory Domain Services (AD DS) domain.

- **Windows 7 Professional:** Windows 7 Professional is intended to be the premium retail version for more advanced home users and small to medium-sized businesses. As a superset of Windows 7 Home Premium, Windows 7 Professional includes a basic array of management features, as well as the ability to join an AD DS domain, but it lacks some of the more advanced networking features, such as BranchCache and DirectAccess. Unlike Windows Vista Business, Windows 7 Professional includes the Windows Media Center application.

- **Windows 7 Enterprise:** Available only through the Microsoft Software Assurance and Enterprise Advantage volume licensing programs, the Enterprise edition includes the complete set of Windows 7 features, making it functionally identical to Windows 7 Ultimate, except for its licensing. The Windows 7 Enterprise license also includes support for all language packs and the right to run as many as four operating systems in virtual machines.

• **Windows 7 Ultimate:** Windows 7 Ultimate is the retail version of the complete Windows 7 operating system, with all of the same features as Windows 7 Enterprise, except those provided by the Enterprise license. Windows 7 Ultimate does not support volume licensing and includes only five years of product support, as opposed to ten years for Windows 7 Enterprise, which makes the latter preferable for business customers.

 Unlike Windows Vista, which drew criticism for excluding in the Business edition certain features found in the Home Premium product, such as Windows Media Center, the Windows 7 editions are true supersets. As you move up from Starter to Ultimate, each higher edition includes all of the features of the next lower edition.

Table 1-2 lists the operating system features and applications that are included in each of the five main Windows 7 editions.

Table 1-2

Feature Support in Windows 7 Editions

	STARTER	HOME BASIC	HOME PREMIUM	PROFESSIONAL	ENTERPRISE	ULTIMATE
Licensing	OEM only	Emerging markets only	Retail/OEM	Retail/OEM/ Volume	Volume only	Retail/ OEM
AD DS domain support	No	No	No	Yes	Yes	Yes
Boot from VHD	No	No	No	No	Yes	Yes
Windows Aero	No	Partial	Yes	Yes	Yes	Yes
Create Homegroups	Join only	Join only	Yes	Yes	Yes	Yes
Remote desktop	Client only	Client only	Client only	Client and host	Client and host	Client and host
Folder redirection	No	No	No	Yes	Yes	Yes
Offline files	No	No	No	Yes	Yes	Yes
Encrypting file system (EFS)	No	No	No	Yes	Yes	Yes
Product support	5 years	5 years	5 years	10 years	10 years	5 years
Network-based backup	No	No	No	Yes	Yes	Yes
DirectAccess	No	No	No	No	Yes	Yes
BranchCache	No	No	No	No	Yes	Yes
BitLocker	No	No	No	No	Yes	Yes
AppLocker	No	No	No	No	Yes	Yes
Multiple User Interface (MUI) language packs	No	No	No	No	Yes	Yes
Windows Media Center	No	No	Yes	Yes	Yes	Yes
Mobility Center	No	No	No	Yes	Yes	Yes

■ Understanding Windows 7 System Requirements

↓ THE BOTTOM LINE

Windows 7 has the same hardware requirements as Windows Vista, making the upgrade process relatively painless. However, an upgrade to Windows 7 from Windows XP is likely to require hardware upgrades, and a thorough understanding of the Windows 7 system requirements is essential for the technical specialist.

CERTIFICATION READY?
Perform a clean installation.
1.1

Because the various Windows 7 editions differ primarily in the number and type of applications included with each product, the basic minimum system requirements are the same for all (except Starter) editions. Table 1-3 shows the minimum hardware requirements for Windows 7.

Table 1-3

Minimum System Requirements for Windows 7

	32-BIT (x86)	**64-BIT (x64)**
Processor speed	1 GHz or faster	1 GHz or faster
System memory	1 GB	2 GB
Available hard disk space	16 GB	20 GB
Graphics adapter	DirectX 9 graphics adapter with WDDM 1.0 or higher driver	DirectX 9 graphics adapter with WDDM 1.0 or higher driver

Microsoft permits PCs conforming to these specifications to display an official logo such as the one shown in Figure 1-15. However, the appearance of the logo on a new computer does not necessarily mean that a license for the Windows 7 operating system is included in the computer's price. You might still have to pay for the operating system separately.

Figure 1-15

The "Compatible with Windows 7" logo

Apart from these minimum system requirements, there are also hardware limitations for each of the Windows 7 editions, as shown in Table 1-4.

Table 1-4

Hardware limitations for Windows 7 editions

	STARTER	**HOME BASIC**	**HOME PREMIUM**	**PROFESSIONAL**	**ENTERPRISE**	**ULTIMATE**
Processor architecture	32-bit only	32-bit or 64-bit	32-bit or 64-bit	32-bit or 64-bit	32-bit or 64-bit	32-bit or 64-bit
Maximum RAM (32-bit)	2 GB	4 GB	4 GB	4 GB	4 GB	4 GB
Maximum RAM (64-bit)	N/A	8 GB	16 GB	192 GB	192 GB	192 GB
Two-processor support	No	No	No	Yes	Yes	Yes
Peer network connections	0	5	10	10	10	10

While the official system requirements that Microsoft provides are a useful starting point, they do not provide the whole picture. Upgrading to Windows 7 is a subject that is sure to be on the minds of many Windows users, ranging from home users with a single computer to corporate executives responsible for thousands of workstations. For these users, simply falling within the system requirements is not enough. They want to be sure that Windows 7 will be an improvement over their previous OS, and that requires them to consider the individual system components carefully:

- **Processor:** Of the major computer components, the processor is likely to have the least effect on overall system performance. The 1 GHz processor called for in the Windows 7 system requirements is relatively outdated by today's desktop standards. Most of the PCs in use today have processors much faster than 1 GHz, and even computers that are four or five years old will most likely meet the required speeds. The benefits derived from a faster processor depend largely on the applications the computer is running. Hardcore gamers are the users most intent on wringing every last GHz from their systems, but for general computer use, the requirements are not so heavy. For the purposes of upgrading to Windows 7, it is probably not worthwhile to purchase a new computer just to get a faster processor.

- **System memory:** The memory requirements of the Windows operating systems have risen precipitously in recent years. The 512 megabyte (MB) minimum required for a Vista Capable PC was pushing the lower limit, and often resulted in disappointing performance levels. Microsoft now treats the 1 GB minimum previously cited for a Windows Vista Premium Ready PC as the minimum for Windows 7. Memory is easy and inexpensive to upgrade, however; no other hardware upgrade will yield a more immediately detectable performance increase. The Windows 7 one GB memory minimum is sufficient for a general-purpose workstation, but memory-intensive applications such as video and image editing, as well as high-end games, will benefit from more. Be sure to check the system documentation to determine what memory upgrades are possible for your computers.

- **Hard disk space:** Windows 7 requires much more hard disk space than earlier versions of Windows, but with the low prices and high capacities of today's hard disk drives, it is not difficult to meet or exceed the system requirements. For most users, the real disk space hog is not operating system files or even applications, but rather the collections of audio and video files that all users seem to accumulate. Another aspect to consider, however, is the performance level of the hard drive(s) in the computer. Older drives that spin at 5400 RPM can lead to palpably poorer performance than drives running at 7200 RPM or faster. In addition, if you plan to upgrade, you might consider using the newer Serial Advanced Technology Attachment (SATA) drives instead of the older Integrated Drive Electronics (IDE) models. If you do upgrade to SATA on older computers, remember that you will probably have to purchase SATA controller cards as well as the drives themselves.

- **Graphics adapter:** The system component that is causing the most upgrade worries for Windows XP users and administrators is the graphics adapter. Windows Vista was the first Windows operating system to require such specific graphics capabilities, compelling many users to take a crash course in graphics adapter specifications as a result. The operating system feature that requires these capabilities is Windows Aero, the interface element that gives the Windows 7 desktop its glass-like, translucent look. On a Windows 7 system with Aero enabled, the edges of the windows are translucent and contain a fuzzy image of the elements behind them. It is the rendering of those fuzzy images that is so graphic intensive, and that, incidentally, consumes significant system resources as well. The result is impressive; an Aero desktop has a slick, modern appearance that enhances the Windows user experience. However, if your existing graphics adapters have been serving you well, you can certainly wait to upgrade them. The Aero features are mostly cosmetic, and your workstations are likely to perform better using the similar but less graphic-intensive Windows 7 Basic interface instead.

For businesses running hundreds or thousands of workstations, the cost of hardware upgrades can be enormous, so you should carefully consider the current state of your computers and what new hardware your organization will need to make a Windows 7 upgrade practical and productive.

■ Running Windows 7 Upgrade Advisor

↓
THE BOTTOM LINE

All technical specialists should be familiar with the Windows 7 Upgrade Advisor application because it is the surest way of determining whether a computer is capable of running Windows 7.

CERTIFICATION READY?
Upgrade to Windows 7
from previous versions
of Windows.
1.2

The easiest way to determine whether a computer is capable of running Windows 7 is to use Microsoft's Upgrade Advisor application, which replaces the Hardware Compatibility List (HCL) associated with earlier Windows versions. Upgrade Advisor is a Windows XP and Windows Vista application that scans an individual computer's hardware and software to determine whether it is capable of running Windows 7 at peak efficiency.

    RUN UPGRADE ADVISOR

GET READY. Before you run Upgrade Advisor, be sure to plug in and turn on any USB devices or other devices such as printers, external hard drives, or scanners that you regularly use with the PC you are evaluating.

1. Insert the Windows 7 installation disc in the drive. The *Install Windows* page appears, as shown in Figure 1-16.

Figure 1-16

The Install Windows page

2. Click the Check compatibility online arrow. Internet Explorer launches and the *Windows 7 Upgrade Advisor* page appears, as shown in Figure 1-17.

TAKE NOTE*

If you do not have a Windows 7 installation disk, you can access the *Windows 7 Upgrade Advisor* page directly by entering the following URL into your browser: http://windows.microsoft.com/en-us/windows/downloads/upgrade-advisor.

Figure 1-17

The Windows 7 Upgrade
Advisor page

3. Click the Download the Windows 7 Upgrade Advisor hyperlink. The *Download Details Windows 7 Upgrade Advisor* page appears, as shown in Figure 1-18.

Figure 1-18

The Windows 7 Upgrade
Advisor Page

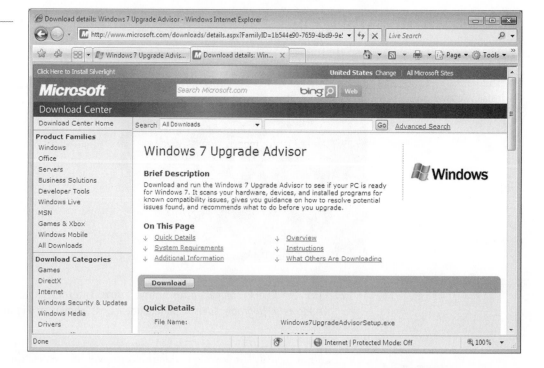

4. Click the Download button. A File Download—Security Warning message box appears.

5. Click the Run button. A progress indicator message box appears. Once the system has finished downloading the file, an Internet Explorer—Security Warning message box appears, asking if you want to run the software.

6. Click the Run button. The *Welcome to the Windows 7 Upgrade Advisor Setup Wizard* page appears, as shown in Figure 1-19.

Figure 1-19

The Welcome to the Windows 7 Upgrade Advisor Setup Wizard page

7. Select the *I Accept the License Terms* option and click Install. The wizard installs the program and the *Installation Complete* page appears, as shown in Figure 1-20.

Figure 1-20

The Installation Complete page

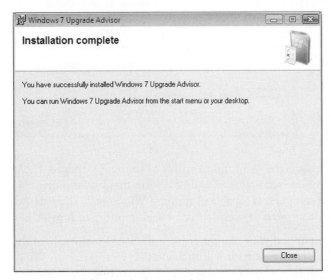

8. Click Close. The wizard closes.

9. On the Start menu, click All Programs > Windows 7 Upgrade Advisor. A User Account Control message box appears.

10. Click Continue. The Windows 7 Upgrade Advisor program loads, as shown in Figure 1-21.

Figure 1-21

The Windows 7 Upgrade Advisor program

11. Click the Start Check button. As it scans the hardware and the software on your computer, Upgrade Advisor displays information about Windows 7.

12. When the scan is completed, a report appears, as shown in Figure 1-22, specifying whether your computer is capable of running Windows 7 and, if so, recommending a specific edition.

Figure 1-22

The Windows 7 Upgrade Advisor report

If your computer is not fully capable of running Windows 7, Upgrade Advisor displays a list of the system requirements and/or devices that would prevent Windows 7 from running. If your computer is capable of running Windows 7, Upgrade Advisor might display system requirements and devices that you could improve, to provide better performance.

For example, if your computer has sufficient memory, hard disk space, and processor speed, Upgrade Advisor will indicate that an upgrade to Windows 7 is possible, but if your graphics adapter is incapable of supporting the Windows Aero interface, the advisor will tell you so.

In addition to evaluating your hardware, Upgrade Advisor also scans the software on your computer and attempts to determine whether it will run with Windows 7. The Programs section lists applications with both major and minor compatibility issues, and also lists the software products that have a Windows 7 logo, indicating that they have been tested with Windows 7.

■ Identifying Upgrade Paths

THE BOTTOM LINE

In many cases, the most convenient way to deploy Windows 7 on existing computers is to perform an upgrade from another operating system. However, there are a multitude of Windows versions, and not all of them support upgrades to Windows 7.

The Windows 7 Upgrade Advisor utility scans computers and specifies whether they are capable of running Windows 7. However, in the strict sense of the word, the utility does not indicate whether you can actually perform an upgrade.

The term upgrade usually refers to an in-place upgrade, in which you install a new operating system over an old one, leaving the existing applications, configuration settings, and personal files intact. *Windows 7 actually only supports in-place upgrades from Windows Vista.*

TAKE NOTE *

When discussing operating system upgrades, it is important to distinguish between the purchase of an upgraded operating system license and the actual installation of the upgraded operating system. The term *in-place upgrade* refers to an installation of Windows 7 on an existing computer, retaining all applications, files, and settings. Some users, however, might be eligible for an upgrade to Windows 7, but can't perform an in-place upgrade. For example, Microsoft allows all licensed Windows XP and Windows Vista users to purchase an upgrade version of Windows 7 at a reduced price, but this does not necessarily mean that they can install Windows 7 with Windows XP or Windows Vista in place. In fact, Windows XP systems always require a clean installation to run Windows 7.

Performing an in-place upgrade from Windows Vista to Windows 7 is a quick and convenient way to provide users with the new operating system without sacrificing the personal files and configuration settings that the users have built up over the years. If you choose to install Windows 7 to the partition that contains the old operating system, the Setup program renames the existing Windows folder to Windows.old, so that the old operating system is still recoverable.

For computers running Windows XP or earlier, you must wipe away the existing operating system and perform a clean Windows 7 installation.

Upgrading Windows 7 Editions

Windows Anytime Upgrade is a program that enables owners of the retail Windows 7 editions to upgrade to a higher Windows 7 edition simply and electronically.

TAKE NOTE *

Windows 7 Enterprise is excluded from Anytime Upgrade because it is only available through volume licensing, and because it already contains the entire set of Windows 7 features.

The idea of allowing users to upgrade their Windows computers to a higher-level edition of their current operating system is an excellent one. However, in Windows Vista, the execution of the idea was flawed. The upgrade paths between the Windows Vista editions were complex, and in many cases, users had to wait for delivery of an upgrade installation disk before they could proceed.

Windows 7 simplifies the Anytime Upgrade process in several ways. First, because each of the Windows 7 editions is a superset of its next lower edition, you can upgrade from any retail Windows 7 product to any higher-level retail product. The available Anytime Upgrade paths are shown in Table 1-5.

Table 1-5

Windows 7 Anytime Upgrade paths

	To Home Premium	To Professional	To Ultimate
From Starter	Anytime Upgrade	Anytime Upgrade	Anytime Upgrade
From Home Premium	N/A	Anytime Upgrade	Anytime Upgrade
From Professional	N/A	N/A	Anytime Upgrade

The second way in which the Windows 7 Anytime Upgrade process is improved is that the entire process is electronic, and no installation disk is needed. Every Windows 7 installation, no matter what the edition, places the entire operating system on the computer's local drive. Therefore, an Anytime Upgrade is really not an upgrade at all, in the true sense of the word; it is just a matter of activating features that are already there.

In Windows 7, Windows Anytime Upgrade is a stand-alone program that you run from the start menu, instead of the Control Panel, as in Windows Vista. When you click Start and select All Programs > Windows Anytime Upgrade, the Windows Anytime Upgrade window appears, as shown in Figure 1-23. From this Window, you can go to the Internet and purchase a higher edition of Windows 7, or enter an upgrade key that you have already purchased.

Figure 1-23

The Windows Anytime Upgrade program

Upgrading from Windows Vista

Windows Vista is the only operating system from which you can perform a true in-place upgrade to Windows 7.

TAKE NOTE*

Windows 7 does not support in-place upgrades of 32-bit to 64-bit operating systems under any circumstances, or vice versa.

To perform an in-place upgrade from Windows Vista to Windows 7, you run the Windows 7 Setup.exe program from within Vista and select the Upgrade option. The editions you can upgrade are limited, however. As a general rule, the allowed upgrade paths separate the home and the business versions of the operating systems, as shown in Table 1-6. The only exception is that you can upgrade any version of Windows Vista to Windows 7 Ultimate.

Table 1-6

Windows Vista to Windows 7 Upgrade paths

	WINDOWS 7 HOME PREMIUM	WINDOWS 7 PROFESSIONAL	WINDOWS 7 ULTIMATE
Windows Vista Home Basic	In-place upgrade	Migration only	In-place upgrade
Windows Vista Home Premium	In-place upgrade	Migration only	In-place upgrade
Windows Vista Business	Migration only	In-place upgrade	In-place upgrade
Windows Vista Ultimate	Migration only	Migration only	In-place upgrade

In theory, an in-place upgrade from Windows Vista to Windows 7 preserves everything you might want to retain on the system, substituting only the new operating system. However, in reality, this is not always the case. Not every application can run properly after an upgrade, and not every customized setting is retained. When planning an in-place upgrade, you should always run the Upgrade Advisor application, and pay particular attention to the compatibility report it provides.

For administrators in an enterprise environment, in-place upgrades take much more time to complete and are often unreliable in their results. Generally speaking, a migration of settings to a clean Windows 7 installation is a much better solution.

Upgrading from Earlier Windows Versions

Windows 7 does not support in-place upgrades from any Windows versions prior to Windows Vista. Instead, you can migrate the user profile data from the existing computer to a new, clean Windows 7 installation.

All Windows XP and Windows Vista owners qualify for the Windows 7 upgrades prices, but Windows 7 only supports the in-place upgrades listed in the previous section. To upgrade a Vista home version to a business version of Windows 7, or to upgrade any version of Windows XP to Windows 7, your only direct option is to perform an operating system migration. It is possible to upgrade Windows XP to Windows Vista and then upgrade Windows Vista to Windows 7, but few people are likely to find this path practical.

For computers running operating system versions prior to Windows XP, including Windows 2000, Windows Me, Windows 98, Windows 95, and Windows 3.1, there is no upgrade pricing available, so you must purchase the full version of Windows 7, and you can only perform a migration.

X REF

For more information on migrating older operating systems to Windows 7, see Lesson 2, "Installing Windows 7."

In an operating system migration, you copy the system configuration settings and personal files from the old operating system to the new one, using a program such as the User State Migration Tool. This process preserves many—but not all—of the existing user settings from the old system. Migration does not preserve third-party applications, so you must re-install and configure them after the Windows 7 installation is completed.

Migrations do not preserve as much of the existing system configuration as in-place upgrades, but they do result in a more uniform, and usually more stable, Windows 7 computer.

■ Understanding the Windows 7 Modular Architecture

↓
THE BOTTOM LINE

Microsoft has increased the number of operating system editions available from two in Windows XP to six in Windows Vista and Windows 7. However, when you begin working with the installation media, you will soon notice that working with six versions of the operating system does not mean working with six different sets of installation disks.

Microsoft has chosen to release Windows 7 only on DVD discs. The amount of code required to install Windows 7 is far too much to fit on one CD, so a single DVD was deemed preferable to a set of CDs.

TAKE NOTE*

There was a five-CD release of Windows Vista, but there is no equivalent for Windows 7. Virtually all new computers sold today come equipped with a DVD reader, and most users who already own computers have DVD support. For those who do not, aftermarket DVD-ROM drives are extremely inexpensive and easy to install. For enterprise administrators or corporate customers with fleets of computers lacking DVD drives, it is possible to install Windows 7 over a network connection by copying the installation files to a USB flash drive, or by creating CD sets using the createspannedshares.cdm script included with the Windows 7 Automated Installation Kit.

However, Microsoft is not distributing a different installation DVD for each Windows 7 edition. Technical specialists working with multiple editions will soon learn that all of the editions are included on a single disk. The operating system setup program determines which edition to install from the product key you enter during the installation process.

These innovations in the Windows 7 distribution method are possible, and practical, because of the modular architecture that Microsoft now uses for the operating system. All of the Windows 7 editions are based on a common core module that is sometimes called **MinWin**. The MinWin module contains approximately 95 percent of the operating system functionality. All Windows 7 setup procedures begin with the installation of the MinWin module; then the secondary module containing the functionality of the edition designated by the product key is installed.

The MinWin module, in addition to lacking all edition-specific code, also lacks all language-specific code. The module is therefore said to be **language-agnostic**. For this reason, Microsoft does not have to produce multiple versions of Windows 7 for different languages. The installer selects the appropriate language during installation, which results in the application of a language module that supplies all of the text the operating system displays. Figure 1-24 illustrates the installation process and the application of the edition-specific and language-specific modules.

Figure 1-24

The Windows 7 modular installation process

The single disc distribution medium also simplifies the process of upgrading Windows 7 to another edition or adding another language to the interface. The Windows Anytime Upgrade process consists of simply activating the appropriate edition in the operating system.

SKILL SUMMARY

IN THIS LESSON YOU LEARNED:

- Windows 7 includes a variety of interface refinements, as well as new and refined features, including BranchCache, DirectAccess, federated search, Explorer Libraries, and Windows PowerShell 2.0.

- Windows 7 is available in six editions: Starter, Home Basic, Home Premium, Professional, Enterprise, and Ultimate. Each successive edition is a superset of the next lower one.

- Upgrade Advisor is an application, capable of running on Windows XP or Windows Vista, that determines whether the computer's hardware and software is compatible with Windows 7.

- Windows 7 is based on a common core module called MinWin. The MinWin module contains approximately 95 percent of the operating system functionality. To create a full installation requires the addition of language-specific and edition-specific modules.

Knowledge Assessment

Fill in the Blank

Complete the following sentences by writing the correct word or words in the blanks provided.

1. The general public in the United States will be able to purchase all of the Windows 7 editions in retail stores except _____, _____, and _____.

2. The core module that provides all of the Windows 7 capability that isn't language- or edition-specific is called _____.

3. When you copy a file to a library, Windows Explorer writes the file to the folder designated as the _____.

4. To use federated search, you must download or create XML files for specific sites called _____.

5. The only operating system edition that you can upgrade in-place to Windows 7 Professional is _____.

6. Upgrading a computer running Windows 7 Starter to Windows 7 Ultimate using Windows Anytime Upgrade requires _____ megabytes of additional hard disk space.

7. To migrate a computer running Windows XP to Windows 7, you can use a utility called _____.

8. The new Windows 7 feature that renders all of the windows on the desktop transparent when you mouse over the right end of the taskbar is called _____.

9. The Windows 7 _____ edition is only available in a 32-bit version.

10. The maximum amount of system memory supported by Windows 7 Enterprise is _____.

True / False

Circle T if the statement is true or F if the statement is false.

T | F 1. Windows 7's ReadyBoost feature requires a USB flash drive.

T | F 2. 1 GB of system memory is sufficient to run any Windows 7 edition.

T | F 3. The Windows 7 Upgrade Advisor application only runs on Windows 7, Windows Vista, and Windows XP SP2.

T | F 4. Only the Professional and Ultimate editions of Windows 7 are capable of joining an AD DS domain.

T | F 5. DirectAccess, BranchCache, and BitLocker are only included with the Enterprise and Ultimate editions of Windows 7.

T | F 6. All of the Windows 7 editions can run on a 64-bit computing platform.

T | F 7. A computer with an inadequate graphics adapter is unlikely to be able to run Windows Aero.

T | F 8. All of the Windows 7 editions have full Homegroup networking support.

T | F 9. The Windows 7 Enterprise and Ultimate editions both contain the same features.

T | F 10. You can upgrade Windows 7 Starter edition to any other edition using Windows Anytime Upgrade.

Review Questions

1. Explain why it is not necessary for Microsoft to create separate installation media for each edition and each language supported by Windows 7.

2. Explain how Windows 7 can utilize a USB flash drive to enhance system performance.

Case Scenarios

Scenario 1-1: Selecting a Windows 7 Edition

You are a private computer consultant, and a new client has approached you about upgrading his small business network. The network currently consists of eight Windows XP workstations and a single server running Windows Server 2003. The server is functioning as a domain controller and the eight workstations are members of an Active Directory domain. The workstations each have 1 gigabyte of memory and a 1.8-gigahertz processor. The video cards support DirectX 9 and have WDDM drivers available from the manufacturer. Three of the workstations are located in a warehouse across town, while the other five in the main office run Microsoft Office applications almost exclusively. The server is also located in the main office. There have been problems with sluggish performance on the warehouse computers when they attempt to access server files. Which edition(s) of Windows 7 would you select for the workstations to provide the features and performance they require most economically? Explain your answers.

Scenario 1-2: Building a Workgroup Network

A business owner called Ortiz approaches you about the possibility of designing a network for deployment at his new branch office in Bolivia. He has already purchased twenty computers and shipped them to the site. Each computer has 1 gigabyte of memory, a 1-gigahertz processor, and an 80-gigabyte hard drive. He wants to connect the computers into a workgroup network that will be used primarily for accessing web-based applications. Because he will be operating the network in a South American country, Mr. Ortiz wants to use Windows 7 Home Basic for his workstations, as this is the most economical solution he can find. Will this be an adequate solution for his needs? Explain why or why not.

Installing Windows 7

OBJECTIVE DOMAIN MATRIX

TECHNOLOGY SKILL	OBJECTIVE DOMAIN	OBJECTIVE NUMBER
Performing a Clean Installation	Perform a clean installation.	1.1
Upgrading to Windows 7	Upgrade to Windows 7 from previous versions of Windows.	1.2
Migrating to Windows 7	Migrate user profiles.	1.3

KEY TERMS

clean installation

dual boot

multilingual user interface (MUI)

side-by-side migration

Windows Preinstallation Environment (PE) 3.0

Windows Recovery Environment (RE)

wipe-and-load migration

■ Selecting Installation Options

THE BOTTOM LINE

Before installing Windows 7, or any operating system, whether on a single computer or a fleet of machines, you must first answer a number of questions to determine what type of installation to perform.

Every Windows 7 installation should begin with a planning phase, which varies depending on the complexity of the installation you are contemplating. For stand-alone home users, installing Windows 7 might mean thinking about what data to preserve, determining whether the existing hardware will work with the new operating system (OS), and finally, purchasing the right Windows 7 edition. For enterprise administrators responsible for hundreds or thousands of computers, an operating system deployment requires a huge amount of testing and preparation, and can represent a massive expense. However, the technicians supporting home users and enterprise technical specialists should ask themselves essentially the same questions, just on a different scale.

Will the Hardware Support the New Operating System?

In Lesson 1, "Introducing Windows 7," you learned about the various Windows 7 editions and their hardware requirements. The first question to ask yourself when contemplating an operating system upgrade is whether the computer's current hardware can run the new software effectively.

In many cases, this question is not just a matter of whether the computer meets the Windows 7 minimum hardware requirements. After all, the user expects the new operating system to run better than the old one, not worse. If the computer does not meet the Windows 7 hardware specifications, you should consider a hardware upgrade.

For the home user, a hardware upgrade might mean purchasing and installing a new memory module or two, or perhaps a graphics adapter. Experienced users might install the hardware themselves, while less savvy users might have a professional do it. Either way, the cost and the time involved are relatively small.

X REF

For more information on deploying Windows 7 in an enterprise environment, see Lesson 3, "Deploying Windows 7."

However, to perform hardware upgrades like these, enterprise administrators must multiply the cost and the installation time by hundreds or thousands of workstations, and factor in other elements such as lost productivity and overtime costs. Therefore, as with all aspects of a large-scale deployment, technical specialists in an enterprise environment must plan and test carefully before even considering an upgrade to Windows 7. For example, you might want to perform a series of test installations on differently configured computers to determine exactly which hardware upgrade provides the best performance at the lowest cost.

TAKE NOTE*

Some of Windows 7's hardware demands are unusual when compared with previous Windows versions. The Windows 7 specifications for graphics capabilities are necessary only to run the Windows Aero user experience. Windows Aero is a selling point for Windows 7, but it is essentially a cosmetic feature, and you should consider your user's needs carefully before recommending hardware upgrades. A home user is likely to want all of the "bells and whistles" that Windows 7 can provide, and replacing a graphics adapter is typically a small enough price to pay for that experience. However, for a corporation considering a mass upgrade to Windows 7, the time and cost of replacing hundreds of graphics adapters is far more substantial, especially when the only result is a cosmetic feature that business users could easily do without.

Will the New Operating System Support the Existing Applications?

The second major consideration for a client contemplating a Windows 7 installation is whether the applications the client already owns will run on the new operating system. The last thing clients want to hear after the successful installation of a new operating system is that they need to purchase additional new software.

As with hardware upgrades, the prospect of upgrading or changing applications is far more daunting in the enterprise environment than for the home user. Home users typically run commercial, off-the-shelf applications, and prices for upgrades supporting new operating systems typically fall soon after the release of the OS.

At the enterprise level, however, you are more likely to find special-purpose or customized applications; these present greater difficulties. It might take time for developers to produce updates for special-purpose applications; for customized applications, it might be necessary to commission additional work from a programmer. Commercial applications can be extremely costly to upgrade, especially when you have to purchase hundreds or thousands of licenses.

X REF

To aid in evaluating and testing applications in the Windows 7 environment, Microsoft provides a free Application Compatibility Toolkit. For more information on using this toolkit and deploying applications on Windows 7, see Lesson 7, "Working with Applications."

In enterprise environments, application testing is as important as hardware testing. Even if an updated version of an application is available, you must test it carefully with the new operating system to ensure that it functions properly. The alternative could be the failure of a mission-critical application across the entire enterprise, resulting in extended down time and lost productivity.

Which Windows 7 Edition Should I Install?

You should select a Windows 7 edition based on several factors, including the tasks the user will be performing and, of course, your budget.

For home users, the choice between Windows 7 Starter and Home Premium is primarily economic. If a client wants to burn DVDs and spends a lot of time working with audio and video files, then Home Premium is generally worth the additional investment. Home Premium provides the Windows Aero user experience; Starter does not. Many new computers ship with Starter installed, so there is likely to be a large number of users upgrading to Home Premium.

Most enterprise installations require their workstations to log on to an Active Directory Domain Services domain, which eliminates Starter and Home Premium as possible choices because they lack domain support. In most cases, the organization's relationship with Microsoft is the deciding factor in the choice between Windows 7 Professional and Enterprise. Windows 7 Professional is a retail product, available in stores everywhere, while Enterprise is only available directly from Microsoft as part of a volume license agreement.

Windows 7 Ultimate edition is a premium product intended for retail users who want all of the features of Windows 7 Enterprise without entering into a volume licensing agreement. Home users for whom price is not a major concern are likely to opt for the Ultimate edition, as are small business customers interested only in retail licensing.

TAKE NOTE *

The Windows 7 Home Basic edition is left out of consideration unless you are located in an emerging market outside of North America, Europe, or Australia.

Should I Perform an Upgrade or a Clean Installation?

The question of whether to install Windows 7 by performing an in-place upgrade or a *clean installation* depends on the amount and type of data stored on the computer, as well as the computer's current efficiency.

Obviously, new computers, or computers with new hard disk drives, require a clean installation in which you boot from the Windows 7 setup disk and create or select a blank partition where the operating system will reside. If the computer is currently running Windows Vista, you must consider whether it is preferable to wipe out the existing operating system and install Windows 7 from scratch or install Windows 7 over the previous operating system.

+ MORE INFORMATION

You can perform an in-place upgrade to Windows 7 only on computers running Windows Vista or another edition of Windows 7. It is not possible to perform an in-place upgrade to Windows 7 from Windows XP, Windows 2000, Windows Me, Windows 98, Windows 95, Windows NT, or Windows 3.1. For computers running these operating systems, you must perform a clean installation.

The primary advantage of performing a clean installation is that Windows 7 will achieve its best possible performance. Installing the operating system files on a blank disk means that they will be unfragmented, improving disk performance. A clean installation ensures that the user retains the maximum amount of disk space for applications and data. Of course, a clean installation also erases all existing data, so you must be careful to back up everything that the user wants to retain.

For home users, there is usually some data to preserve, such as image, audio, and video files, as well as data files for specific applications. Fortunately, writable CDs and DVDs, USB flash drives, and external hard drives make it relatively easy to back up a user's essential data. What can be more problematic in a case like this is the loss of important configuration settings, such as usernames, passwords, and customized application templates. Be sure to preserve this type of information before wiping out a partition to perform a clean installation.

Performing an in-place upgrade to Windows 7 means that whatever disk and registry clutter is present under the previous operating system will remain in place. Files might be extensively fragmented, even to the point of executing poorly, and outdated applications and data files could occupy significant amounts of disk space.

The advantage of performing an in-place upgrade is that all of the user's applications, data files, and configuration settings remain intact, but even this could be a problem. Upgrades can generate incompatibilities with drivers or applications that you must rectify before the computer can run properly.

In an enterprise environment, it is more typical for users to store their data files on servers, as opposed to local drives. Also, a properly maintained enterprise network should document all configuration settings and logon credentials. This minimizes the problem of potential data loss when performing a clean installation.

Clean installations are generally preferable in an enterprise environment because they ensure that all of the computers are running an identical system configuration. This eliminates many of the technical support problems that can occur when computers are running different configurations.

Should I Perform a Single or Dual Boot Installation?

One other solution to the problem of whether to perform an upgrade or a clean installation is to create a *dual boot* environment, in which you retain the old operating system installation on one disk partition and create a clean installation of Windows 7 on another.

Dual booting enables a user to run either operating system at any time. The original operating system installation retains all of its existing applications and settings, but you must configure the new Windows 7 installation from scratch and install all of your applications.

The disadvantages of dual booting include the following:

- You must have a separate disk partition available to install Windows 7.
- Two operating systems require twice as much disk space as one.
- Switching from one operating system to another to perform a specific task requires a computer restart, which can take several minutes.

Dual booting is not commonly found in enterprise computing environments, except as a makeshift compatibility solution, but some home users employ it to test new operating systems or maintain configurations to support different applications.

Do I Have to Install Multiple Languages?

Before Windows Vista, each language-specific version of a Windows operating system had to be developed, maintained, and distributed separately. Starting with Vista, however, and now with Windows 7, it is possible to install multiple language packs on a single computer so that individuals can work in multiple languages.

The main problems for multilingual users in the past have been the availability of the languages they need and the complex procedure for implementing multiple languages on a single computer. To use multiple languages on a Windows XP computer, you must begin with an installation of the English language Windows XP version. Then you install the *multilingual user interface (MUI)* pack and whatever additional language packs you need. Unfortunately, some of the language packs provide more complete support than others.

Windows 7 contains an MUI architecture that makes it easier to install multilingual support on a computer. In Windows 7, the binary code that makes up the operating system is entirely language neutral. During the operating system installation process, the Setup program installs the operating system and then applies a language pack containing the information needed to provide the localized user interface.

Because the language packs for Windows 7 contain no binary code, they are interchangeable. Therefore, it is no longer necessary for technicians to consider localization issues before installing the operating system. You can change a Windows 7 installation from one language to another at any time, or install multiple language packs that utilize the same binary code.

➕ **MORE INFORMATION**

Because the Windows 7 binaries are language neutral there is no need for language-specific service packs or other updates. Microsoft is therefore able to release each update in one generic version suitable for all Windows 7 computers around the world, regardless of the language they use.

■ Understanding the Windows 7 Boot Environment

⬇ **THE BOTTOM LINE**

Windows 7 eliminates DOS from the installation process and provides a new boot environment.

Those who have performed clean installations of stand-alone Windows XP systems should recall that the very beginning of the process, immediately after the system boots from the installation disk, consists of several character-based (that is, nongraphical) screens, like that shown in Figure 2-1. On these screens, you opt to perform the installation, agree to the terms of the End User License Agreement (EULA), select the drive partition on which you want to install Windows XP, and then watch as the program copies the installation files from the CD-ROM to a temporary folder on the hard disk.

Figure 2-1

A character-based screen from the MS-DOS phase of a Windows XP installation

```
Windows XP Professional Setup

  Welcome to Setup.

  This portion of the Setup program prepares Microsoft(R)
  Windows(R) XP to run on your computer.

     •  To set up Windows XP now, press ENTER.

     •  To repair a Windows XP installation using
        Recovery Console, press R.

     •  To quit Setup without installing Windows XP, press F3.




  ENTER=Continue   R=Repair   F3=Quit
```

These screens are character-based because all of the Windows operating systems up to and including Windows XP required an MS-DOS boot at the beginning of the installation process. The MS-DOS boot was necessary because the computer required an operating system to run the installation program and to gain access to the disk drives.

For original equipment manufacturers (OEMs) and enterprise installations, deploying Windows on a large number of computers typically required a boot from an MS-DOS system disk to provide access to the computer's drives and to provide access to a network share where the Windows installation files or a disk image was located.

This need for an MS-DOS boot became increasingly problematic over the years for several reasons, including the following:

- **Limited disk support:** MS-DOS can provide access only to disk drives formatted using one of the File Allocation Table (FAT) formats. MS-DOS cannot provide access to the NTFS drives that most of today's Windows computers use.

- **No internal networking support:** MS-DOS has no internal networking support, and because it is a 16-bit operating system, administrators had to obtain and load 16-bit real mode network adapter drivers (as compared to the 32-bit drivers that current Windows versions use), as well as a TCP/IP client, before they can access a share containing Windows installation files.

- **Limited script support:** MS-DOS has no internal support for any scripting languages other than rudimentary batch files.

- **Boot device limitations:** Many computers today, especially those in corporate environments, do not have floppy disk drives, and creating bootable MS-DOS CD-ROMs can be problematic.

Introducing Windows PE

Ever since Windows Me was retired, Microsoft has eliminated the need for MS-DOS as an underlying operating system for Windows, but Windows 7 is only the second operating system (after Vista) to completely eliminate MS-DOS from the installation process. To replace the MS-DOS boot, Windows 7 includes Windows Preinstallation Environment 3.0 (Windows PE).

Windows PE 3.0 is a stripped-down operating system, based on the Windows 7 kernel, that enables system administrators to boot a computer that has no operating system installed and initiate the operating system setup process. When compared to MS-DOS, Windows PE has a number of distinct advantages, including the following:

- **Native 32-bit or 64-bit support:** Windows PE is a native 32-bit or 64-bit operating system that enables the computer to address memory just as the full Windows 7 operating system does. MS-DOS is a 16-bit OS and is relatively limited in its memory addressing capabilities.

- **Native 32-bit or 64-bit driver support:** Because Windows PE is a 32-bit or 64-bit OS, it can use the same drivers as a full Windows 7 installation. System administrators therefore do not have to search for antiquated 16-bit real mode network drivers as they did with MS-DOS.

- **Internal networking support:** Windows PE includes its own internal TCP/IP networking stack and is capable of functioning as a Windows file-sharing client. This means that after booting Windows PE, an administrator only has to supply a driver for the network adapter and the networking stack is complete.

- **Internal NTFS support:** Windows PE includes internal support for the NTFS file system used by Windows 7, as well as the FAT file systems that MS-DOS supports. This means that when you boot a system using Windows PE, you can read from and write to existing NTFS drives in the computer, as well as create and format new NTFS partitions. It is even possible to create and manage dynamic volumes using Windows PE.

- **Scripting language support:** Windows PE includes internal support for a subset of the Win32 application programming interface (API), meaning that it is possible to run some Windows programs in the preinstallation environment. Windows PE also includes support for Windows Management Instrumentation (WMI) and Windows Script Host that makes it possible for administrators to create scripts that are far more powerful than MS-DOS batch files.

- **Flexible boot options:** Windows PE can boot from a variety of media, including CD-ROMs, DVD-ROMs, USB devices, such as flash disks and floppy drives, or a Windows Deployment Services (WDS) server. The computer can then run the Windows PE operating system from a variety of media, including the DVD, a temporary folder on a hard disk, a USB flash drive, a RAM disk, or a network share.

> **➕ MORE INFORMATION**
>
> Windows PE 3.0 is available in both 32-bit and 64-bit versions. You must use the 32-bit version of Windows PE to install the 32-bit version of Windows 7 and the 64-bit version of Windows PE to install the 64-bit version of Windows 7.

What's New in Windows PE 3.0?

> The latest version of Windows PE, version 3.0, is more readily available than previous versions and includes a variety of tools you can use to customize the Windows PE environment.

The most important new development in Windows PE 3.0 is that anyone can get it. Prior to Windows 7, Microsoft made Windows PE available only to customers with service agreements. Now, it's available for free in a stand-alone version as part of the Windows 7 Automated Installation Kit (AIK).

Some of the other new features of Windows PE 3.0 are as follows:

- **Windows Imaging format:** Windows 7 AIK provides Windows PE in the Windows Imaging (.wim) file-based image format. Unlike sector-based (iso) images, file-based images are editable.
- **Size reduction:** Windows PE 3.0 omits some of the optional components found in version 2.1, reducing the overall size of the image.
- **Customization:** Windows 7 AIK includes the Deployment Image Servicing and Management (DISM.exe) tool, which enables you to mount the Windows PE image file and customize it by adding device drivers and other components.
- **Hyper-V support:** Windows PE 3.0 includes all of the drivers needed to run in the hyper-V hypervisor environment.
- **Scratch space:** You can customize the Windows PE RAM scratch space to sizes ranging from 32 to 512 megabytes.

TAKE NOTE *
> Windows 7 AIK, including Windows PE 3.0, is available free of charge from the Microsoft Download Center at http://www.microsoft.com/downloads/details.aspx?familyid=696DD665-9F76-4177-A811-39C26D3B3B34&displaylang=en.

Understanding Windows PE 3.0 Limitations

> Microsoft intends Windows PE to be a reduced subset of the Windows 7 operating system, only providing sufficient capability to perform certain installation, diagnostic, and recovery functions while running from a minimized hardware environment, such as a RAM drive.

Because there was never any intention for Windows PE to function as a full-time operating system, and to facilitate its rapid deployment and execution, there are certain inherent limitations in the product, such as the following:

- Windows PE does not support the entire collection of Win32 APIs as a full installation of Windows 7 does. Microsoft limits the APIs in Windows PE primarily to those providing disk and network input/output functions, as well as certain APIs that make it possible to run basic programs. Reducing the API support enables Windows PE to run in a smaller memory space than Windows 7.

➕ MORE INFORMATION

Because Windows PE requires a relatively small memory space, the entire operating system can run from a RAM disk. A RAM disk is a driver that allocates a section of active memory for use as a virtual disk drive, complete with drive letter. Because the RAM disk is based in memory it is much faster than a hard disk drive, but it is also volatile; all of its contents are lost when the computer restarts. Running the Windows 7 Setup program from a RAM disk allows all the operating system file handles to remain open throughout the installation process, allowing you to remove the boot device, if necessary. By contrast, running the Setup program directly from a DVD makes it impossible to remove the disk (e.g., to load third-party drivers) without interrupting the installation procedure. In the same way, running the Setup program from a temporary folder on a hard disk interferes with partition creation and management functions that might be needed during the installation.

- Windows PE automatically stops and reboots the computer after 72 hours of continuous operation. This deliberate limitation prevents individuals from using the product as a permanent operating environment.
- Windows PE will not fit on a floppy disk, but it is possible to create bootable Windows PE CD-ROMs, DVD-ROMs, and USB flash drives.
- Windows PE networking support is limited to the TCP/IP and NetBIOS Over TCP/IP (NetBT) protocols. There is no support for IPX/SPX or any other network/transport layer protocols.
- You must use the 32-bit version of Windows PE to install the 32-bit version of Windows 7, and the 64-bit version of Windows PE to install the 64-bit Windows 7.
- While it is possible to modify the Windows PE registry when the operating system is running, all registry keys are reset to their default values each time the operating system restarts. It is possible to make permanent changes to the registry, but to do so you must make the changes offline by manually editing the registry while Windows PE is not running.
- You can create drive letter assignments in a Windows PE session, but these assignments are not persistent between sessions.
- Windows PE does not have file server or Terminal Server capabilities, nor does it support the Microsoft .NET Framework or the Common Language Runtime (CLR), Windows on Windows 32 (WOW32), Windows on Windows 64 (WOW64), Virtual DOS Machine (VDM), OS/2, or POSIX subsystems.
- Windows PE does not support the installation of Windows Installer package (.msi) files.
- Windows PE can access Distributed File System (DFS) folders, but only those in stand-alone DFS roots.

Using Windows PE

> In addition to functioning as a platform for individual installations of Windows 7, Windows PE is useful for other scenarios that require a basic operating system with minimal resource usage.

Some of the other scenarios that can make use of Windows PE are as follows:

- **Custom deployments:** Windows 7 uses Windows PE during the default installation procedure, but it is possible for administrators to build their own unattended installation routines using Windows PE as a platform to run scripts and deploy customized disk images on fleets of workstations. You can even use Windows PE to deploy operating systems other than Windows 7.

* **System troubleshooting:** If a Windows 7 computer fails to start, or if it crashes repeatedly, a technician can launch the *Windows Recovery Environment* (Windows RE), which is simply another name given to Windows PE on a computer with Windows 7 already installed. In the Windows RE environment, the technician can use Windows' built-in troubleshooting utilities or run third-party or custom diagnostic tools.

* **System recovery:** OEMs who build their own computers typically supply their customers with a system recovery disk rather than an operating system installation disk. A system recovery disk contains image files that can restore the computer to its original state, just as it was when it left the factory. OEMs can use Windows PE to build recovery solutions that automate the process of setting up Windows 7, installing specific drivers, installing applications, and configuring the entire system to create a standardized environment.

■ Performing a Clean Installation

THE BOTTOM LINE

A clean installation is the simplest way to deploy Windows 7 on a new computer or a computer with a partition that you are willing to reformat (losing all of the data on the partition in the process).

CERTIFICATION READY?
Perform a clean
installation.
1.1

If a computer is brand new and has no operating system installed on it, then it cannot start until you supply a boot disk, such as the Windows 7 installation disk. During the installation you will select the disk partition on which you want to install Windows, and the Setup program will copy the operating system files there.

If the computer has an operating system installed on it, and you have already backed up all the data that you want to preserve, then you are ready to boot the computer from the Windows 7 installation disk. During the setup process you can erase a partition on the disk in preparation for installing Windows there.

TAKE NOTE*

The following procedure is for an installation of Windows 7 Professional edition. Although the installation procedure for the other editions is nearly identical, you might see minor differences in the procedure.

 PERFORM A CLEAN INSTALLATION

GET READY. Prepare the computer for the Windows 7 installation by making sure that all of its external peripheral devices are connected and powered on.

1. Turn on the computer and insert the Windows 7 installation disk into the DVD drive.
2. Press any key to boot from the DVD (if necessary). A progress indicator screen appears as Windows is loading files.

+ MORE INFORMATION

The device that a PC uses to boot is specified in its system (or BIOS) settings. In some cases, you might have to modify these settings to enable the computer to boot from the Windows 7 DVD. If you are not familiar with the operation of a particular computer, watch the screen carefully as the system starts and look for an instruction specifying what key to press to access the system settings.

3. The computer switches to the Windows graphical interface and the *Install Windows* page appears, as shown in Figure 2-2.

Figure 2-2

The Install Windows page

TAKE NOTE*

At this point, the computer is running Windows PE as its operating system, providing it with the means to execute the Setup program and to load drivers providing access to the disk drives and other hardware resources.

4. Using the drop-down lists provided, select the appropriate Language to install, Time and currency format, and Keyboard or input method and then click Next. The *Windows 7 Install now* page appears, as shown in Figure 2-3.

Figure 2-3

The Windows 7 Install now page

5. Click the Install now button. The *Please read the license terms* page appears, as shown in Figure 2-4.

Figure 2-4

The Please read the license terms page

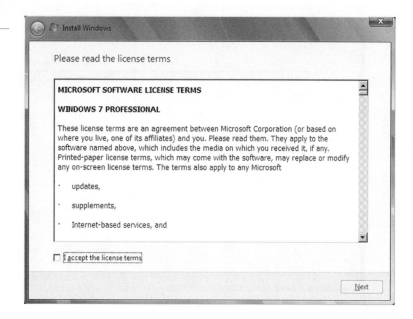

6. Select the I accept the license terms check box and click Next. The *Which type of installation do you want?* page appears, as shown in Figure 2-5.

Figure 2-5

The Which type of installation do you want? page

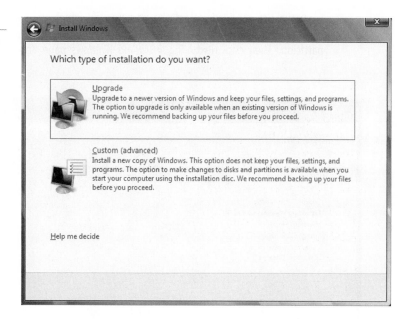

7. Click the Custom (advanced) option. The *Where do you want to install Windows?* page appears, as shown in Figure 2-6.

Figure 2-6

The Where do you want to install Windows? page

The Upgrade option is currently disabled because you booted the computer using the Windows 7 installation disk. For the Upgrade option to function, you must boot an existing Windows Vista operating system and start the Windows 7 installation program from there. See "Upgrading to Windows 7" later in this lesson for more information.

TAKE NOTE*

8. From the list provided, select the partition on which you want to install Windows 7, or select an area of unallocated disk space where the Setup program can create a new partition. Then click Next. The *Installing Windows* page appears, as shown in Figure 2-7.

Figure 2-7

The Installing Windows page

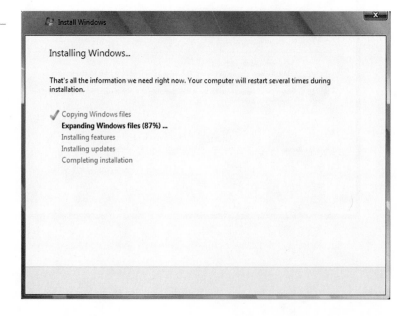

9. After several minutes, during which the Setup program installs Windows 7, the computer reboots twice and the *Set Up Windows* page appears, as shown in Figure 2-8.

Figure 2-8

The Set Up Windows page

10. In the Type a user name text box, enter a name for the first user account on the system.

11. In the Type a computer name text box, enter a name, no more than fifteen characters long, by which the computer will be known on the network.

12. Click Next to continue. The *Set a password for your account* page appears, as shown in Figure 2-9.

Figure 2-9

The Set a password for your account page

13. In the Type a password and Retype your password text boxes, enter a password for the user name you specified earlier.

14. In the Type a password hint text box, type a phrase to remind you of the password.

15. Click Next to continue. The *Type your Windows product key* page appears, as shown in Figure 2-10.

Figure 2-10

The Type your Windows product key page

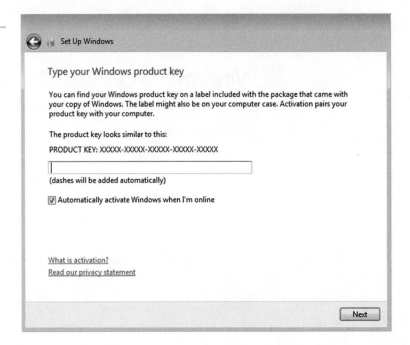

16. In the Product key text box, type the key code supplied with your copy of Windows 7. Leave the Automatically activate Windows when I'm online check box selected, unless you know you will have to activate your computer by telephone or some other means.

17. Click Next to continue. The *Help protect your computer and improve Windows automatically* page appears, as shown in Figure 2-11.

Figure 2-11

The Help protect your computer and improve Windows automatically page

18. Select one of the three options specifying what security settings you want the computer to use. The *Review your time and date settings* page appears, as shown in Figure 2-12.

Figure 2-12

The Review your time and date settings page

> **TAKE NOTE***   As with most of the settings you configure during the Windows 7 installation, you can also select a different security option at a later time.

19. From the Time zone drop-down list, select the time zone in which the computer will be running. If the date and time specified in the calendar and clock are not accurate, or you want to prevent the computer from adjusting itself during Daylight Savings Time, correct the settings and click Next. The *Select your computer's current location* page appears, as shown in Figure 2-13.

Figure 2-13

The Select your computer's current location page

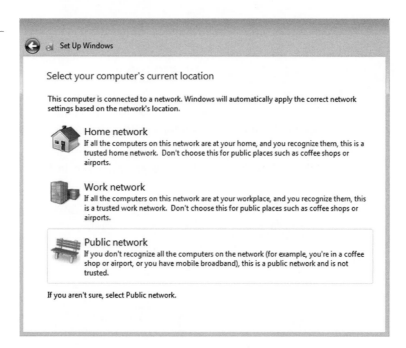

TAKE NOTE[*] The *Select your computer's current location* page appears only when the Setup program successfully detects and configures a network connection. Otherwise, the Setup program skips it.

20. Click the appropriate option specifying the computer's normal location. The system completes its new startup routine and the Windows desktop appears.

At this point, you can remove the installation disk from the drive.

Installing Third-Party Device Drivers

During the Windows 7 installation procedure, the Setup program enables you to select a disk partition or an area of unallocated disk space where you want to install the operating system.

The *Where do you want to install Windows?* page lists the partitions on all the hard disks that the Setup program detects with its default drivers. In most cases, all of the computer's hard disks will appear in the list; if they do not, it is probably because Windows PE does not include a driver for the computer's drive controller.

If the hard disk drives in the computer are connected to a third-party controller, rather than the one integrated into the motherboards, the list of partitions might appear empty, and you will have to supply a driver before the Setup program can see the disks. Check the controller manufacturer's Web site for a driver supporting Windows 7. If none is available, use the most recent Windows Vista driver.

+ MORE INFORMATION

There are several reasons why a computer might employ a third-party disk controller, rather than the one integrated into the motherboard. The computer might have a relatively old motherboard and more modern drives whose capabilities are not supported by the older controller. The computer might also be using SCSI (Small Computer Systems Interface) rather than SATA (Serial ATA) or IDE (Integrated Drive Electronics) hard drives, and a SCSI controller that is not supported by Windows PE. Finally, the computer might be using a specialized controller that provides advanced disk management technologies, such as RAID (Redundant Array of Independent Disks).

To install a driver, use the following procedure:

INSTALL A THIRD-PARTY DISK DRIVER

GET READY. If, during a Windows 7 installation, no disk partitions or unallocated space appear on the *Where do you want to install Windows?* page, you must install the appropriate driver for your disk controller using the following procedure before the installation can continue.

1. On the *Where do you want to install Windows?* page, click the Load Driver button. A Load Driver message box appears, as shown in Figure 2-14.

Figure 2-14

The Load Driver message box

2. Insert the storage medium containing the driver into the computer. You can supply drivers on a CD, DVD, USB flash drive, or floppy disk.

TAKE NOTE*

Because Windows PE is running on a RAM drive, it is possible to remove the Windows 7 installation disk from the DVD drive and insert another disk containing drivers. You will later have to re-insert the Windows 7 disk to complete the installation.

3. Click OK if the driver is in the root directory of the storage medium, or Browse if it is necessary to locate the driver in the directory structure of the disk. When the driver loads, the partitions and unallocated space on the associated disks appear in the list on the *Where do you want to install Windows?* page.

4. Select the partition or area of unallocated space where you want to install Windows 7 and then continue with the rest of the installation procedure, as covered earlier in this lesson.

Working with Installation Partitions

In addition to installing disk drivers, the *Where do you want to install Windows?* page enables you to create, manage, and delete the partitions on your disks.

Clicking the Drive options (advanced) button on the page causes four additional buttons to appear, as shown in Figure 2-15. These buttons have the following functions:

- **Delete:** Removes an existing partition from a disk, permanently erasing all of its data. You might want to delete partitions to consolidate unallocated disk space, enabling you to create a new, larger partition.

- **Extend:** Enables you to make an existing partition larger, as long as there is unallocated space available immediately following the selected partition on the disk.

- **Format:** Enables you to format an existing partition on a disk, thereby erasing all of its data. There is no need to format any new partitions you create for the install, but you might want to format an existing partition to eliminate unwanted files prior to installing Windows 7 on it.

- **New:** Creates a new partition of a user-specified size in the selected area of unallocated space.

Figure 2-15

Additional buttons on the Where do you want to install Windows? page

■ Migrating to Windows 7

THE BOTTOM LINE

Performing a clean installation of Windows 7 on a user's workstation does not necessarily mean that the user has to lose his or her personal files and folders, operating system and application settings, and Internet favorites. Using tools supplied with Windows 7 or the Windows 7 AIK, you can migrate these elements from one operating system to another.

CERTIFICATION READY?
Migrate user profiles.
1.3

In some cases, performing a clean installation of Windows 7 is a perfectly adequate solution. You might be working with a brand new computer, or the user might not have any important data to carry over from the previous operating system. However, most experienced computer users have settings and data they want to keep, data that is typically stored in a Windows user profile.

A user profile is a series of folders, associated with a specific user account, that contain personal documents, user-specific registry settings, Internet favorites, and other personalized information—everything that provides a user's familiar working environment. On a stand-alone Windows XP workstation, user profiles are stored in the Documents and Settings folder, in subfolders named for the user accounts. On a Windows Vista or 7 workstation, the subfolders are found in the Users folder. On a workstation that is joined to an Active Directory Domain Services (AD DS) domain, the user profiles are also stored on a network server.

MORE INFORMATION

User profiles consist of files, such as a user's personal documents and Internet favorites, stored in appropriate profile folders and settings stored in a registry file. The registry settings include basic display parameters, such as the colors, themes, and images you have designated for your Windows desktop, as well as configuration parameters for specific applications. Windows loads the profile information into memory each time that particular user logs on to Windows and saves any changes the user has made to the profile when that user logs off. User profiles make it possible for different users to maintain their own individual settings on one Windows computer.

There are two basic methods for deploying Windows 7 to a client while retaining the user profile settings: upgrade and migration. In an upgrade, you install Windows 7 on the computer running an earlier operating system. Windows 7 overwrites the old OS, but all of the user profiles already on the computer remain in place. In a migration, you copy the user profile information from the old operating system to some temporary medium and transfer it to a new, clean installation of Windows 7.

Microsoft has created two different tools for migrating files and settings to new computers:

- **Windows Easy Transfer:** Designed for the migration of a single computer, Easy Transfer is a wizard-based utility that makes it possible to migrate user profile information for multiple users from one computer to another.
- **User State Migration Tool 4.0:** Designed for large-scale enterprise deployments, User State Migration Tool is a command line utility that can migrate profile information for multiple users on multiple computers.

In the following sections, you learn the procedure for using Windows Easy Transfer to migrate user profile settings from an existing Windows Vista workstation to a new Windows 7 workstation. You also learn some basic facts about using the User State Migration Tool.

Using Windows Easy Transfer

Windows Easy Transfer is a tool that migrates user profile information from an existing Windows computer to a new computer with a clean installation of Windows 7.

Windows Easy Transfer migrates user profile data from one computer to another in a variety of scenarios. As long as you are working with the user accounts from one single computer, Windows Easy Transfer can function in virtually any hardware configuration. Some of the options you can select include:

- **Number of computers:** Windows Easy Transfer supports both side-by-side and wipe-and-load migrations. In a ***side-by-side migration***, you have two computers running simultaneously; one is the source computer containing the user profile information you want to transfer, and the other is the destination computer running Windows 7 to which you want to transfer the profile information. In a ***wipe-and-load migration***, you have only one computer, which initially contains the user profile settings you want to transfer. After saving the profile information to a removable storage medium, you perform a clean Windows 7 installation to wipe out all data on the computer's hard disk and then transfer the profile data from the removable medium back to the computer.
- **Direct or indirect:** When you are performing a side-by-side migration, you can use Windows Easy Transfer with the computers connected together directly, using a cable or a network, or connected indirectly, using a removable storage medium.
- **Storage medium:** Windows Easy Transfer can use virtually any storage medium to transfer profile data between computers, as long as it provides sufficient storage space and is accessible by both machines. You can use a writable CD or DVD, a USB flash drive, an external hard drive, or a network share. Floppy disks are not supported because they have insufficient capacity.

The procedure for migrating files consists of two basic elements: saving the user profile information on the existing computer and transferring the information to the new computer. Using the capabilities of Windows Easy Transfer, you should be able to satisfy the requirements of almost any stand-alone user that wants to move to Windows 7 without performing an upgrade. The most common scenarios are likely to be these:

- **Scenario 1:** A user purchases a new computer on which he wants to run Windows 7, but he also wants to retain the files and settings from his existing Windows Vista computer.
- **Scenario 2:** A user wants to install Windows 7 on her existing Windows Vista computer and retain all of her files and settings, but she wants to avoid performing an upgrade to maximize her Windows 7 performance.

The following sections describe the Windows Easy Transfer procedures for each of these scenarios.

Performing Migration Scenario 1

Ed is a longtime Windows Vista user with a small network in his home. He has just purchased a new computer with Windows 7 preinstalled on it and wants to migrate his files and settings from his Vista computer to the Windows 7 computer. The new computer came with recovery disks, but no Windows 7 installation disk.

In this scenario, you perform a side-by-side migration with both computers connected to the user's home network. However, because you do not have access to a Windows 7 installation disk, you must add a third element to the procedure, in which you provide the Vista computer with access to the Windows Easy Transfer program.

 PERFORM MIGRATION SCENARIO 1

GET READY. Both computers must be powered up and connected to the home network. Create a network share on one of the two computers and make sure that both systems can access it.

1. On the Windows 7 computer, click Start > All Programs > Accessories > System Tools and then select Windows Easy Transfer. The *Welcome to Windows Easy Transfer* page appears, as shown in Figure 2-16.

Figure 2-16

The Welcome to Windows Easy Transfer page

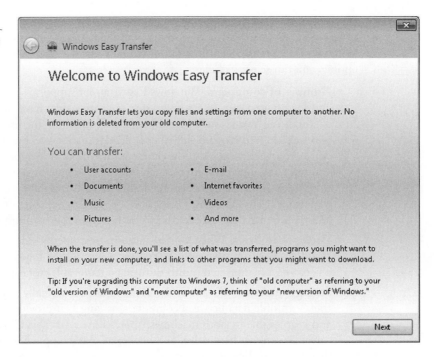

2. Click Next. The *What do you want to use to transfer items to your new computer?* page appears, as shown in Figure 2-17.

Figure 2-17

The What do you want to use to transfer items to your new computer? page

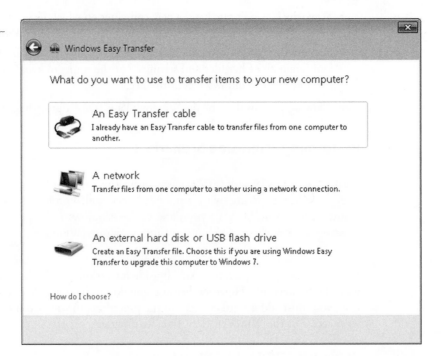

➕ **MORE INFORMATION**

An Easy Transfer cable is a special USB cable that you can use to connect two Windows computers together solely for the purpose of using the Windows Easy Transfer utility. In this particular scenario, the user has a network available, which performs the same function.

3. Click A network. The *Which computer are you using now?* page appears, as shown in Figure 2-18.

Figure 2-18

The Which computer are you using now? page

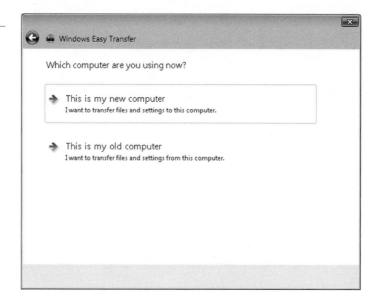

4. Click This is my new computer. The *Do you need to install Windows Easy Transfer on your old computer?* page appears, as shown in Figure 2-19.

Figure 2-19

The Do you need to install Windows Easy Transfer on your old computer? page

 WARNING To transfer user profile information to a Windows 7 computer, you must use the Windows Easy Transfer program supplied with Windows 7. Windows Vista has its own version of Windows Easy Transfer, but this version is not compatible with Windows 7 user profiles.

5. Click I need to install it now. The *How do you want to install Windows Easy Transfer on your old computer?* page appears, as shown in Figure 2-20.

Figure 2-20

The How do you want to install Windows Easy Transfer on your old computer? page

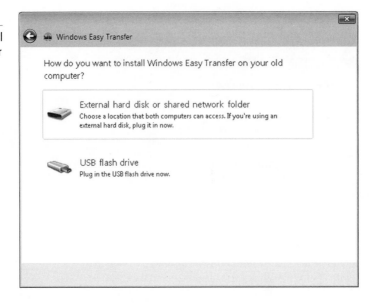

6. Click External hard disk or shared network folder. A *Browse for Folder* dialog box appears, as shown in Figure 2-21.

Figure 2-21

The Browse for Folder dialog box

7. Browse to the location of the network share you created before beginning the procedure and click OK. The wizard copies Windows Easy Transfer to the location you specified and the *Install Windows Easy Transfer on your old computer* page appears, as shown in Figure 2-22.

TAKE NOTE*

You can use any other storage medium to transfer the Windows Easy Transfer program to the Windows Vista computer, such as a writable CD or DVD or a USB flash drive, as long as the Vista computer is capable of reading it.

Figure 2-22

The Install Windows Easy
Transfer on your old computer
page

8. Switch to the Windows Vista computer, click Start > All Programs > Accessories, and then select Windows Explorer. A Windows Explorer window appears.

9. Browse to the location on the network you selected earlier and double click the Windows Easy Transfer shortcut. An Open File—Security Warning dialog box appears.

10. Click Open. A User Account Control message box appears.

11. Click Continue. The *Welcome to Windows Easy Transfer* page appears.

12. Click Next. The *What do you want to use to transfer items to your new computer?* page appears.

13. Click A network. The *Which computer are you using now?* page appears, as shown in Figure 2-23.

Figure 2-23

The Which computer are you
using now? page

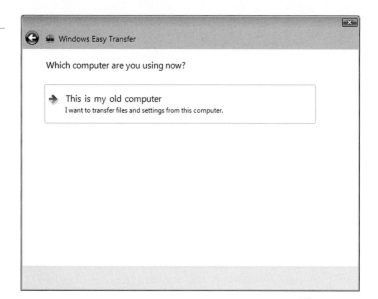

> **TAKE NOTE** ★   Now that you are running Windows Easy Transfer on Windows Vista, the program recognizes that this must be the old computer.

14. Click This is my old computer. The *Go to your new computer and enter your Windows Easy Transfer key* page appears, as shown in Figure 2-24. Take note of the key number that appears.

Figure 2-24

The Go to your new computer and enter your Windows Easy Transfer key page

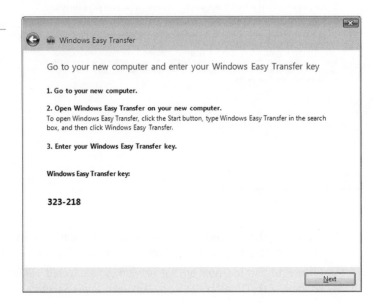

15. Switch back to the new computer and click Next. The *Enter your Windows Easy Transfer key* page appears, as shown in Figure 2-25.

Figure 2-25

The Enter your Windows Easy Transfer key page

16. In the Windows Easy Transfer Key text box, type the key that appeared on your old computer and click Next. The new computer establishes a connection with the old computer, scans it for files and settings it can transfer, and displays the results in the *Choose what to transfer* page, as shown in Figure 2-26.

Figure 2-26

The Choose what to transfer page

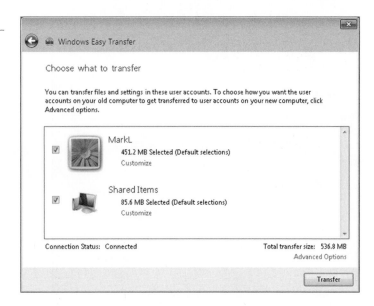

17. Select the items you want to copy to the new computer and click Transfer. The program transfers the selected items to the new computer, and then the *Your transfer is complete* page appears, as shown in Figure 2-27.

Figure 2-27

The Your transfer is complete page

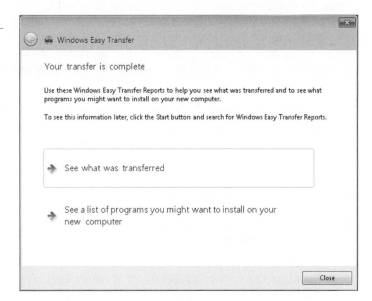

18. Click See what was transferred. A Windows Easy Transfer Reports window appears, as shown in Figure 2-28.

Figure 2-28

A Windows Easy Transfer
Reports window

19. Close the Windows Easy Transfer Reports window and, on the *Your transfer is complete* page, click Close.

20. On the Windows Vista computer, on the *The transfer is complete* page, click Close.

Performing Migration Scenario 2

Alice has a Windows Vista computer that she has been sharing with her roommates for several years. She recently purchased the retail version of Windows 7, which came bundled with a free external hard drive. Alice wants to install Windows 7 on her existing computer, retaining the files and settings she has accrued and omitting the files and settings created by her roommates. However, she does not want to perform an upgrade, because she has recently noticed that the computer's performance has degraded, possibly due to file fragmentation and registry clutter.

In this scenario, you perform a wipe-and-load migration using the external hard drive to temporarily store the files and settings from the Windows Vista operating system. Then, after performing a clean installation of Windows 7, you transfer the files and settings from the external drive back to the computer.

⊙ PERFORM MIGRATION SCENARIO 2

GET READY. Plug the external hard drive into a USB port on the computer and make sure that it is connected and operating. Then make a secondary backup of the client's important files as a safety measure, in case there is a problem with the migration procedure.

1. Download the appropriate version of Windows Easy Transfer from the Microsoft Download Center and install it by executing the Microsoft Update Standalone Installer (.msu) file.

TAKE NOTE*

Windows Easy Transfer is not accessible from the Windows 7 installation disk as it is from the Windows Vista disk. To perform a wipe-and-load migration without an existing computer running Windows 7, you have to download Windows Easy Transfer from the Microsoft Download Center Web site. The http://windows.microsoft.com/en-us/windows7/ products/features/windows-easy-transfer page has links to versions for Windows Vista and Windows XP in 32-bit and 64-bit versions.

2. Click Start > All Programs > Windows Easy Transfer 7. A User Account Control message box appears.

3. Click Continue. The *Welcome to Windows Easy Transfer* page appears.

4. Click Next. The *What do you want to use to transfer items to your new computer?* page appears.

5. Click An external hard disk or USB flash drive. The *Which computer are you using now?* page appears.

6. Click This is my old computer. The program scans the computer for files and settings it can transfer and displays the results in the *Choose what to transfer from this computer* page.

7. Select the items you want to copy to the new computer and click Next. The *Save your files and settings for transfer* page appears, as shown in Figure 2-29.

Figure 2-29

The Save your files and settings
for transfer page

8. In the Password and Confirm Password text boxes, type a password to protect the data to be transferred and click Save. The *Save Your Easy Transfer File* combo box appears.

9. Browse to the external hard drive and click Save. The program transfers the selected items to the external drive and the *These files and settings have been saved for your transfer* page appears, as shown in Figure 2-30.

Figure 2-30

The These files and settings
have been saved for your
transfer page

10. Click Next. The *Your transfer file is complete* page appears, specifying the name and location of the file containing the transferred data.

11. Click Next. The *Windows Easy Transfer is complete on this computer* page appears.

12. Click Close.

13. Disconnect the external hard drive from the computer.

14. Perform a clean installation of Windows 7 on the computer, as detailed earlier in this Lesson, erasing the partition on which Windows Vista was installed.

15. Reconnect the external hard drive to the computer and make sure that it is functioning.

16. On the newly installed Windows 7 computer, click Start > All Programs > Accessories > System Tools and select Windows Easy Transfer. The *Welcome to Windows Easy Transfer* page appears.

17. Click Next. The *What do you want to use to transfer items to your new computer?* page appears.

18. Click An external hard disk or USB flash drive. The *Which computer are you using now?* page appears.

19. Click This is my new computer. The *Has Windows Easy Transfer already saved your files from your old computer to an external hard disk or USB flash drive?* page appears.

20. Click Yes. The Open an Easy Transfer File combo box appears.

21. Browse to the external hard drive, select the Windows Easy Transfer—Items From Old Computer file and click Open. The *Enter the password you used to help protect your transfer file and start the transfer* page appears, as shown in Figure 2-31.

Figure 2-31

The Enter the password you used to help protect your transfer file and start the transfer page

22. Type the password you specified earlier and click Next. The *Choose what to transfer from this computer* page appears.

23. Select the items you want to copy to the Windows 7 computer and click Transfer. The program transfers the selected items to the computer, and then the *Your transfer is complete* page appears.

24. Click See what was transferred. A *Windows Easy Transfer Reports* window appears.

25. Close the Windows Easy Transfer Reports window and, on the *Your transfer is complete* page, click Close.

Using User State Migration Tool

The User State Migration Tool (USMT) has the same basic capabilities as Windows Easy Transfer. The primary difference between the two is that USMT is a command line program that lacks a graphical interface.

USMT's command line interface is not a disadvantage, although individuals who prefer graphical utilities might perceive it as such. The command line interface enables administrators to incorporate USMT tasks into scripts, making it more suitable for large-scale deployments than Windows Easy Transfer.

For example, Microsoft Deployment Toolkit 2010 enables administrators to incorporate migration tasks into an installation script called a task sequence. A properly configured task sequence can save the user data on a workstation to a network share, perform a clean Windows 7 installation on the workstation, and then load the saved user data, all with little or no user interaction required.

USMT includes two separate command line programs: Scanstate.exe, which saves user profile data; and Loadstate.exe, which restores previously saved user profile data. Each program supports a variety of command line parameters that enable you to specify a storage location and control what data the programs save and restore.

In addition to the command line interface, the other big advantage to using USMT for large-scale deployments is the ability to customize the migration process. USMT uses XML (Extensible Markup Language) files to control the migration process. The default XML files supplied with the program enable it to migrate the most common user data sources, but it is also possible to create your own XML files to migrate specific application settings and data.

■ Upgrading to Windows 7

THE BOTTOM LINE

To the workstation user, performing an in-place upgrade to Windows 7 is a relatively simple procedure, but the activities the Setup program performs behind the scenes are highly complex.

CERTIFICATION READY?
Upgrade to Windows 7 from previous versions of Windows.
1.2

During the upgrade process, the Setup program creates a new Windows folder and installs the Windows 7 operating system files into it. This is only half of the process, however. The program must then migrate the applications, files, and settings from the old OS. This calls for a variety of procedures, such as importing the user profiles, copying all pertinent settings from the old registry to the new one, locating applications and data files, and updating device drivers with new versions.

While in-place upgrades often proceed smoothly, the complexity of the upgrade process and the large number of variables involved means that there are many things that can potentially go wrong. To minimize the risks involved, it is important for a technical specialist to take the upgrade process seriously, prepare the system beforehand, and have the ability to troubleshoot any problems that might arise. The following sections discuss these subjects in greater detail.

TAKE NOTE*

An in-place upgrade from Windows Vista to Windows 7 is much more complex than an upgrade from one Windows 7 edition to another. All of the Windows 7 editions use the same basic core files and architecture. Upgrades are primarily a matter of activating additional applications, which is not as invasive or dangerous.

X REF

For more information on Windows 7's hardware requirements, and on running the Upgrade Advisor program, see Lesson 1, "Introducing Windows 7."

Preparing to Upgrade

Before you begin an in-place upgrade to Windows 7, you should perform a number of preliminary procedures to ensure that the process goes smoothly and that the user data is protected.

Consider the following before you perform any upgrade to Windows 7:

- **Run Upgrade Advisor:** To be sure that the computer is capable of running the Windows 7 edition that you plan on installing, run Upgrade Advisor and take note of its advisories regarding the computer's hardware and software. If it is necessary to perform hardware upgrades, do so before installing Windows 7, making sure that the new hardware is operational before proceeding.

- **Check hardware compatibility:** The Upgrade Advisor program can point out hardware inadequacies in the computer, especially regarding Windows 7 system requirements. If it is necessary to upgrade hardware, make certain that the products you purchase are certified for use with Windows 7. The Upgrade Advisor program can also identify devices that might not function under Windows 7. However, it is sometimes possible to make such devices run properly with a driver or firmware upgrade. It is a good idea to perform an inventory of the computer's primary components and consider the age and capabilities of each one before you perform the upgrade. It is always best to locate potential hardware incompatibilities before you perform the upgrade procedure.

- **Search for updated drivers:** As part of your hardware inventory, be sure to consider the age of the device drivers installed on the computer. Check hardware manufacturers' Web sites for driver updates, especially those that are specifically intended to provide support for Windows 7. In some cases it might be preferable to install the new drivers while Vista is still running, but if the manufacturer provides separate Vista and Windows 7 drivers wait until you have installed Windows 7. Even if no updates are available, it is a good idea to gather all of the drivers for the computer's hardware together and copy them to a removable storage medium, such as a writable CD or flash drive. This way, if the Setup program requires a driver during the upgrade process, you have it available.

- **Check application compatibility:** Upgrade Advisor can point out possible application compatibility problems, but you can sometimes solve these problems by updating or upgrading the application. Create an inventory of the software products installed on the computer and check the manufacturers' Web sites for updates, availability of upgrades, and announcements regarding support for Windows 7. For example, if the computer is running Microsoft Office, use the Office Online Web site to download the latest updates. Check the applications' system requirements as well. Install any free updates that are available and consider the need for paid upgrades. In an enterprise environment, you should test all applications for Windows 7 compatibility, no matter what the manufacturer says, before you perform any operating system upgrades. However, for stand-alone clients, testing usually isn't practical. The best you can do is to inform the user that there might be problems with specific applications and warn them that there might be additional costs involved for new versions or different products.

- **Check disk space:** Make sure that there is at least 15 gigabytes of disk space free on the partition where the old operating system is installed. During the upgrade procedure, sufficient disk space is needed to hold both operating systems simultaneously. After the upgrade is complete, you can remove the old Vista files, freeing up some additional space.

- **Ensure computer functionality:** Make sure that Windows Vista is running properly on the computer before you begin the upgrade process. You must start an in-place upgrade from within Windows Vista, so you cannot count on Windows 7 to correct any problems that prevent the computer from starting or running the Setup program.

- **Perform a full backup:** Before you perform any upgrade procedure you should back up the entire system, or at the very least the essential user files. You can use Windows Easy

Transfer if no other tool is available. Removable hard drives make this a simple process, even if the client does not have a suitable backup device in the computer.

- **Purchase Windows 7:** Be sure to purchase the appropriate Windows 7 edition for the upgrade, and have the installation disk and product key handy.

Upgrading from Windows Vista

Once you complete the steps in the previous section, you are ready to perform an in-place upgrade from Windows Vista to Windows 7.

To upgrade a Windows Vista computer to Windows 7 while preserving all files and settings, use the following procedure.

 UPGRADE WINDOWS VISTA TO WINDOWS 7

GET READY. Turn on the computer running Windows Vista and make sure you have the Windows 7 installation disk and product key ready.

1. Insert the Windows 7 installation disk into the DVD drive. An Autoplay dialog box appears.
2. Click Run setup.exe. A User Account Control message box appears.
3. Click Continue. The Install Windows screen appears.
4. Click Install now. The Get important updates for *installation* page appears.
5. Click Do not get the latest updates for installation. The *Please read the license terms* page appears.

TAKE NOTE*

If the computer is connected to the Internet, you might want to click *Go online to get the latest updates for installation* to ensure that the computer's drivers and other software are up to date.

6. Select the I accept the license terms check box and click Next. The *Which type of installation do you want?* page appears, as shown in Figure 2-32.

Figure 2-32

The Which type of installation do you want? page

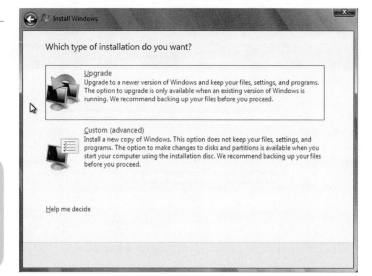

TAKE NOTE*

Note that unlike the previous Windows 7 installation procedures in this Lesson, the Upgrade option is activated.

7. Click Upgrade. The *Upgrading Windows* page appears.
8. After a delay, during which the Setup program installs Windows 7, the computer reboots and the *Type your Windows product key* page appears.

TAKE NOTE

Depending on the applications installed and the complexity of the system configuration, an in-place upgrade can take anywhere from several minutes to several hours.

9. Type your product key in the text box provided and click Next. The *Help protect your computer and improve Windows automatically* page appears.

10. Select one of the three options specifying what security settings you want the computer to use. The *Review your time and date settings* page appears.

11. From the Time Zone drop-down list, select the time zone in which the computer will be running and then click Next. The *Select your computer's current location* page appears.

12. Click the appropriate option specifying the computer's normal location. A *Welcome* page appears as Windows 7 prepares and loads the desktop.

Upgrading Windows 7 Editions

One of the main advantages of the new architecture that Microsoft devised for Windows 7 is that it makes upgrades to other editions incredibly simple.

There are three ways to upgrade a Windows 7 computer to another edition, as follows:

TAKE NOTE *

While it is possible to upgrade Windows 7 to a different edition, you cannot upgrade a 32-bit version of Windows 7 to a 64-bit version, or vice versa.

- **Purchase a retail version of a higher level Windows 7 edition:** When you purchase a full retail version of Windows 7 at a higher level, you can perform an in-place upgrade just as you would on a computer running Windows Vista.
- **Purchase a Windows 7 product upgrade package from a retailer:** The Windows 7 product upgrade package does not contain any software at all, just the upgrade key you need to activate the higher-level version of Windows 7.
- **Use the Windows Anytime Upgrade tool included with Windows 7:** The Windows Anytime Upgrade feature in Windows 7 enables you to select and purchase the upgrade key for a higher-level edition of Windows 7 in less than 10 minutes.

USE WINDOWS ANYTIME UPGRADE

GET READY. Log on to Windows 7, using an account with administrative privileges.

1. Click Start > Control Panel. The Control Panel window appears.
2. Click System and Security > Windows Anytime Upgrade. The Windows Anytime Upgrade Wizard appears, displaying the *How do you want to begin?* page, as shown in Figure 2-33.

Figure 2-33

The How do you want to begin? page

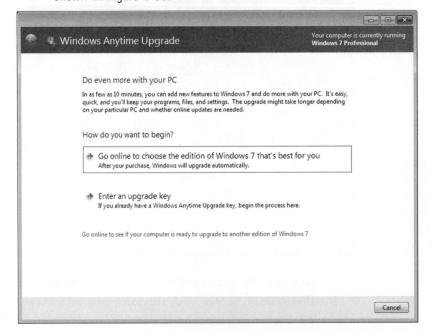

3. Click Go online to choose the edition of Windows 7 that's best for you. A *Compare* page appears showing the upgrades that are available to you, as shown in Figure 2-34.

Figure 2-34

The Compare page

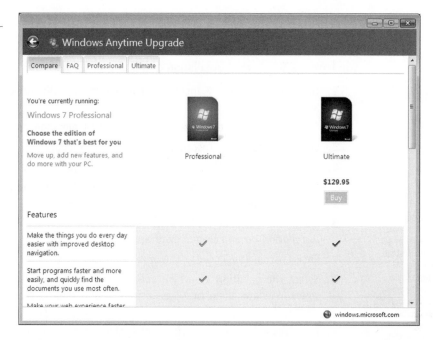

4. Click the Buy button for the upgrade that you want to purchase. A Microsoft Store Wizard appears to step you through the process of purchasing the upgrade.

5. Follow the instructions to purchase and install the upgrade.

■ Performing a Dual Boot Installation

THE BOTTOM LINE

When a user wants to test Windows 7 without making a full commitment, or needs to maintain an older operating system for compatibility with specific applications, a dual boot environment can be ideal.

TAKE NOTE*

If you have sufficient disk space for a Windows 7 installation on your computer's only hard disk, but you have only one partition on that disk, there is no way to create a new primary partition out of that disk space using the tools in Windows Vista or XP without erasing the entire drive. You must use a third-party tool, such as Norton Partition Magic, to create the partition.

Although it has drawbacks, mainly in terms of disk space, many users rely on a dual boot environment to provide access to two independent operating system installations. In a dual boot environment, both operating systems are completely independent of each other, so restrictions regarding upgrade paths do not apply. You can dual boot any edition of Windows 7 with Windows Vista or Windows XP.

To create a dual boot environment, you must have all of the following:

- **Two disk partitions:** Windows does not support multiple operating systems on a single disk partition. Therefore, you must have two partitions to dual boot, one for the computer's original operating system, and one for the Windows 7 installation. In addition, be aware that Windows 7 must be installed on a primary partition, not on a logical disk in an extended partition. Make sure that the partition where you intend to install Windows 7 has sufficient disk space for a full installation.

- **Two full product licenses:** From a licensing standpoint, a dual boot environment is a full Windows 7 installation, not an upgrade. Do not purchase an upgrade license for Window 7, which requires Windows Vista or XP to be running to start the installation. As far as Windows 7 knows, it is the sole operating system on the computer.

- **A full system backup:** Dual booting is something of a hack, and not an officially supported environment. As a result, the behavior of the operating systems can sometimes be unpredictable. Be sure that you have a full backup of your existing installation before you attempt the following procedure.

INSTALL WINDOWS 7 IN A DUAL BOOT ENVIRONMENT

GET READY. Turn on the computer running Windows Vista or Windows XP and make sure you have the Windows 7 installation disk and product key ready.

1. Insert the Windows 7 installation disk into the DVD drive. An Autoplay dialog box appears.

2. Click Run setup.exe. A User Account Control message box appears.

3. Click Continue. The Install Windows screen appears.

4. Click Install now. The *Get important updates for installation* page appears.

5. Click Do not get the latest updates for installation. The *Please read the license terms* page appears.

6. Select the I accept the license terms check box and click Next. The *Which type of installation do you want?* page appears.

7. Click Custom (advanced). The *Where do you want to install Windows?* page appears.

8. Select the partition on which you want to install Windows 7 (not the partition where Windows Vista or XP is installed) and then click Next. The *Installing Windows* page appears.

9. After several minutes, during which the Setup program installs Windows 7, the computer reboots twice and the *Set Up Windows* page appears.

10. Complete the installation process by following the "Perform a Clean Installation" procedure described earlier in this lesson, starting at Step 10.

⚠ **WARNING** If you select the partition on which Windows Vista or XP is installed, you will not get a dual boot environment. Instead, the Windows 7 Setup program will rename the Windows folder to Windows.old and create a new Windows folder for the Windows 7 files. This is still a clean installation, however. The Setup program will not import the Vista or XP files and settings, and once the process is completed, you will no longer be able to boot to Windows Vista or XP.

Rebooting the system after completing the Windows 7 installation process causes the screen shown in Figure 2-35 to appear. From this menu, you select the operating system you want to start. "Earlier Version of Windows" refers to Windows Vista or XP. To switch between operating systems, you have to completely shut down the one that is running, and then restart the computer.

Figure 2-35

The Windows Boot Manager page

SKILL SUMMARY

IN THIS LESSON YOU LEARNED:

- Windows 7 includes a new preinstallation environment called Windows PE.

- In a clean installation, you boot from the Windows 7 Setup disk and create or select a blank partition where Windows 7 will reside.

- It is possible to migrate files and settings from an existing Windows installation to a newly installed Windows 7 installation using either Windows Easy Transfer or User State Migration Tool.

- Windows 7 supports in-place upgrades only from Windows Vista or another Windows 7 edition.

- To perform an in-place upgrade, you must launch the Windows 7 Setup program from within Windows Vista.

- To upgrade from one Windows 7 edition to another, you can use the Windows Anytime Upgrade tool found in the Windows 7 Control Panel.

- A dual boot installation is one in which two operating systems are installed on separate disk partitions, providing access to both at boot time.

■ Knowledge Assessment

Fill in the Blank

Complete the following sentences by writing the correct word or words in the blanks provided.

1. Windows Easy Transfer supports two types of migrations, called _____ and _____.

2. When a serious problem occurs with Windows 7, you might be able to repair it by starting the Windows PE operating system and running diagnostic tools. In this scenario, Windows PE is called by another name, which is _____.

3. To migrate user profile information from one computer to another, you can use either _____ or _____.

4. A computer running Windows PE will automatically reboot after _____.

5. Windows Easy Transfer supports migration using any removable storage medium common to the two computers except _____.

6. The Windows 7 component that enables the computer to support more than one language is called the _____.

7. The reason it is possible to remove the Windows 7 installation disk to supply the Setup program with drivers is that Windows PE runs on a _____.

8. To upgrade Windows XP to Windows 7, you must perform a _____.

9. The files and settings that Windows Easy Transfer can migrate to a Windows 7 computer are primarily stored in _____.

10. As a preinstallation environment, Windows PE is a vast improvement over MS-DOS because it includes internal support for _____ and _____.

True / False

Circle T if the statement is true or F if the statement is false.

T | F 1. Windows PE is the latest version of the MS-DOS operating system.

T | F 2. It is possible to perform an in-place upgrade from any 32-bit version of Windows Vista to the 32-bit version of Windows 7.

T | F 3. To create a dual boot environment with Windows 7, you must have two primary partitions on your computer.

T | F 4. Windows 7 Home Premium users can perform in-place upgrades to Windows 7 Professional without obtaining a new installation disk.

T | F 5. One way to perform an in-place upgrade from Windows Vista to Windows 7 is to boot from the Windows 7 installation disk, choose the Custom option, and then select the partition on which Windows Vista is installed.

T | F 6. To create a Windows 7 workstation that supports multiple languages, you must begin by installing the English language version.

T | F 7. It is not possible to "upgrade" a computer running the Windows 7 Ultimate edition to the Enterprise edition without performing a clean installation.

T | F 8. Windows XP users are eligible to purchase an upgrade version of Windows 7, but they cannot perform an in-place upgrade.

T | F 9. To migrate the user profiles of multiple user accounts located on the same computer, you must use the User State Migration Tool.

T | F 10. Any program that can run on Windows 7 can run on Windows PE.

Review Questions

1. Give two detailed reasons why Windows PE is a better installation environment for Windows 7 than MS-DOS.

2. Explain the difference between a side-by-side migration and a wipe-and-load migration, using Windows Easy Transfer.

■ Case Scenarios

Scenario 2-1: Upgrading Windows 7 Editions

You are working as a desktop support technician at a computer store, and a customer approaches you with a laptop computer he purchased three years ago. The computer came with Windows XP Home Basic installed on it, and the customer now wants to upgrade to Windows 7 and also use the computer to log on to the Active Directory Domain Services domain at his office. He knows he cannot do this with the Windows 7 Home Premium edition, so he wants you to upgrade the computer to Windows 7 Professional, without affecting his files and settings. Explain in detail the procedure you would have to use to fulfill the customer's request.

Scenario 2-2: Updating Graphics

When you run Windows Upgrade Advisor on a client's computer, the report's only recommendation is that you upgrade the graphics adapter after you upgrade the operating system to Windows 7. What is likely to be the result immediately after you install Windows 7 on the computer and before you upgrade the graphics adapter?

4 LESSON

Working with Disks and Devices

OBJECTIVE DOMAIN MATRIX

TECHNOLOGY SKILL	OBJECTIVE DOMAIN	OBJECTIVE NUMBER
Working with VHDs	Configure a VHD.	2.4
Working with Devices and Drivers	Configure devices.	3.1
Working with Disks	Manage disks.	7.2

KEY TERMS

basic disk

Diskpart.exe

dynamic disk

exFAT

FAT (file allocation table)

FAT32

globally unique identifier (GUID)

GUID (globally unique identifier) partition table (GPT)

master boot record (MBR)

mirrored volume

native boot

NTFS

simple volume

spanned volume

striped volume

Virtual Hard Disk (VHD)

■ Working with Disks

↓ THE BOTTOM LINE

Hard disks are nearly always the primary storage medium in a computer running Windows 7, but in many cases, technician specialists must prepare a hard disk to store data by performing certain tasks before the computer can use it. Once you prepare the hard disk, you can keep the data stored on the disk secure with tools and features provided by Windows 7.

When you install Windows 7 on a computer, the setup program automatically performs all of the preparation tasks for the hard disks in the computer. However, adding another disk is a common upgrade, and after you install the hardware, you must perform the following tasks before the user can begin storing data on it:

- **Select a partitioning style:** In Windows 7, two hard disk partition styles are available for both x86- and x64-based computers. The *master boot record (MBR)* partition style has been around as long as Windows and is still the default partition style. *GUID (globally unique identifier)* partition table (GPT) has been around for a while also, but no x86 version of Windows prior to Vista supports it. (Windows XP Professional x64 edition does support GPT.) You must choose one of these partition styles for a drive; you cannot use both.

- **Select a disk type:** Two disk types are available in Windows 7—basic disks and dynamic disks. Both the MBR and the GPT partition styles support basic and dynamic disks. You cannot use both types on the same disk drive. You have to decide which is best for the computer.

- **Divide the disk into partitions or volumes:** Although many professionals use the terms partition and volume interchangeably, it is correct to refer to creating partitions on basic disks, and volumes on dynamic disks.

- **Format the volumes with a file system:** Because of the high capacities of the hard drives on the market today, NTFS is the preferred file system for Windows 7. However, the *FAT (File Allocation Table)* file system is also available, in the form of *FAT32* and *exFAT*.

CERTIFICATION READY?
Manage disks.
7.2

Understanding Partition Styles

The term *partition style* refers to the method that Windows operating systems use to organize partitions on the disk.

There are two hard disk partition styles that you can use in Windows 7:

- **Master boot record (MBR):** This is the default partition style for x86-based and x64-based computers.
- **GUID (globally unique identifier) partition table (GPT):** First introduced in Windows Vista, you can now use the GPT partition style on x86-, as well as x64-based, Windows 7 computers.

Before Windows Vista, all x86-based computers used the MBR partition style only. Computers based on the x64 platform could use either the MBR or GPT partition style, as long as the GPT disk was not the boot disk.

MBR uses a partition table to point to the locations of the partitions on the disk. Windows selected this style automatically on x86-based workstation computers because, prior to Windows Vista, this was the only style available to them. The MBR disk partitioning style supports volumes up to 2 terabytes in size, and up to either four primary partitions or three primary partitions and one extended partition. Data critical to platform operations is stored in hidden (unpartitioned) sectors.

Table 4-1 lists the Windows operating systems that can use either the MBR or the GPT partition style for their disks:

Table 4-1

Windows Operating Systems Supporting MBR and GPT Partition Styles

OPERATING SYSTEM	x86-BASED	x64-BASED	IA-64-BASED
Windows XP	No	Yes	Yes
Windows Server 2003 SP1 (or later)	Yes	Yes	Yes
Windows Vista	Yes	Yes	N/A
Windows Server 2008	Yes	Yes	Yes
Windows 7	Yes	Yes	N/A
Windows Server 2008 R2	Yes	Yes	Yes

+ MORE INFORMATION

As far as the Windows 7 disk management tools are concerned, there is no difference between creating partitions or volumes in MBR and in GPT. You create partitions and volumes for both by using the same tools in the same ways.

Bear in mind, however, that unless the computer's architecture provides support for an Extensible Firmware Interface (EFI)-based boot partition, it is not possible to boot from GPT disks. In this case, the operating system must reside on an MBR disk, and GPT must reside on an entirely separate, nonbootable disk, used for data storage only.

One of the ways that GPT differs from MBR is that data critical to platform operation is stored in partitions rather than in hidden sectors. Additionally, GPT partitioned disks use redundant primary and backup partition tables for improved integrity. Although GPT specifications permit an unlimited number of partitions, the Windows implementation is restricted to 128 partitions per disk. The GPT disk partitioning style supports volumes up to 18 exabytes in size (1 exabyte = 1 billion gigabytes, or 2^{60} bytes).

Table 4-2 compares some of the characteristics of the MBR and GPT partition styles.

Table 4-2

MBR and GPT Partition Style Comparison

MASTER BOOT RECORD (MBR)	GUID PARTITION TABLE (GPT)
Supports up to four primary partitions or three primary partitions and one extended partition, with unlimited logical drives on the extended partition	Supports up to 128 primary partitions
Supports volumes up to 2 terabytes in size	Supports volumes up to 18 exabytes in size
Data critical to platform operations is stored in hidden (unpartitioned) sectors	Data critical to platform operation is stored in partitions rather than in hidden sectors
Replication and CRC are not features of MBR's partition table	Replication and cyclical redundancy check (CRC) protection of the partition table provide increased reliability

Understanding Disk Types

Windows 7 supports two disk types: basic disks and dynamic disks.

Most Windows computers use basic disks because they are the easiest to manage. A **basic disk** uses primary partitions, extended partitions, and logical drives to organize data. A primary partition appears to the operating system as though it is a physically separate disk and can host an operating system. A primary partition that hosts an operating system is marked as the *active partition*.

During the Windows 7 operating system installation, the setup program creates a *system partition* and a *boot partition*. The system partition contains hardware-related files that the computer uses to start. The boot partition contains the operating system files, which are stored in the Windows folder. In Windows 7, the system partition is the active partition, which the computer uses when starting.

When you use the Disk Management snap-in to work with basic disks using the MBR partition style, you can create up to three primary partitions. The fourth partition you create must be an extended partition, after which you can create as many logical drives as you need from the space in the extended partition. You can format and assign drive letters to logical drives, but they cannot host an operating system. Table 4-3 compares some of the characteristics of primary and extended partitions.

Table 4-3

Comparison of Primary and Extended Partitions

PRIMARY PARTITIONS	EXTENDED PARTITIONS
A primary partition functions as if it is a physically separate disk and can host an operating system.	Extended partitions cannot host an operating system.
A primary partition can be marked as an active partition. You can have only one active partition per hard disk. The system BIOS looks to the active partition for the boot files it uses to start the operating system.	You cannot mark an extended partition as an active partition.
You can create up to four primary partitions or three primary partitions and one extended partition.	A basic disk can contain only one extended partition, but an unlimited number of logical partitions.
You format each primary partition and assign a unique drive letter.	You do not format the extended partition itself, but the logical drives it contains. You assign a unique drive letter to each of the logical drives.

When you use DiskPart, a command-line utility included with Windows 7, to manage a basic disk, you can create up to four primary partitions or three primary partitions and one extended partition.

TAKE NOTE *

The DiskPart command-line utility contains a superset of the commands that the Disk Management snap-in supports. In other words, DiskPart can do everything Disk Management can do, and more. The Disk Management snap-in prohibits you from unintentionally performing actions that may result in data loss. DiskPart does not have the built-in protections that Disk Management possesses, and so does not prohibit you from performing such actions. For this reason, Microsoft recommends that only advanced personnel use DiskPart and that they use it infrequently and with due caution because, unlike Disk Management, DiskPart provides absolute control over partitions and volumes.

The alternative to using a basic disk is to convert it to a **dynamic disk**. The process of converting a basic disk to a dynamic disk creates a single partition that occupies the entire disk. You can then create an unlimited number of volumes out of the space in that partition. The advantage of using dynamic disks is that they support several different types of volumes, as described in the next section.

Understanding Volume Types

Dynamic disks can support five types of volumes: simple, spanned, striped, mirrored, and RAID-5 (Redundant Array of Independent Disks, level 5). Windows 7 only supports four of these volume types, however: simple, spanned, striped, and mirrored.

A dynamic disk is able to contain an unlimited number of volumes that function like primary partitions on a basic disk. However, you cannot access a dynamic disk from any operating system instance other than the one that converted it from basic to dynamic, which means you cannot use dynamic disks on multiboot systems.

When you create a volume on a dynamic disk in Windows 7, you can choose from the following four volume types:

- *Simple volume:* Consists of space from a single disk. Once you have created a simple volume, you can later extend it to multiple disks to create a spanned or striped volume, as long as it is not a system volume or boot volume. Windows 7 supports simple volumes on both basic and dynamic disks.

- *Spanned volume:* Consists of space from at least 2, to a maximum of 32, physical disks, all of which must be dynamic disks. A spanned volume is essentially a method for combining the space from multiple dynamic disks into a single large volume. Windows 7 writes to the spanned volume by filling all of the space on the first disk, and then filling each of the additional disks in turn. You can extend a spanned volume at any time by adding additional disk space. Creating a spanned volume does not increase the read/write performance, nor does it provide fault tolerance. In fact, if a single physical disk in the spanned volume fails, all of the data in the entire volume is lost.

- *Striped volume:* Consists of space from at least 2, to a maximum of 32, physical disks, all of which must be dynamic disks. The difference between a striped volume and a spanned volume is that in a striped volume, the system writes data one stripe at a time to each successive disk in the volume. Striping provides improved performance because each disk drive in the array has time to seek the location of its next stripe while the other drives are writing. Striped volumes do not provide fault tolerance, and you cannot extend them after creation. If a single physical disk in the striped volume fails, all of the data in the entire volume is lost.

- *Mirrored volume:* Consists of an equal amount of space from 2 disks, both of which must be dynamic disks. In a mirrored volume, each disk holds an identical copy of the data written to the volume as a fault tolerance measure. If one disk fails, the data remains accessible from the second disk. Because of the data redundancy, a mirrored volume only provides half as much storage space as any of the other volume types.

TAKE NOTE*

The disk volume limitations described here are those of Windows 7 itself. It is also possible to implement these disk technologies using third-party hardware and software products that have their own capabilities and limitations. For example, while Windows 7 does not support RAID-5, there are many disk adapter products on the market that enable you to create RAID volumes of various types on computers running Windows 7.

Windows 7 does not support dynamic disks in the following environments:

- portable computers
- removable disks
- detachable disks that use the Universal Serial Bus (USB) or IEEE 1394 (FireWire) interface
- disks connected to shared Small Computer System Interface (SCSI) buses
- computers running Windows 7 Starter, Home Basic, or Home Premium

The type of disk configuration you choose for a Windows 7 computer depends on the user's needs. While stand-alone systems for home or small business users might benefit from striped, spanned, or mirrored volumes, for most Windows 7 workstations in an enterprise environment, basic disks are adequate. If the client's computer stores data that requires additional performance or protection against failure, dynamic disks can fill the bill.

Understanding File Systems

To organize and store data or programs on a hard drive, you must install a file system. A file system is the underlying disk drive structure that enables you to store information on your computer. You install file systems by formatting a partition or volume on the hard disk.

In Windows 7, there are two basic file system options to choose from: NTFS and FAT. *NTFS* is the preferred file system for Windows 7; its main benefits being improved support for larger hard drives and better security in the form of encryption and permissions that restrict access by unauthorized users.

Because the FAT file systems lack the security that NTFS provides, any user who gains access to your computer can read any file without restriction. Additionally, most of the various FAT file systems have disk size limitations that render them impractical.

The FAT file systems that Windows 7 supports are as follows:

- *FAT:* The original 16-bit FAT file system for hard disks, also known as FAT16, is limited to partitions no larger than 4 GB, which makes it virtually useless for today's computers.
- *FAT32:* Using the 32-bit version of FAT, called FAT32, Windows 7 can create partitions up to 32 GB in size, with individual files up to 4 GB. Although these limits at one time seemed outlandishly large, they make FAT32 an impractical file system solution on computers today. The 32 GB maximum partition size is a deliberate restriction in Windows 7, not an inherent limitation of FAT32. In fact, Windows 7 can access FAT32 partitions up to 2 TB in size; it just can't create them. This limitation is intended to prevent Windows performance degradation caused by large FAT32 partitions.
- *exFAT:* Introduced in Windows Vista SP1, the Extended File Allocation Table (exFAT) file system, also known as FAT64, is a 64-bit FAT implementation that is intended primarily for large USB flash drives. The theoretical limitations of exFAT are partitions and files of up to 64 zettabytes in size. (1 zettabyte equals 1 billion terabytes or 10^{21} bytes.) The recommended maximum size for an exFAT partition in Windows 7 is 512 TB. The exFAT file system does not support the encryption and permission features found in NTFS, and is therefore not recommended for use on Windows 7 hard disks.

When you create or format a partition or volume using the Disk Management snap-in, the interface displays only the file system options that are available to you, based on the size of the partition or volume. Because of these size limitations, the only viable reason for using any of the FAT file systems on Windows 7 hard disks is the need to multiboot the computer with an operating system that does not support NTFS.

Using the Disk Management Snap-In

Disk Management is the primary Windows 7 graphical utility for creating and manipulating hard disk partitions and volumes.

Disk Management is a Microsoft Management Console (MMC) snap-in that you use to perform disk-related tasks, such as:

- Initializing disks.
- Selecting a partition style.

TAKE NOTE *

You can also use command-line utilities, such as the DiskPart command, to perform Disk Management tasks.

- Converting basic disks to dynamic disks.
- Creating partitions and volumes.
- Extending, shrinking, and deleting volumes.
- Formatting partitions and volumes.
- Assigning and changing driver letters and paths.
- Examining and managing physical disk properties, such as disk quotas, folder sharing and error-checking.

Opening the Disk Management Snap-In

The Disk Management snap-in is a graphical tool you use to manage hard disks.

To access the Disk Management snap-in, use the following procedure:

OPEN THE DISK MANAGEMENT SNAP-IN

GET READY. Log on to Windows 7 using an account with Administrator privileges.

1. Click Start, then click Control Panel. The Control Panel window appears.
2. Click System and Security, and then, under Administrative Tools, click Create and Format Hard Disk Partitions. The Disk Management window appears, as shown in Figure 4-1.

Figure 4-1

The Disk Management window

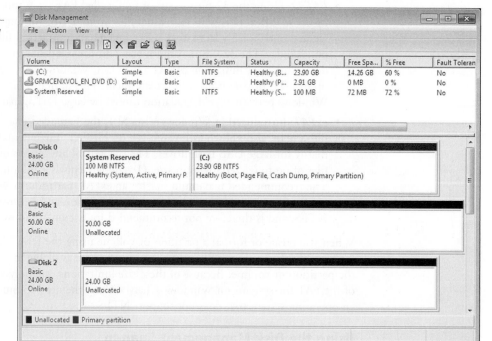

The Disk Management console is divided into two customizable panes: the Top view and the Bottom view, which display disk and volume information, respectively. Although Disk Management can display only two views at any one time, three views are available:

- **Disk List:** As shown in Figure 4-2, this view provides a summary about the physical drives in the computer. This information includes the disk number; disk type, such as basic or DVD; disk capacity; size of unallocated space; the status of the disk device, such as online, offline, or no media; the device interface, such as small computer system interface (SCSI) and integrated device electronics (IDE); and the partition style, such as MBR or GPT.

Figure 4-2

Disk Management's Disk List view

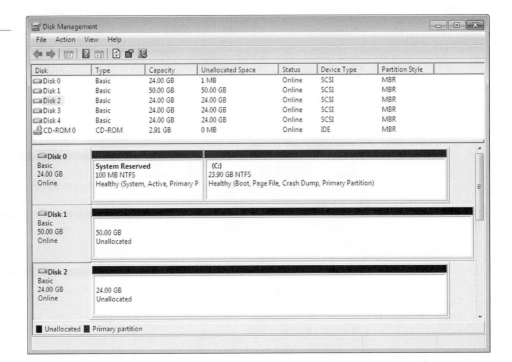

• **Volume List:** As shown in Figure 4-3, this view provides a more detailed summary of all the drives on the computer. This information includes the volume name; the volume layout, such as simple; the disk type, such as basic or dynamic; the file system in use, such as NTFS or CDFS; the hard disk status, such as healthy, failed, or formatting; the disk capacity and available free space; the percentage of the hard disk that is free; whether the hard disk is fault tolerant; and the disk overhead percentage.

Figure 4-3

Disk Management's Volume List view

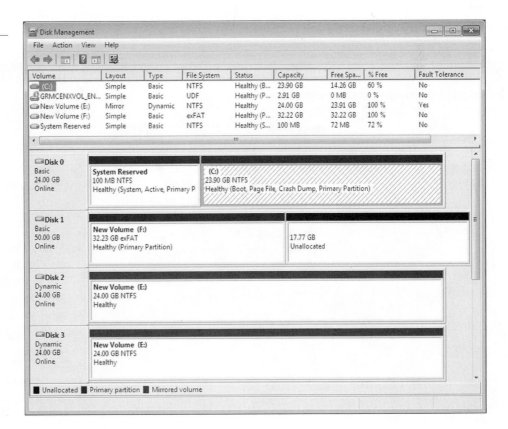

Figure 4-4

Disk Management's Graphical View

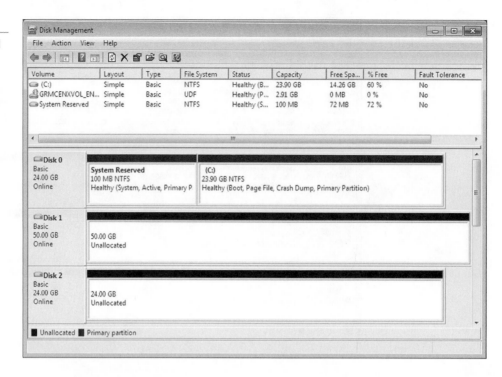

- **Graphical View:** As shown in Figure 4-4, this view displays a graphical representation of all the physical disks, partitions, volumes, and logical drives available on the computer. The graphical view is divided into two columns: the disk status column (located on the left) and the volume status column (located on the right). The information displayed in these columns and the commands available in the context menu produced by right clicking them, are shown in Table 4-4.

Table 4-4

Disk Management Graphical View Information

	DISK STATUS COLUMN	VOLUME STATUS COLUMN
Information displayed	Disk number Disk type Disk capacity Disk status	Volume name Volume size File system Volume status
Context menu commands	Convert a basic disk to a dynamic disk Convert an MBR disk to a GPT disk Create a new spanned, striped, or mirrored volume Take the disk offline Open the disk's Properties sheet	For a mounted partition or volume: • Mark a basic disk as active • Change the drive letter and paths • Format the partition or volume • Extend the volume • Shrink the volume • Add a mirror • Delete the volume • Open the volume's Properties sheet For unallocated space: • Create a new simple volume • Create a new spanned volume • Create a new striped volume • Create a new mirrored volume • Open the disk's Properties sheet

By default, the Top view pane depicts the Volume List view, and the Bottom view pane depicts the Graphical View. You can change the views of both the Top view and Bottom view to suit your purposes by clicking the View menu, selecting either Top or Bottom, and then selecting the desired view. You can hide the Bottom view by clicking the Hidden menu option.

ANOTHER WAY

You can circumvent using Control Panel to access the Disk Management console by clicking the Start button, right clicking Computer, and then clicking Manage. The Computer Management console appears. Under the Storage node, click Disk Management. You can also click Start, and use the Run dialog box to execute the Compmgmt.msc file.

VIEWING PHYSICAL DISK PROPERTIES

To view and configure certain properties and settings for the physical disk, right click the disk status column in Disk Management's graphical view and then select Properties from the context menu. A Properties sheet appears as shown in Figure 4-5, with the General tab active.

Figure 4-5

The General tab on a disk's Properties sheet

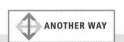

ANOTHER WAY

You can open a disk's Properties sheet by right clicking a drive in the Disk List view, and then clicking Properties.

The disk's Properties sheet contains the following tabs:

- **General:** Lists the device type, drive manufacturer, device status, and physical location of the device, including the bus number or the SCSI identifier.
- **Volumes:** Lists the volumes contained on the disk, as well as the disk number, disk type, status, partition style, capacity, unallocated space, and reserved space. If you highlight a volume in the Volumes list, you can click the Properties button to display the Properties sheet for the partition or volume.
- **Driver:** Displays driver details, and enables you to update, roll back, disable, and uninstall the driver for this device.
- **Details:** Displays a Property drop-down list that enables you to display extensive information about the disk.

VIEWING PARTITION OR VOLUME PROPERTIES

To view or configure the properties of a partition or volume, right click the volume status column in Disk Management's Graphical View and then select Properties from the context menu. The volume's Properties sheet appears, as shown in Figure 4-6.

Figure 4-6

The General tab on a volume's Properties sheet

ANOTHER WAY

You can also open a volume's Properties sheet by right clicking a drive in the Volume List view and selecting Properties from the context menu.

The Properties sheet for a partition or volume contains the following tabs:

- **General:** Lists the volume label, type of disk, file system, used space, free space, and provides a graphical representation of the total disk capacity. For drives formatted with the NTFS file system, you can choose to compress the drive and to have the Indexing Service index the disk for faster file searching. Additionally, you can run the Disk Cleanup tool to delete unnecessary files, clearing up disk space.

- **Tools:** Enables you to check the partition or volume for errors and fragmentation, and to back up files on the volume.

- **Hardware:** Enables you to view properties for all of the disk drives on the computer, including their manufacturers, bus locations, and device status.

- **Sharing:** Enables you to share the drive or specific folder(s) on the drive, set permissions for the share, and specify the type of caching for the share.

- **Security:** Enables you to set NTFS permissions to secure files and folders by assigning permissions that allow or deny users or groups to perform specific actions on that object. (Appears only on NTFS drives and in the Windows 7 Professional, Enterprise, and Ultimate editions).

- **Previous Versions:** Displays shadow copies that Windows automatically saves to your computer's hard disk as part of a restore point. A restore point represents a specific point in time of your computer's system files. You can use these previous versions of files to restore files that users have accidentally deleted or modified.

- **Quota:** Enables you to configure disk quota management on the computer, which limits the amount of disk space a user can consume. You must format the disk with the NTFS file system in order for this tab to be available.

ADDING A NEW DISK

To add a new secondary disk, shut down your computer and install or attach the new physical disk per the manufacturer's instructions. Use the following procedure to initialize the new disk.

 ADD A NEW DISK

GET READY. Log on to Windows 7 using an account with Administrator privileges.

1. Open the Disk Management snap-in.
2. If the disk does not have a disk signature, the console automatically displays the Initialize Disk dialog box, as shown in Figure 4-7.

Figure 4-7

The Initialize Disk dialog box

3. Select the partition style (MBR or GBT) that you want to use for the disk and click OK. The disk is ready to be partitioned.

CHANGING THE PARTITION STYLE

If you are running an x86-based computer, Disk Management has most likely selected the MBR partition style by default. You can quickly check which partition style the hard disk is assigned by right clicking the disk status column in the Graphical view. If the context menu contains the Convert to GPT Disk menu item, then the disk is using the MBR partition style.

You can also check the volume's information by opening the Properties sheet for disk and clicking the Volumes tab, as shown in Figure 4-8. This tab displays information such as disk type, disk status, and partition style.

Figure 4-8

The Volumes tab of a disk's Properties sheet

To convert the partition style for a disk, use the following procedure.

CONVERT THE DISK PARTITION STYLE

GET READY. Log on to Windows 7 using an account with Administrator privileges.

1. Open the Disk Management snap-in.
2. In Disk List view, right click the disk you need to convert and, from the context menu, select Convert to GPT Disk or Convert to MBR Disk. The system then proceeds with the conversion. The length of time this process takes depends on the size of the hard disk.

CONVERTING A BASIC DISK TO A DYNAMIC DISK

When you create a striped, spanned, or mirrored volume on a basic disk, the Disk Management snap-in automatically converts the basic disk (and any additional disks needed to create the volume) to a dynamic one. Therefore, it usually is not necessary to manually convert disks yourself. However, you can convert a basic disk to a dynamic disk at any time, without affecting the data stored on it. Before you convert a basic disk to a dynamic disk, you must be aware of the following conditions:

- Make sure that you have enough hard disk space available for the conversion. The basic-to-dynamic conversion will fail if the hard drive does not have at least 1 MB of free space at the end of the disk. The Disk Management console reserves this free space when creating partitions and volumes, but you cannot presume that other disk management tools you might use will also preserve that space.

- You should not convert a basic disk to a dynamic disk if you are multibooting the computer. If you convert to a dynamic disk, you will not be able to start installed operating systems from any volume on the disk except the current boot volume.

- You cannot convert removable media to dynamic disks. You can configure them only as basic disks with primary partitions.

- You cannot convert drives that use an allocation unit size (sector size) greater than 512 bytes unless you reformat the drive with a smaller sector size before the conversion.

- Once you change a basic disk to a dynamic disk, the only way you can change it back again is to back up the entire disk and delete the dynamic disk volumes. When you delete the last volume, the dynamic disk automatically reverts back to a basic disk.

To manually convert a basic disk to a dynamic disk, use the following procedure.

CONVERT A BASIC DISK TO A DYNAMIC DISK

GET READY. Log on to Windows 7 using an account with Administrator privileges.

1. Open the Disk Management snap-in.
2. In Disk List view, right click the basic disk that you want to convert and, from the context menu, select Convert to Dynamic Disk. The Convert to Dynamic Disk dialog box appears, as shown in Figure 4-9.

WARNING Converting the disk partition style is a destructive process. You can only perform the conversion on an unallocated disk, so if the disk you want to convert contains data, you must back up the disk, verify the back up, and then delete all existing partitions or volumes, before you begin the process.

Figure 4-9

The Convert to Dynamic Disk dialog box

3. Select the check boxes for the disks you want to convert, and click OK. If the disks you selected do not contain formatted partitions, clicking OK immediately converts the disks, and you do not need to follow the remaining steps. If the disks you are converting to dynamic disks do have formatted partitions, clicking OK displays the Disks to Convert dialog box, as shown in Figure 4-10, which means that you need to follow the remaining steps to complete the disk conversion.

Figure 4-10

The Disks to Convert dialog box

4. The Disks to Convert dialog box lists the disks you chose for conversion for your confirmation. Check the value in the Will Convert column. It should be set to Yes for each of the disks that you are converting. If any of the disks have the value No, then they may not meet Windows conversion criteria.

5. Click Details. The Convert Details dialog box appears, as shown in Figure 4-11. This dialog box lists the partitions on the selected drives that Disk Management will convert.

Figure 4-11

The Convert Details dialog box

6. Click OK when you are ready to continue with the conversion.

7. On the Disks to Convert dialog box, click Convert to start the conversion. A Disk Management information box appears, as shown in Figure 4-12, to warn you that once you convert the disks to dynamic disks, you will not be able to boot installed operating system from any volume other than the current boot volume.

Figure 4-12

A Disk Management information box

8. Click Yes to continue. Disk Management completes the conversion. If a selected drive contains the boot partition, the system partition, or a partition that is in use, Disk Management will prompt you to restart the computer.

When you convert from a basic disk to a dynamic disk, Disk Management performs the following tasks:

- Basic disk partitions are converted to dynamic disk volumes of equal size.
- Basic disk primary partitions and logical drives in the extended partition are converted to simple volumes.
- Any free space in a basic disk extended partition is marked as unallocated.

CREATING PARTITIONS AND VOLUMES

The Disk Management console creates both partitions and volumes with one set of dialog boxes and wizards. To create a new partition on a basic disk, or a new volume on a dynamic disk, use the following procedure.

 TAKE NOTE

> Technically speaking, the Disk Management snap-in creates partitions on basic disks and volumes on dynamic disks. However, in recent Windows versions, including Windows 7, the interface tends to use the terms interchangeably. In most instances, the snap-in refers to volumes on both basic and dynamic disks, but it still uses the term *partition* when referring to formatting and making a partition active.

➔ CREATE A VOLUME

GET READY. Log on to Windows 7 using an account with administrator privileges.

1. Open the Disk Management snap-in.
2. In the Graphical view, right click the unallocated area on the volume status column for the disk on which you want to create a volume and, from the context menu, select New Simple Volume. The New Simple Volume Wizard appears.
3. Click Next to bypass the Welcome page. The *Specify Volume Size* page appears, as shown in Figure 4-13.

Figure 4-13

The Specify Volume Size page

4. In the Simple Volume Size in MB spin box, specify the size for the new volume, within the maximum and minimum limits stated on the page, and then click Next. The *Assign Drive Letter or Path* page appears, as shown in Figure 4-14.

Figure 4-14

The Assign Drive Letter or Path page

5. Configure one of the following three options, and then click Next. The *Format Partition* page appears, as shown in Figure 4-15:

- **Assign the following drive letter:** If you select this option, click the associated drop-down list for a list of available drive letters, and then select the desired letter you want to assign to the drive.

- **Mount in the following empty NTFS folder:** If you select this option, you are required to either type the path to an existing NTFS folder, or click Browse to search for or create a new folder. The entire contents of the new drive will appear in the folder you specify.

- **Do not assign a drive letter or drive path:** Select this option if you want to create the partition, but are not ready to use it yet. When you do not assign a volume a drive letter or path, the drive is left unmounted and inaccessible. When you want to mount the drive for use, assign a drive letter or path to it.

Figure 4-15

The Format Partition page

6. Specify whether and how the wizard should format the volume. If you do not want to format the volume at this time, select the *Do not format this volume* option. If you do want to format the volume, select the *Format this volume with the following settings* option, and then configure the associated options, which are as follows:

- **File system:** Select the desired file system—NTFS, FAT, FAT32, or exFAT. The options that appear in the drop-down list are based on the size of the partition or volume you are creating.

- **Allocation unit size:** Specify the file system's cluster size. The cluster size specifies the size of the basic unit that the system will use to allocate disk space. The system calculates the default allocation unit size based on the size of the volume. You can override this value by clicking on the associated drop-down list and then selecting one of the values in the list. For example, if your client uses consistently small files, you may want to set the allocation unit size to a smaller cluster size.

- **Volume label:** Specify a name for the partition or volume. The default name is New Volume, but you can change the name to anything you want.

- **Perform a quick format:** When selected, the wizard formats the disk without checking for errors. This is certainly a faster formatting method, but it is not the Microsoft recommended method. When you check for errors, the system looks for and marks bad sectors on the disk so that the system will not use them.

- **Enable file and folder compression:** When selected, file and folder compression for the disk is turned on. This option is available for the NTFS file system only.

Then click Next. The Completing the *New Simple Volume Wizard* page appears, as shown in Figure 4-16.

Figure 4-16

The Completing the New Simple Volume Wizard page

7. Review the settings to confirm your options, and then click Finish. The wizard creates the volume according to your specifications.

EXTENDING AND SHRINKING VOLUMES

The ability to shrink and extend volumes was first introduced in Windows Vista. To extend or shrink a partition or volume, you simply right click a partition or volume and select Extend Volume or Shrink Volume from the context menu, or from the Action menu.

Windows 7 extends existing primary partitions, logical drives, and simple volumes by expanding them into adjacent unallocated space on the same disk. When you extend a simple volume across multiple disks, the simple volume becomes a spanned volume. You cannot extend striped volumes.

To extend a partition on a basic disk, the system must meet the following requirements:

- A basic partition must be either unformatted or formatted with the NTFS file system.

- If you extend a logical drive, the console first consumes the contiguous free space remaining in the extended partition. If you attempt to extend the logical drive beyond the confines of its extended partition, the extended partition expands to any unallocated space left on the disk.

TAKE NOTE *

You must be a member of the Backup Operator or the Administrators group to extend or shrink any partition or volume.

- You can extend the partition of logical drives, boot volumes, or system volumes only into contiguous space, and only if the hard disk can be upgraded into a dynamic disk. The operating system will permit you to extend other types of basic volumes into noncontiguous space, but will prompt you to convert the basic disk to a dynamic disk.

To extend a simple or spanned volume on a dynamic disk, the system must meet these requirements:

- When extending a simple volume, you can only use the available space on the same disk, if the volume is to remain simple.
- You can extend a simple volume across additional disks if it is not a system volume or a boot volume. However, once you expand a simple volume to another disk, it is no longer a simple volume but becomes a spanned volume.
- You can extend a simple or spanned volume if it does not have a file system (a raw volume) or if you formatted it using the NTFS file system. (You cannot extend FAT volumes.)

When shrinking partitions or volumes, the Disk Management console frees up space at the end of the volume, relocating the existing volume's files, if necessary. The console then converts that free space to new unallocated space on the disk. To shrink a basic disk partition or any kind of dynamic disk volume except for a striped volume, the system must meet the following requirements:

- The existing partition or volume must not be full and must contain the specified amount of available free space for shrinking.
- The partition or volume must not be a raw partition (one without a file system). Shrinking a raw partition that contains data mighty destroy the data.
- You can shrink a partition or volume only if you formatted it using the NTFS file system. (You cannot shrink FAT volumes.)

CREATING SPANNED, STRIPED, AND MIRRORED VOLUMES

Spanned, striped, or mirrored volumes require dynamic disks. When you create a spanned, striped, or mirrored volume, you create a single dynamic volume that extends across multiple physical disks.

To create a spanned, striped, or mirrored volume, use the following procedure.

 CREATE A SPANNED OR STRIPED VOLUME

GET READY. Log on to Windows 7 using an account with administrator privileges.

1. Open the Disk Management snap-in.
2. In the Graphical view, right click an unallocated area on a disk and, from the context menu, select New Spanned Volume, New Striped Volume, or New Mirrored Volume. A wizard appears, named for the volume type.
3. Click Next to bypass the *Welcome* page. The *Select Disks* page appears.
4. On the Select Disks page, under the Available standard list box, select each disk you want to use in the volume and then click Add. For a spanned or striped volume, you can add up to 31 additional disks; for a mirrored volume, you can add only 1.
5. Specify the space you want to use on each disk by selecting the disk in the Selected standard list box, and then, using the *Select the amount of space in MB* spin box, specify the amount of disk space that you want to include in the volume. For spanned or striped volumes, you can use different amounts of space on each drive. For mirrored volumes, you must use the same amount of space on both disks. Then click Next. The *Assign Drive Letter or Path* page appears.

6. Specify whether you want to assign a drive letter or path, and then click Next. The *Format Partition* page appears.

7. Specify whether or how you want to format the volume, and then click Next. The *Completing* page appears.

8. Review the settings to confirm your options, and then click Finish. If one or more of the disks you selected is a basic disk, a Disk Management message box appears, informing you that the wizard will convert the basic disk(s) to dynamic disk(s). Click Yes to continue. The wizard creates the volume according to your specifications.

Once the wizard has created the volume, it appears in the Graphical view with a single color on each of the disks contributing to the volume space, as shown in Figure 4-17.

Figure 4-17

A spanned volume in the Disk Management snap-in

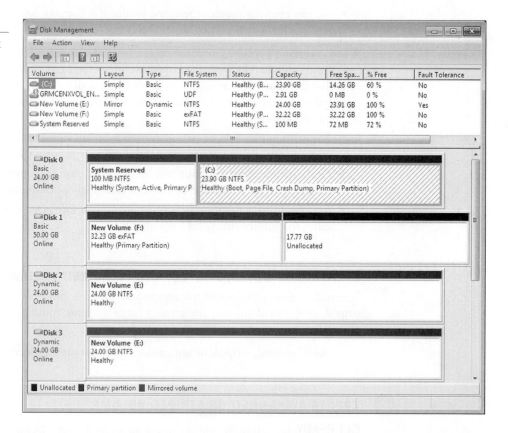

Windows Server 2008 R2, in addition to simple, spanned, striped, and mirrored volumes, also supports RAID-5 volumes. RAID-5 stripes data and parity blocks across three or more disks, making sure that a block and its parity information are never stored on the same disk. Parity is a bit-level fault tolerance mechanism that enables the system to reconstruct the data from any one of the disks in the array that fails. During the development process, Microsoft considered including support for RAID-5 volumes in Windows 7. However, in the final release, RAID-5 support is disabled under all conditions, despite its appearance in the Disk Management interface.

TAKE NOTE *

Using Diskpart.exe

In addition to the graphical interface in the Disk Management snap-in, Windows 7 also includes a command-line tool called *Diskpart.exe*, which you can use to manage disks.

Diskpart.exe is a powerful utility that can perform any task the Disk Management snap-in can and more. For example, Diskpart enables you to create a fourth primary partition on a basic disk, rather than an extended partition and a logical disk.

Diskpart.exe has two operational modes: a script mode and an interactive mode. If you choose to create Diskpart scripts, you can run them from the command prompt using the following syntax:

`Diskpart.exe /s scriptname`

When you run Diskpart.exe from the Windows 7 command prompt without any parameters, a DISKPART> prompt appears, from which you execute additional commands. The typical working method is to shift the focus of the program to the specific object you want to manage, and then execute commands on that object.

For example, the `list disk` command displays a list of the disk drives in the system, as shown in Figure 4-18. The `select disk 1` command then shifts the focus to Disk 1. The program will now apply any disk-specific commands that you execute to Disk 1. The `create partition primary size=10000` command therefore creates a new 10 GB primary partition on Disk 1.

Figure 4-18

Shifting object focus in Diskpart.exe

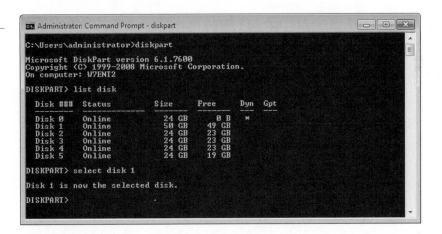

TAKE NOTE *

Unlike the Disk Management snap-in, the Diskpart.exe program is particular about disk terminology. When you are working with a basic disk, for example, you can only create partitions, not volumes, unless you convert the basic disk to a dynamic disk first.

Using Disk Tools

Windows 7 provides a selection of tools that you can use to free up disk space, defragment volumes, and check disks for errors. These tools are simple and safe enough for most end users and still powerful enough for technical specialists.

The Windows 7 disk tools are all accessible from each volume's Properties sheet. You can therefore access the tools from any Windows Explorer window or from the Disk Management snap-in.

USING DISK CLEANUP

When a disk starts to run low on storage space, it is often possible to reclaim space occupied by unnecessary files, such as temporary files, setup logs, and files in the Recycle Bin. Windows 7 refers to the process of deleting these files as cleaning up a disk.

To clean up a Windows 7 volume, use the following procedures.

CLEAN UP A VOLUME

GET READY. Log on to Windows 7 using an account with administrator privileges.

1. Open the Disk Management snap-in.
2. In the Graphical view, right click a volume and, from the context menu, select Properties. The Properties sheet for the volume appears.
3. On the General tab, click Disk Cleanup. After a scan of the volume, the Disk Cleanup dialog box appears, as shown in Figure 4-19. The dialog box lists the types of files that are available for cleanup and specifies the amount of disk space you can reclaim.

Figure 4-19

The Disk Cleanup dialog box

4. Select the check boxes for the files you want to delete, and then click OK. A Disk Cleanup message box appears.
5. Click Delete Files to confirm that you want to delete the selected files. Disk Cleanup deletes the selected files.
6. Click OK to close the volume's Properties sheet.

Once you delete files using the Disk Cleanup tool, you cannot reclaim them from the Recycle Bin.

DEFRAGMENTING DISKS

Hard disk drives write data in clusters, units of a standard size designated when you format the disk. Initially, when you save a file to a hard disk, the drive writes it to contiguous clusters, that is, a sequence of clusters that are next to each other. Over time, however, as files are written and rewritten to the disk, the contiguous spaces grow smaller, and the drive is forced to split files into clusters located at different places on the disk. This process is called *fragmentation*.

Fragmentation reduces the efficiency of the disk because it forces the drive to relocate its heads many times to read a single file. The effect is the same as if you were forced to read a book with pages not in numerical order. You would spend a lot of time looking for each page and less time actually reading.

Windows 7 includes a tool that enables you to defragment your volumes by recopying fragmented files to contiguous space on the disk. The Disk Defragmentation tool in Windows 7 is changed substantially from the one in Windows Vista.

⚠️ **WARNING** It is strongly recommended that you perform a full backup of your volumes before you defragment them. While the Windows 7 Disk Defragmenter is a reliable tool, defragmentation is a hardware-intensive process, and drive failures can conceivably occur.

To defragment a volume, use the following procedure.

 DEFRAGMENT A VOLUME

GET READY. Log on to Windows 7 using an account with administrator privileges.

1. Open the Disk Management snap-in.
2. In the Graphical view, right click a volume and, from the context menu, select Properties. The Properties sheet for the volume appears.
3. Select the Tools tab, as shown in Figure 4-20.

Figure 4-20

The Tools tab of a volume's Properties dialog box

4. Click Defragment now. The Disk Defragmenter dialog box appears, as shown in Figure 4-21.

Figure 4-21

The Disk Defragmenter dialog box

5. In the Current Status box, select the volume you want to work with and click Analyze Disk, The Current Status box displays the percent of the volume that is fragmented.

6. In the Current Status box, select the volume you want to work with and click Defragment Disk, The Disk Defragmenter manipulates the files on the volume to eliminate as much fragmentation as possible. When the process is completed, the Current Status box displays the new fragmentation percentage for the volume.

7. Click Close to close the Disk Defragmenter dialog box.

8. Click OK to close the volume's Properties dialog box.

The time required for the defragmentation process depends on the size of the volume, the number of files stored there, the amount of free space, and the degree to which the volume is fragmented. The process can easily take several hours. In addition to the graphical interface, it is also possible to defragment disks from the command prompt, using the Defrag.exe program. This enables you to incorporate defragmentation into scripts. The syntax for the command line interface is as follows:

```
Defrag.exe volume [/C][/E volumes][/A][/X][/T][/H][/M][/U][/V]
```

- *volume:* Specifies the drive letter or mount point of the volume to defragment.
- /C: Defragments all local volumes on the computer.
- /E *volumes:* Defragments all local volumes on the computer except those you specify.
- /A: Displays a fragmentation analysis for the volume without performing a defragmentation.
- /X: Consolidates the free space on the volume.
- /T: Tracks the operation currently in progress.
- /H: Runs the operation at normal priority, instead of the default low priority.
- /M: Defragments multiple volumes simultaneously.
- /U: Displays the progress of the operation currently in progress.
- /V: Displays information in verbose mode, with additional detail and statistics.

CHECKING FOR DISK ERRORS

Windows 7 includes a tool that can check disks for errors and, in many cases, repair them. If, for example, one of a system's volumes is unavailable for defragmentation, it could be due to errors that you must repair first.

To check a volume for errors, use the following procedure.

CHECK FOR DISK ERRORS

GET READY. Log on to Windows 7 using an account with administrator privileges.

1. Open the Disk Management snap-in.

2. In the Graphical view, right click a volume and, from the context menu, select Properties. The Properties sheet for the volume appears.

3. Select the Tools tab.

4. Click Check now. The Check Disk dialog box for the selected volume appears, as shown in Figure 4-22.

Figure 4-22

The Check Disk dialog box

5. Configure the following options and click Start to begin scanning for errors:
   - **Automatically fix file system errors:** Selected by default, this option configures the program to repair any errors that it finds. Clearing this check box causes the program to scan for errors only.
   - **Scan for and attempt recovery of bad sectors:** Cleared by default, this option configures the program to scan the disk for bad sectors and mark any that it finds, to prevent the drive from using them. Depending on the size of the disk, this option can take from several minutes to several hours.

6. When the scan is completed, the *Your device or disk was successfully scanned* dialog box appears. Click the See Details down-arrow to display the verbose record of the scan, as shown in Figure 4-23.

Figure 4-23

The expanded Checking Disk dialog box

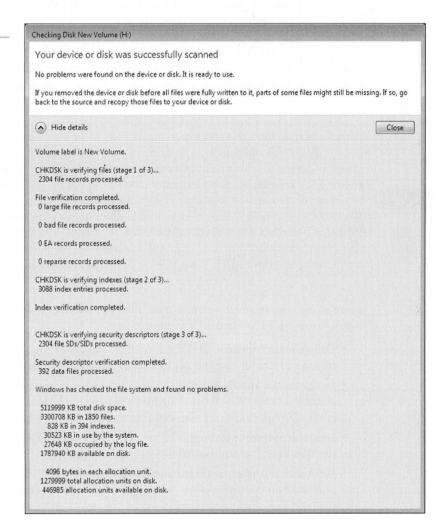

7. Click Close.
8. Click OK to close the volume's Properties dialog box.

If you select the boot volume for error checking, the program defers the check until the next time you start the computer. This is because the program cannot check a disk with open files stored on it.

■ Working with VHDs

Windows 7 supports the native use of VHD files, which enables technical specialists to access their contents and even boot from them without installing a virtual machine manager or hypervisor.

CERTIFICATION READY?
Configure a VHD.
2.4

Microsoft created the *Virtual Hard Disk (VHD)* format to support its Virtual PC, Virtual Server, and Hyper-V products. A VHD file contains the entire contents of a hard disk in a single, portable file that administrators can use to move entire virtual machines (VMs) from one host computer to another. In the logical environment of a virtual machine, a VHD functions exactly like a hard disk drive does in a physical machine.

Since its introduction, Microsoft has found other uses for the VHD file format, such as the backup products in the Windows operating systems and System Center Data Protection Manager. The Windows 7 Enterprise and Ultimate editions also include support for VHD files, using a feature called *native boot*, which enables you to create and modify VHDs in Windows 7 and even boot Windows 7 from a VHD, all without having to run a virtual machine manager product such as Virtual PC or a hypervisor-based product such as Hyper-V.

TAKE NOTE * Virtual machine managers and hypervisors always incur a certain amount of overhead because the system must dedicate some of its resources to running the VM hosting environment, on top of which run the separate VMs. To access a single VHD for maintenance and testing purposes, installing Virtual PC on a workstation or Hyper-V on a server can be a waste of resources. A workstation with the processor and memory resources to run Windows 7 reasonably well by itself would be likely to perform relatively poorly with Virtual PC installed and a VHD loaded in a virtual machine. The ability to access VHDs natively in Windows 7 provides technical specialists with a convenient platform for tasks requiring basic access to VHDs without excessive hardware requirements.

Some of the ways in which technical specialists can take advantage of the native boot capabilities of Windows 7 include the following:

- **Offline image updates:** VHDs mounted in Windows 7 are accessible by all standard file management tools, enabling administrators to update and service the images stored in them.
- **Image format standardization:** In an enterprise environment that relies on virtual machine or hypervisor technology for its servers, the VHD capability in Windows 7 can enable administrators to avoid .wim files entirely and use VHDs for all of their image files.
- **Image deployment testing:** Prior to large-scale image deployments, administrators can use Windows 7 to test the viability of their images.
- **Workstation configuration management:** By booting to VHDs without incurring the overhead of a host operating system and virtual machine manager or hypervisor, administrators can easily deploy alternative application configurations to workstation computers as needed.

Creating a VHD

Windows 7 can create VHDs using the Disk Management snap-in.

To create a new VHD in Windows 7, you can use the Disk Partition snap-in, accessible from the Computer management console, or the Diskpart.exe command-line program.

To create a new VHD file, use the following procedure.

CREATE A VHD

GET READY. Log on to Windows 7, using an account with administrative privileges.

1. Click Start, and then click Control Panel > System and Security > Administrative Tools. The Administrative Tools control panel appears.
2. Double click Computer Management. The Computer Management console appears.
3. Select Disk Management. The Disk Management snap-in appears, as shown in Figure 4-24.

Figure 4-24

The Disk Management snap-in

4. Right click Disk Management and, from the context menu, select Create VHD. The *Create and Attach Virtual Hard Disk* dialog box appears, as shown in Figure 4-25.

Figure 4-25

The Create and Attach Virtual Hard Disk dialog box

5. In the Location text box, type the path and filename of the VHD you want to create.
6. In the Virtual Hard Disk Size text box, specify the size of the VHD you want to create, in megabytes (MB), gigabytes (GB), or terabytes (TB).

7. Select the *Virtual hard disk format* option you want to use and click OK. The new VHD appears in the graphical view pane of the Disk Management snap-in.

8. Right click the new disk in the graphical view and, from the context menu, select Initialize Disk. The Initialize Disk dialog box appears, as shown in Figure 4-26.

Figure 4-26

The Initialize Disk dialog box

9. Click OK to accept the default MBR (master boot record) partition style. The VHD appears in the graphical view as a basic, online disk.

Once you have created and initialized the VHD, you can create a volume on it in the usual manner, format it, and assign it a drive letter, which makes it accessible through the Windows Explorer interface. Copying files to the drive adds them to the VHD.

You can also create a VHD using the Diskpart.exe utility from the command line. To perform the same tasks described in this procedure using Diskpart, use commands like the following:

```
diskpart
create vdisk file=e:\filename.vhd maximum=20000
select vdisk file=e:\filename.vhd
attach vdisk
```

Attaching and Detaching VHDs

Before you can work with a VHD in Windows you must attach it to the file system.

Creating a new VHD automatically mounts it into the Windows 7 file system, a process called attachment. However, unlike physical hard disks, mounting a VHD is not persistent. Each time you restart Windows 7, you must attach the VHD using the Disk Management snap-in before you can access its contents.

To attach a VHD, use the following procedure.

 ATTACH A VHD

GET READY. Log on to Windows 7, using an account with administrative privileges.

1. Click Start, and then click Control Panel > System and Security > Administrative Tools. The Administrative Tools control panel appears.

2. Double click Computer Management. The Computer Management console appears.

3. Select Disk Management. The Disk Management snap-in appears.

4. Right click Disk Management and, from the context menu, select Attach VHD. The *Attach Virtual Hard Disk* dialog box appears, as shown in Figure 4-27.

Figure 4-27

The Attach Virtual Hard Disk dialog box

5. Type the name or browse to the location of the VHD file you want to mount and click OK. The VHD is added to the Disk Management snap-in.

Once attached, the VHD is accessible from the Windows Explorer interface. To detach a VHD, which you must do before you move it to another location, right click the disk in the Disk Management snap-in and, from the context menu, select Detach VHD. A *Detach Virtual Hard Disk* dialog box appears, as shown in Figure 4-28, which allows you to delete the VHD file as well.

Figure 4-28

The Detach Virtual Hard Disk dialog box

Booting from VHDs

The ability to boot from a VHD is a major new feature that enables administrators to deploy virtual machines to Windows 7 computers without using a virtual machine manager or hypervisor. You can create a bootable VHD by deploying an image to a VHD file you have created in the Disk Management snap-in and then adding the VHD to the boot menu of the computer running Windows 7.

The process of deploying an image to a VHD is no different from deploying it to a physical disk. You can use the ImageX.exe utility from the command line, Windows Deployment Services, or any of the other Windows deployment tools. Once you have deployed the image, you must add it to the Windows 7 boot menu before you can select it when the system starts. To do this, you use the BCDedit.exe utility from the command line.

 ADD A VHD TO THE BOOT MENU

GET READY. Log on to Windows 7 using an account with administrative privileges. This procedure assumes that you have already created or attached a VHD called filename.vhd, on which you have deployed an image file.

1. Click Start, and then click All Programs > Accessories. Right click Command Prompt and, from the context menu, select Run as administrator. An Administrator: Command Prompt window appears.

2. From the command prompt, copy an existing boot entry and disclose its globally unique identifier (GUID) by typing the following command and pressing Enter, as shown in Figure 4-29:

```
bcdedit /copy {default} /d "vhs boot (locate)"
```

TAKE NOTE*

If you are working on a computer that is a member of a workgroup, a User Account Control message box appears, in which you must click Yes to continue.

Figure 4-29

Copying a boot entry

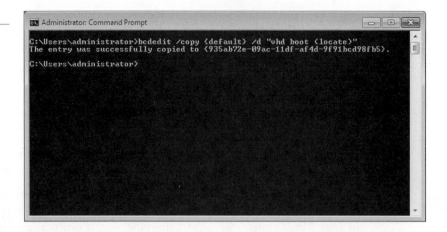

➕ **MORE INFORMATION**

A **_globally unique identifier (GUID)_** is a 128-bit hexadecimal value that Windows uses to identify a particular operating system component. The value consists of five numerical groups, with 8, 4, 4, 4, and 12 hexadecimal digits, respectively, surrounded by curly brackets. When you use the GUID in subsequent commands, you must type the entire value precisely, including the brackets.

3. Using the GUID value displayed by the previous command, type the following two commands, pressing Enter after each one to modify the boot entry you just copied, as shown in Figure 4-30:

```
bcdedit /set {guid} device vhd=[locate]\filename.vhd
bcdedit /set {guid} osdevice vhd=[locate]\filename.vhd
```

Figure 4-30

Modifying a boot entry

4. To configure the system to detect the computer's hardware abstraction layer automatically during startup, type the following command and press Enter:

```
bcdedit /vbcedit /set {guid} detecthal on
```

5. Close the Administrator: Command Prompt window.

Now when you restart the computer, a boot menu appears from which you can select whether you want to boot the system from the active hard disk partition or from the VHD. You can also view and configure the new boot menu entry from the Boot tab of the System Configuration tool (Msconfig.exe), as shown in Figure 4-31.

Figure 4-31

The new boot entry in the
System Configuration tool

Working with Devices and Drivers

THE BOTTOM LINE

A computer is a collection of hardware devices, each of which requires a piece of software called a device driver in order to function. Windows 7 includes a large library of device drivers, but it is still sometimes necessary to obtain them yourself.

CERTIFICATION READY?
Configure devices.
3.1

As most people know, a PC is a collection of hardware devices, all of which are connected together and installed in a single case. Disk drives, keyboards, mice, modems, and printers are all types of devices. To communicate with the operating system running on the computer, each device also requires a software element called a *device driver*. The device driver provides the operating system with information about a specific device.

For example, when you use a word processing application to save a file to a hard disk, the application issues a generic WriteFile function call to the operating system. The application knows nothing specific about the disk drive hardware; it just issues an instruction to store a particular file there. When the operating system processes the function call, it accesses the device driver for the hard disk drive, which provides detailed information about how to communicate with the drive. If the user selects a different target location for the file, the operating system accesses the device driver for that location, whether it's a hard drive, a floppy drive, or USB flash drive.

In most cases, the information the device driver provides is integrated into the Windows interface. For example, the Properties sheet for a printer includes generic system information, such as which port the printer is connected to and who is permitted to use it. Other tabs, and particularly the Device Settings tab, as shown in Figure 4-32, are based on hardware-specific information provided by the device driver.

In addition to providing information about a device, drivers also permit the operating system to modify the hardware configuration settings of the device. For example, when you configure a printer to print a document in landscape mode instead of portrait mode, the printer device driver generates the appropriate command and sends it to the hardware.

Figure 4-32

The Device Settings tab of a printer's Properties sheet

Understanding Device Drivers

> The process of installing a hardware device consists primarily of identifying the device and installing a device driver for it. This process can occur during the operating system installation or at a later time, but the steps are fundamentally the same.

A major part of the Windows 7 installation process consists of identifying the devices in the computer and installing the appropriate drivers for them. The Windows 7 installation package includes hundreds of drivers for many different devices, which is why many installations finish without any user intervention. Sometimes, however, you might have to supply device drivers yourself.

UNDERSTANDING DRIVER COMPLEXITY

Virtually every component in a PC requires a device driver, but they can vary greatly in complexity. Many of the standard computer devices are so standardized that their drivers operate virtually invisibly. When was the last time you had a problem with a keyboard driver, for example? Nearly every computer has a keyboard and the generic keyboard driver included with Windows 7 functions properly in almost every case. If you have a keyboard with special features, you might need a special driver to access them, but the basic keyboard functions will still function even without it.

At the other end of the scale are more complex drivers, such as those for graphics adapters. Many of the graphics adapters on the market are really self-contained computers in themselves, with their own processors and memory. The drivers for these complex devices are equally complex, and are often much more problematic than simple keyboard drivers, for the following reasons:

- **The device driver is likely to be revised more often:** Drivers that are required to do more are more likely to have problems. Generic keyboard drivers can go for years without upgrades, because keyboards rarely change. Manufacturers often release new graphics adapters, however, and therefore require new drivers as well.

- **The device driver is less likely to be included with the operating system:** The Windows 7 installation disk includes hundreds of device drivers, but the older the operating system gets, the less likely it is to include the latest drivers for the newest

+ MORE INFORMATION

With a few exceptions, the device drivers included with the Windows 7 operating system, as well as all other Windows versions, are supplied by the hardware manufacturers themselves, not by Microsoft. Therefore, if you experience driver problems for a specific device, you are much more likely to get help from the hardware manufacturer than from Microsoft.

devices. In these cases, you must obtain the drivers you need from the hardware manufacturer and install them yourself.

- **The device driver is more likely to cause compatibility or functionality problems:** New devices are often rushed to market, and as a result, the drivers that ship with them might not be fully debugged. This is particularly true, again, with graphics drivers. It is always a good idea to check the manufacturer's Web site for the latest drivers before installing new hardware.

CREATING A DRIVER UPDATE POLICY

As a technical specialist, you are likely to be working with many different computers, each containing many devices. Keeping up with the drivers for all of these devices can be difficult, and you also must consider whether installing each driver update is necessary and, above all, safe.

There are two basic schools of thought when it comes to updating drivers. The "latest is the greatest" school advocates downloading and installing every new driver that is released, while the "if it ain't broke, don't fix it" school prefers to leave things as they are until they experience a problem. Both of these philosophies have their advantages and disadvantages, and unfortunately, this is not likely to be a question that can be answered with a hard-and-fast rule or a company policy.

There are three main reasons why hardware manufacturers release new driver updates:

- To address problems with the previous driver release(s)
- To implement new features
- To enhance performance of the device

The question of whether to update a driver is most easily answered for the first of these reasons. If you are experiencing the problem that the update is designed to address, then you should install it. Otherwise, you probably should not. As to the other two reasons, new features and enhanced performance are certainly desirable, but you should be sure that the driver update does not introduce new problems at the same time.

As a general rule, it is a good idea to test all driver updates before deploying them, especially in an enterprise environment. Another good safety measure is to avoid installing driver updates as soon as they are released. Waiting at least a week or so gives the manufacturer time to address any major issues that arise.

Above all, the question of whether to install driver updates should depend on the hardware devices involved and the policies and reputation of the hardware manufacturer. Some manufacturers release driver updates frequently and haphazardly, while others are more careful. Examining the manufacturer's support Web site is a good way to ascertain how they deal with hardware problems and how often they release driver updates.

UNDERSTANDING DRIVER SIGNING

As with any other software, device drivers have the potential to damage a computer configuration. Unscrupulous programmers can conceivably alter device drivers by adding their own malware, and the average user, downloading the driver from the Internet, would never know the difference. For that reason, Microsoft has instituted the practice of digitally signing the device drivers they have tested and approved.

A signed driver is a device driver that includes a digital signature. The signer uses a cryptographic algorithm to compute the digital signature value and then appends that value to the device driver. A *signer* is an organization, or publisher, that uses a private key to create the digital signature for the device driver. This process ensures that the device driver does come from the authentic publisher and that someone has not maliciously altered it.

+ MORE INFORMATION

Public key cryptography is an encryption method based on a pair of keys, called the public key and the private key. As the names imply, the public key is freely available to anyone, and the private key is kept secret by its owner. Any code that is digitally encrypted using the public key can only be decrypted by the holder of the private key. In the same way, any code that is encrypted using the private key can only be decrypted by the public key. It is the latter example that publishers use for driver signing. The signer encrypts the device driver using its private key. The fact that the user can decrypt the driver using that signer's public key confirms that the software has not been modified.

Generally, the process the publisher uses to create the digital signature starts by running the device driver files through a hash algorithm and then using the publisher's private key to transform the hash result cryptographically. The resulting value is the digital signature of the device driver.

The digital signature value is a protected checksum. A protected checksum is the value of an algorithmic function that is dependent on the contents of the data object with which it is stored. Its purpose is to protect the data object against active attacks that attempt to change the checksum to match changes that a malicious individual has made to the data object. Thus, the properties of a cryptographic hash ensure that when a malicious individual attempts to change the data object, the digital signature no longer matches the object.

If Windows 7 perceives a problem with a digital signature of a device driver, it alerts you with one of the following messages during the installation attempt:

- **Windows can't verify the publisher of this driver:** Either a certification authority has not verified the digital signature or the driver does not contain a digital signature. Only install this driver if you obtained it from the original manufacturer's disk.

- **This driver has been altered:** Someone has altered this driver after the verified publisher has digitally signed it, possibly with malicious intent. The driver package may now include malware that could harm your system or steal information. Only install this driver if you obtained it from the original manufacturer's disk.

- **Windows cannot install this driver:** x64-based versions of Windows 7 cannot install a device driver that someone has altered after the verified publisher has digitally signed it or one that lacks a valid digital signature altogether.

SUPPLYING DRIVERS DURING WINDOWS 7 INSTALLATION

As mentioned earlier, one of the primary functions of the Windows 7 installation program is to identify the hardware devices in the computer and install the appropriate device drivers for them. For most devices, this process occurs invisibly. There are occasions, however, when the installation program fails to identify a device. When this occurs, one of three things happens:

- **The installation program installs a generic driver instead:** For devices that are essential to system operation, such as keyboards and graphics adapters, Windows 7 includes generic drivers that support nearly all hardware devices. If Windows 7 does not include a driver for your specific graphics adapter, for example, it installs a generic VGA (video graphics array) driver. This VGA driver won't support the esoteric features of your graphics adapter, but it will at least display an image on your screen, albeit a low-resolution one. After the operating system installation is completed, you can obtain a driver for your hardware and install it in place of the generic driver.

- **The installation program leaves the device without a driver and completes the installation:** If the hardware device is not essential to basic system operation, such as an audio adapter, Windows 7 leaves the hardware uninstalled and proceeds with the rest of the installation. When the installation is completed, the hardware appears in Device Manager with a warning icon, indicating that it has no driver.

X REF

To install a device driver after the installation is complete, you must use the Device Manager utility as described later in this lesson in "Using Device Manager."

- **The installation program permits you to supply an alternate driver or, failing that, halts:** The sole exception to the preceding condition is when the installation program cannot access a disk drive with sufficient free space to install Windows 7. When this happens, the setup program halts, unless you are able to supply the device driver for an unrecognized mass storage hardware device. For example, if your hard drives are connected to an interface card that Windows 7 does not recognize, you can click Load Driver on the installation program's *Where Do You Want to Install Windows?* page, and specify the location of a driver for the interface card.

UPDATING DRIVERS WITH WINDOWS UPDATE

The Windows Update Web site was originally designed to provide users with operating system updates, but it now includes a large library of device driver updates as well. The drivers distributed through Windows Update have all undergone Windows Hardware Quality Labs (WHQL) testing and have received the Windows logo.

When you access the Windows Update Web site manually, Windows 7 transmits a list of installed hardware and device version numbers to the site. If there are any updated drivers available for your hardware, the Web site makes them available, usually as an optional download.

If Windows 7 is configured to use automatic updating, the system will download device drivers only for hardware that does not have a driver installed. If you use Device Manager to search for updated drivers, Windows 7 examines the drivers that are available and only downloads a new driver if it is a better match for the device than the driver that is currently installed.

Using Device Manager

The primary Windows 7 tool for managing devices and their drivers is called Device Manager. You can use Device Manager to get information about the devices installed on the computer, as well as to install, update, and troubleshoot device drivers.

Although it is not immediately apparent, Device Manager is a snap-in for the Microsoft Management Console (MMC). This means that there are many ways that you can access Device Manager, including the following:

- Open the hardware and Sound control panel and click the Device Manager link.
- Open the Computer Management console from the Administrative Tools program group in the System and Security control panel and click Device Manager in the scope (left) pane.
- Run the Microsoft Management Console shell application (Mmc.exe), select File > Add/Remove Snap-in, and select Device Manager from the list of snap-ins provided.
- Open the Start menu, type the filename of the Device Manager snap-in (Devmgmt.msc) in the Search programs and files box, and then execute the resulting file.

Each of these procedures launches the Device Manager and displays a window with an interface like that shown in Figure 4-33.

Figure 4-33

The Windows 7 Device Manager

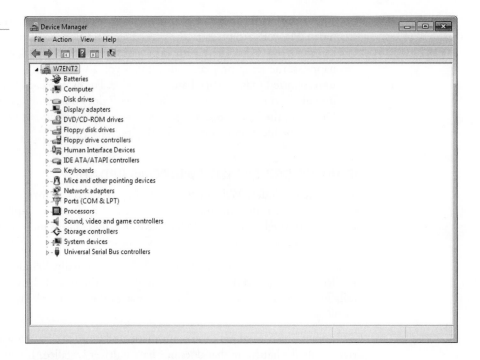

VIEWING DEVICE PROPERTIES

Device Manager is capable of displaying information in the following four modes:

- **Devices by type:** Displays a list of device categories, which you can expand to show the devices in each category. This is the default Device Manager view, as shown in Figure 4-34.

Figure 4-34

Device Manager's Devices by Type display, expanded

- **Devices by connection:** Displays a list of the interfaces that hardware devices use to communicate with the computer. Expanding a connection shows the devices using that connection.
- **Resources by type:** Displays a list of resource types, including Direct Memory Access (DMA), Input/Output (I/O), Interrupt Request (IRQ), and Memory, which you can expand to show the resources of each type and the devices that are using them.

- **Resources by connection:** Displays a list of resource types, including Direct Memory Access (DMA), Input/Output (I/O), Interrupt Request (IRQ), and Memory, which you can expand to show the connection associated with each individual resource and the device using each connection.

To examine the properties of a device, simply locate it in the tree display and double click it to open its Properties sheet, as shown in Figure 4-35.

Figure 4-35

A Device Manager Properties sheet

The tabs on the Properties sheet vary depending on the nature of the device you select, but virtually all devices have the following four tabs:

- **General:** Displays the name of the device, its type, manufacturer, and location in the system. The Device Status box indicates whether the device is functioning and, if not, provides troubleshooting help.
- **Driver:** Displays the device driver's provider, date, version, and digital signer. The tab also provides buttons you can use to display driver details, update, roll back, or uninstall the driver, and enable or disable the device.
- **Detail:** Displays extensive information about the driver and its properties.
- **Resources:** Displays the hardware resources being used by the device and indicates whether there are any conflicts with other devices in the computer.

ENABLING AND DISABLING DEVICES

With Device Manager, you can disable any device in the computer, using any of the following procedures:

- Select the device and choose Disable from the Action menu.
- Right click the device and choose Disable from the context menu.
- Open the device's Properties sheet and click the Disable button on the Driver tab.

Disabling a device does not affect the hardware in any way or uninstall the device driver, it simply renders the device inoperative until you enable it again. Obviously, you cannot disable devices that are necessary for the system to function, such as the processor, and some devices that are in use require you to restart the system before they can be disabled.

TAKE NOTE *

Disabling a device releases the hardware resources it was using back to the operating system. If you restart the computer with the device disabled, Windows might reassign those hardware resources to other devices. If you re-enable the device, the computer might allocate different hardware resources to it than it had originally.

UPDATING DRIVERS

When you update a driver using Device Manager, you can point to a location on your computer where you have already saved the new driver, or you can run a search of your computer and the Internet. To update a device driver, use the following procedure.

 UPDATE A DEVICE DRIVER

GET READY. Log on to Windows 7 using an account with administrator privileges.

1. Open Device Manager and locate the device that you want to update.
2. Double click the device you want to update, so that its Properties sheet appears.
3. Click the Driver tab, and then click the Update Driver button. The *How do you want to search for driver software?* page appears, as shown in Figure 4-36.

Figure 4-36

The How do you want to search for driver software? page

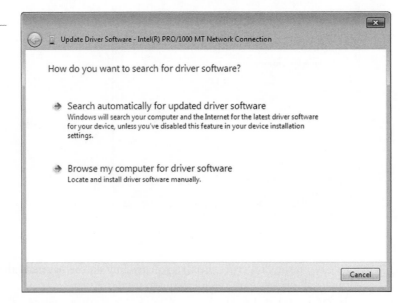

4. Click Browse my computer for driver software to specify a location for the driver or select from a list of installed drivers, as shown in Figure 4-37. Click Search automatically for updated driver software to initiate a search for a driver.

Figure 4-37

The Browse for driver software on your computer page

5. Click Next when you locate the driver you want to install. The *Windows Has Successfully Updated Your Driver Software* page appears.

6. Click Close.

7. Close the Device Manager window.

ROLLING BACK DRIVERS

When you update a device driver in Windows 7, the operating system does not discard the old driver completely. It is not uncommon for new drivers to cause more problems than they solve, and many users find that they would prefer to go back to the old version. Windows 7 makes this possible with the Roll Back feature, which you initiate by clicking the Roll Back Driver button on the Driver tab of the device's Properties sheet. This procedure uninstalls the current driver and reinstalls the previous version, returning the device to its state before you performed the most recent driver update.

TROUBLESHOOTING DRIVERS

Installing a new hardware device or a new device driver is a risky undertaking. There is always the possibility of a problem that, depending on the devices involved, could be trivial or catastrophic. For a peripheral device, such as a printer, a hardware misconfiguration or faulty driver would probably just cause the new device to malfunction. However, if the device involved is a graphics adapter, a bad driver could prevent the system from functioning.

To troubleshoot hardware or driver problems, consider some of the following techniques:

- Open the Properties sheet for the device and check the Device Status box on the General tab. If the device is malfunctioning, this tab informs you of its status and enables you to launch a troubleshooter.

- Open the Device Manager and delete the device entirely. Then restart the system and allow Windows 7 to detect and install the device over again. This process will cause Windows to re-allocate hardware resources to the device, which could resolve the problem if it was caused by a hardware resource conflict.

- If the device or driver malfunction prevents the system from running properly, as in the case of a bad graphics driver that prevents an image from appearing on the screen, you can start the computer in Safe Mode by pressing the F8 key as the system starts. Safe Mode loads the operating system with a minimal set of generic device drivers, bypassing the troublesome ones, so you can uninstall or troubleshoot them.

SKILL SUMMARY

IN THIS LESSON YOU LEARNED:

- There are two hard disk partition styles that you can use in Windows 7: MBR and GPT.

- Windows 7 supports two disk types: basic disks and dynamic disks.

- Basic disks can have up to four partitions: three primary partitions and the fourth usually being an extended partition, on which you can create multiple logical drives.

- Windows 7 supports four types of dynamic volumes: simple, spanned, striped, and mirrored.

- You use the Disk Management snap-in for MMC to manage disks.

- The Virtual Hard Disk (VHD) format defines a file that contains the entire contents of a hard disk in a single, portable file that administrators can use to move entire virtual machines (VMs) from one host computer to another.

(continued)

SKILL SUMMARY (*continued*)

- The Windows 7 Enterprise and Ultimate editions also include support for a feature called native boot, which enables you to create and modify VHDs and even boot Windows 7 from a VHD, all without having to run Virtual PC or Hyper-V.

- Device drivers are software components that enable applications and operating systems to communicate with specific hardware devices. Every hardware device you install in a computer must have a corresponding driver.

- Plug and Play (PnP) is a standard that enables computers to detect and identify hardware devices, and then install and configure drivers for those devices. PnP dynamically assigns hardware resources to each device, and can reconfigure devices at will to accommodate each component's special needs.

- The drivers included with Windows 7 have all been digitally signed to ensure that they have not been modified since they were published.

- Device Manager is an MMC snap-in that lists all hardware devices in the computer and indicates problems with hardware identification or driver configuration. Using Device Manager, you can enable and disable devices, update and roll back drivers, and manage devices and device driver properties.

■ Knowledge Assessment

Fill in the Blank

Complete the following sentences by writing the correct word or words in the blanks provided.

1. By default, Windows 7 standard users are permitted to install Plug and Play devices only if their drivers are _____.

2. The debilitating condition in which files are stored as clusters scattered all over a disk is called _____.

3. The file system included in Windows 7 that is specifically designed for use on flash drives is called _____.

4. Technically speaking, you create _____ on basic disks and _____ on dynamic disks.

5. In Windows 7, the _____ file system is limited to volumes no larger than 32 gigabytes.

6. The digital signature of a driver consists of a _____ that is appended to the driver itself before publication.

7. To create a fourth primary partition on a basic disk, you must use the _____ utility.

8. To extend or shrink a partition on a basic disk, you must be a member of the _____ or _____ group.

9. The default partition style used by Windows 7 on an x86 computer is _____.

10. All digitally signed drivers have undergone _____ testing.

True / False

Circle T if the statement is true or F if the statement is false.

T | F **1.** There is no way to create a fourth primary partition on a basic disk in Windows 7.

T | F **2.** Striped volumes provide greater fault tolerance than simple volumes.

T | F **3.** All dynamic disks have only one partition on them.

T | F **4.** By default, all device drivers must be digitally signed to be installed on a computer running Windows 7.

T | F **5.** Windows Update dynamically updates device drivers only when a hardware device has no driver installed.

T | F **6.** Disabling a device in Device Manager causes its device driver to be uninstalled.

T | F **7.** The x64-based versions of Windows 7 do not permit the installation of unsigned drivers under any circumstances.

T | F **8.** You cannot convert an MBR disk to a GPT disk without erasing all data on the disk.

T | F **9.** You cannot extend a striped volume unless it is on a dynamic disk.

T | F **10.** Windows 7 can access VHDs without the use of a hypervisor.

Review Questions

1. Explain the difference between a spanned volume and a striped volume, and specify which (if any) provides increased performance and/or fault tolerance.

2. List the three main reasons why manufacturers release driver updates.

■ Case Scenario

Scenario 4-1: Troubleshooting Graphics Drivers

A user asks you to troubleshoot his Windows 7 workstation, which is behaving erratically. He has recently purchased and installed a new graphics adapter, and since then, he sees occasional wavy lines in the display. You run Device Manager on the system and note the manufacturer, model, and version number of the device driver for the graphics adapter. Then, you check the adapter manufacturer's Web site and discover that there is a new driver available for the adapter. After downloading and installing the driver update, you restart the system. The system appears to start normally, except that the graphical interface has been replaced by incomprehensible noise. Because you can't see the display, you can't work with the system. What should you do to return the computer to an operational state?

5 LESSON
Connecting to a Network

OBJECTIVE DOMAIN MATRIX

TECHNOLOGY SKILL	OBJECTIVE DOMAIN	OBJECTIVE NUMBER
Configuring IPv4 Settings	Configure IPv4 network settings.	4.1
Configuring IPv6 Settings	Configure IPv6 network settings.	4.2
Managing Network Connections	Configure networking settings.	4.3

KEY TERMS

classless inter-domain routing (CIDR)

connectionless protocol

connection-oriented protocol

data encapsulation

datagram

8P8C connectors

firewall

frame

Internet Protocol (IP)

IP address

Link Local Multicast Name Resolution (LLMNR)

media access control (MAC) addresses

network address translation (NAT)

open systems interconnection (OSI) reference model

packet-switching networks

ports

protocols

router

socket

stateless address autoconfiguration

subnet mask

Transmission Control Protocol (TCP)

unshielded twisted pair (UTP)

■ Networking Basics

THE BOTTOM LINE

The networking modifications introduced in Windows Vista were the most significant changes to the Windows networking engine since it was first incorporated into the operating system in Windows 95. Windows 7 networking now includes a revamped TCP/IP stack and a variety of new tools that simplify the networking process, for both users and administrators.

Networking is one of the primary functions of Windows 7. Most Windows computers are connected to either a private local area network (LAN) or to the Internet, and many are connected to both. These connections provide users with access to remotely stored data, shared resources, network-attached hardware, and the virtually unlimited information and services available on the Internet.

Most Windows users are unaware of how computer networks function or even of when they are accessing a network resource, as opposed to a local one. Users expect Windows to provide a seamless network experience, wherever they happen to be located, and Windows 7 includes many new networking features that help to provide this experience.

To promote interoperability between hardware manufacturers' products, computer networks are, for the most part, based on independent standards. The networking capabilities built into Windows 7 are implementations of those standards. Before you work directly with the Windows 7 networking tools, it is helpful to have a firm grasp of the underlying principles on which they were designed.

Computer networking is a highly complex process, but most of the technology operates invisibly, both to the user and the administrator. Computers on a network communicate using *protocols*, which are nothing more than languages that all of the computers understand. These protocols operate on different levels, forming what is commonly known as a networking stack or protocol stack. The most common method for illustrating the operations of the networking stack is the ***Open Systems Interconnection (OSI) reference model***, which consists of seven layers, as shown in Figure 5-1.

Figure 5-1

The OSI reference model

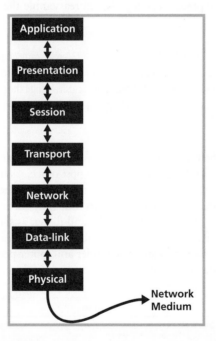

The Physical Layer

At the bottom of the OSI model is the physical layer, which represents the hardware that forms the network.

The physical layer of the OSI model consists of the cable or the radio signals that carry data from one system to another and the network interface adapters, which are the hardware components in the computers that provide the connection to the physical network.

Most cabled networks use a type of cable called ***unshielded twisted pair (UTP)***, which is similar to the cable used for telephone wiring. UTP cable consists of four pairs of wires, with

X REF

For more information on wireless networking, see Lesson 12, "Using Mobile Computers."

each pair twisted individually. At either end of each cable run are modular **8P8C connectors** (often incorrectly referred to as RJ45 connectors), which are similar to the RJ11 connectors used for telephones.

A network interface adapter is the component that provides the connection to the network. Most of the computers manufactured today have Ethernet network interface adapters integrated into their motherboards, but the adapter can also take the form of an expansion card that you install into the computer or an external device that connects to a Universal Serial Bus (USB) port. For wireless networking, the cables and cable connectors are replaced by radio transceivers that transmit the same data using a different kind of signal.

The Data-Link Layer

As you move up beyond the physical layer, the subsequent layers of the OSI model are realized in software, as protocols that provide different types of communications.

Most Windows networks use a protocol called Ethernet at the data-link layer. Local area networks are sometimes described as **packet-switching networks** because the messages generated by each computer are divided up into small pieces called packets, which the computer transmits individually over the network. A single file might be divided into hundreds or thousands of packets, each of which is transmitted separately. The packets might take different routes to the destination, and might even arrive there in a different order. The receiving computer is responsible for putting the pieces back together to reassemble the file.

> **+ MORE INFORMATION**
>
> The cable on a packet-switching network, at any given moment, can be carrying packets generated by dozens of different computers. The alternative to a packet-switching network is called a circuit-switching network, in which two systems establish a dedicated connection that they use exclusively until their transaction is completed. The most common example of a circuit-switching network is the public switched telephone network (PSTN), the standard telephone system.

For the packets to reach their destination, they have to know where they are going; therefore, they need an address. Just like letters mailed in the post office, each packet needs an address identifying the computer that will be its destination. Ethernet is the protocol responsible for addressing the packets at the data-link layer, which it does by surrounding the data it receives from the network layer just above it with a header and footer, as shown in Figure 5-2. This header and footer and the data they contain are collectively called a **frame**, and the process of applying it is called **data encapsulation**. The header and footer perform the same functions as the envelope does for a letter, protecting the contents and displaying the address of the recipient.

Figure 5-2

Data-link layer data encapsulation

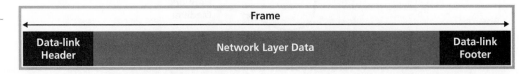

Frame

| Data-link Header | Network Layer Data | Data-link Footer |

> **TAKE NOTE** *
>
> There are other data-link layer protocols, such as Token Ring, but the vast majority of LANs today use Ethernet. Two computers must both be running the same data-link layer protocol to communicate.

The addresses computers use at the data-link layer are six-byte hexadecimal sequences, hard-coded into each network interface adapter by the manufacturer. These sequences are called hardware addresses or **media access control (MAC) addresses**. The first three bytes of a hardware address identify the manufacturer of the network interface adapter, and the last three bytes identify the adapter itself.

➕ MORE INFORMATION

The standards on which Ethernet networks are based are published by the Institute of Electrical and Electronics Engineers (IEEE) and are known as IEEE 802.3, which refers to the number of the working group that produced the standards. The IEEE 802.3 standard defines three elements of an Ethernet network: a frame format for the packets transmitted over the network, a media access control mechanism called Carrier Sense Multiple Access with Collision Detection (CSMA/CD), and a series of physical layer specifications that describe the types of cables and other media that can be used to build an Ethernet network. For more information on Ethernet and for access to the standards, see http://www.ieee802.org/3.

In addition to addresses, the Ethernet header contains other information that helps to direct and protect the data in the packet. Each Ethernet frame contains a code that identifies the network-layer protocol that generated the data in the packet and a checksum that the receiving system will use to confirm that the packet has not been altered in transit.

The Network Layer

The protocols that Windows uses by default at the network and transport layers are collectively called TCP/IP. TCP is the **Transmission Control Protocol** and IP is the **Internet Protocol**. Early versions of Windows used a different protocol called NetBIOS, but TCP/IP is the native protocol of the Internet, and the explosive growth in the Internet's popularity eventually led developers of all network operating systems to adopt TCP/IP as their default protocol.

IP is the network layer protocol that performs many important networking functions. These functions are described in the following sections.

TAKE NOTE *

There are other network layer protocols that perform functions similar to those of IP, such as Internetwork Packet Exchange (IPX), a proprietary protocol developed by Novell for use with its NetWare operating system. However, the ubiquity of TCP/IP on the Internet has lead to the almost universal adoption of IP at the network layer.

IP ROUTING

The term internet (with a lowercase "i") literally means a network of networks. The Internet as we know it (with a capital "I") is a huge conglomeration of networks, all connected together by devices called routers. A **router** is simply a device that connects one network to another. When you install a LAN in a home or office, and connect it to the Internet, you are actually installing a router that connects your network with another network, that of your Internet service provider (ISP).

➕ MORE INFORMATION

Windows 7 itself can function as a router. When a Windows 7 computer is connected to two networks, such as a LAN and an ISP's network, you can activate the Internet Connection Sharing (ICS) feature, which enables Windows 7 to route packets between the networks. In most cases, however, routers are not general-purpose computers, but rather specialized devices that are dedicated to routing functions.

IP is the primary end-to-end protocol used on most data networks. Data-link layer protocols like Ethernet are actually LAN protocols; they are designed to send packets from one system to another system on the same local network. An *end-to-end protocol* like IP is responsible for the complete transmission of a packet from its source to its final destination on another network.

To get to that final destination, packets must be passed from router to router, through many different networks. A single packet might pass through dozens of routers before it reaches its destination network. The IP protocol is responsible for this routing process. Every TCP/IP system maintains a routing table that functions as the road map to other networks. By examining the destination address on each packet, and comparing it with the information in the routing table, IP decides which router to send the packet to next. The next router to receive the packet does the same thing, and step-by-step, the packet makes its way to the destination. Actually, each router the packet passes through is called a *hop*, so it is really a hop-by-hop process.

Of course, this process occurs much more quickly than this text can describe it. When you type a URL into your web browser and press the Enter key, in the time it takes for the web page to begin appearing on your screen, dozens of packets have traveled back and forth through dozens of routers to and from a destination that might be in another city or another country.

+ MORE INFORMATION

To see how many routers there are between your Windows 7 computer and a destination on the Internet, open a Command Prompt window and type **tracert *destination***, where *destination* is the name of a server on the Internet, such as www.microsoft.com. The Tracert.exe program will gradually compile a list of the routers as they process the packets on the way to the destination.

IPv4 ADDRESSING

IP has its own addressing system, which it uses to identify all of the devices on a network. Every network interface in a computer, and every device that is directly connected to a TCP/IP network, must have an *IP address*. IP addresses are independent of the hardware addresses assigned to network interface adapters. A Windows 7 computer that is connected to a LAN has both a hardware address and an IP address.

As mentioned earlier, data-link layer protocols like Ethernet are LAN protocols; their addresses are only used to transmit packets to other systems on the same local network. The IP address in a given packet, on the other hand, always identifies the packet's final destination, even if it is on another network. This is why IP is called an end-to-end protocol. When you use your web browser to connect to a site on the Internet, the packets your computer generates contain the IP address of the destination site, but at the data-link layer, they carry the hardware address of a router on the local network that they can use to access the Internet. Thus, the data-link layer and the network layer both have their own addressing systems, and the two addresses do not have to point to the same destination.

The current standard for IP is version 4 (IPv4), which defines a 32-bit address space. Each address is split into two parts:

- **Network identifier:** As the name implies, specifies the network on which a particular system is located.
- **Host identifier:** Specifies a particular network interface (also called a *host*) on the network.

Unlike hardware addresses, however, which always use three bytes for the network and three bytes for the interface, IP addresses can have variable numbers of network bits and host bits. To locate the division between the network identifier and the host identifier, TCP/IP systems use a mechanism called a *subnet mask*.

+ MORE INFORMATION

The TCP/IP protocols are defined by public domain documents that are published by a body called the Internet Engineering Task Force (IETF). When they are first published, these documents are known as Requests For Comments (RFC). They then proceed through a lengthy ratification process before being declared Internet standards. The original IP standard, published as RFC 791, "Internet Protocol: DARPA Internet Program Protocol Specification" in September 1981, is a relatively short document that concentrates largely on IPv4 addressing. There are numerous other RFCs that define other aspects of the IP protocol, all of which are available from the IETF Web site at http://www.ietf.org.

Subnet Masking

IPv4 addresses are expressed in dotted decimal notation, that is, four eight-bit numbers, separated by dots (or periods), such as 192.168.3.64. An eight-bit binary number, when expressed in decimal form, can have any value from 0 to 255. A subnet mask is also a 32-bit number, expressed in dotted decimal notation, such as 255.255.255.0. The difference between a subnet mask and an IPv4 address is that a subnet mask consists, in binary form, of a series of consecutive 1s followed by a series of consecutive 0s. When you compare the binary values of the subnet mask to those of the IPv4 address, the 1 bits in the mask represent the network identifier, while the 0 bits represent the host identifier.

For example, a Windows 7 computer might be configured with the following IPv4 address and subnet mask:

- **IP address:** 192.168.3.64
- **Subnet mask:** 255.255.255.0

The whole concept of the subnet mask is easier to understand if you convert both values from decimal to binary, as follows:

- **IP address:** 11000000 10101000 00000011 100000000
- **Subnet mask:** 11111111 11111111 11111111 00000000

In binary form, you can see that the first 24 bits of the subnet mask are ones. Therefore, the first 24 bits of the IPv4 address form the network identifier. The last eight bits of the mask are zeroes, so the last eight bits of the address are the host identifier. As a result, in decimal form, the network identifier is 192.168.3 and the host identifier is 64.

The original IP standard defines three classes of IP addresses, based on the byte divisions of their subnet masks. These classes, and their characteristics, are shown in Table 5-1.

Table 5-1

IPv4 Address Classes

	CLASS A	CLASS B	CLASS C
Subnet mask	255.0.0.0	255.255.0.0	255.255.255.0
First bit values (binary)	0	10	110
First byte value (decimal)	0–127	128–191	192–223
Number of network identifier bits	8	16	24
Number of host identifier bits	24	16	8
Number of possible networks	126	16,384	2,097,152
Number of possible hosts	16,777,214	65,534	254

Classless Inter-Domain Routing (CIDR)

In practical use, the IP address classes proved to be wasteful, and when the Internet first experienced a massive period of growth in the 1990s, it was feared that there might at some time be a shortage of addresses. To avoid assigning entire addresses of a particular class to networks that didn't have that many hosts, the IETF eventually published a new standard for assigning IP addresses called *classless inter-domain routing (CIDR)*.

CIDR differs from traditional addressing (now called *classful addressing*) by allowing the division between the network identifier and the host identifier to fall anywhere in an IPv4 address; it does not have to fall on one of the eight-bit boundaries. For example, a subnet mask of 255.255.240.0 translates into a binary value of 11111111 11111111 11110000 00000000, meaning that the network identifier is 20 bits long and the host identifier is 12 bits. This falls between a Class B and a Class C address, and enables ISPs to assign clients only the number of addresses they need, which conserves the IP address space.

CIDR also introduced a new syntax for IP network address references. In classful notation, an address like 172.23.0.0 was assumed to be a Class B address and use the standard 255.255.0.0 Class B subnet mask.

In CIDR notation, the network address is followed by a slash and the number of bits is the network identifier. Therefore, 172.23.0.0/16 would be the CIDR equivalent of a Class B address. An address that used the 255.255.240.0 subnet mask described earlier would therefore look something like 172.23.0.0/20.

Private IP Addressing

Computers that are connected directly to the Internet must use IPv4 addresses that are registered with the Internet Assigned Numbers Authority (IANA). This is to prevent the duplication of IP addresses on the Internet. The IANA assigns blocks of network identifiers to ISPs, who assign them in turn to their customers. Once an organization is assigned a network identifier, it is up to the network administrators to assign a unique host identifier to each computer on the network.

Private LANs do not need registered addresses, so they can use network identifiers from three special ranges of private addresses that are reserved for that purpose. The three private address ranges are shown in Table 5-2.

Table 5-2

IPv4 Private Addresses

ADDRESS CLASS	IPv4 PRIVATE ADDRESS RANGE	SUBNET MASK
Class A	10.0.0.0 through 10.255.255.255	255.0.0.0
Class B	172.16.0.0 through 172.31.255.255	255.255.0.0
Class C	192.168.0.0 through 192.168.255.255	255.255.255.0

Internet routers do not forward these private addresses, so computers that use them are theoretically not accessible from the Internet. However, most networks today that use private IP addresses provide their computers with Internet access using a technology such as *network address translation (NAT)*.

NAT is a feature built into many routers that takes the packets destined for the Internet that are generated by the computers on a private network, substitutes a registered address for the computer's private address, and then forwards the packets to the Internet destinations. When the Internet servers send replies, the NAT router does the same thing in reverse. As a result, an entire private network can share a single registered address.

Assigning IP Addresses

Windows 7 computers can acquire IP addresses in the following three ways:

- **Manual configuration:** It is possible for administrators to manually assign IP addresses to hosts and configure each computer to use the address assigned to it. However, this method requires much more time and effort than the other alternatives and is prone to error.

- **Dynamic Host Configuration Protocol (DHCP):** DHCP is a client/server application and protocol that enables clients to obtain IP addresses from a pool provided by a server. It then returns the addresses to the pool when the clients no longer need them. Windows 7 includes a DHCP client, which it uses by default. The Windows server products all include a full-featured DHCP server, which you can configure to assign any range of addresses in a variety of ways. Windows 7 also includes a DHCP server, which is incorporated into the ICS feature, but it has only rudimentary capabilities and is not configurable.

- **Automatic Private IP Addressing (APIPA):** When a Windows 7 computer with no IP address starts, and it fails to locate a DHCP server on the network, the TCP/IP client automatically configures itself using an address in the 169.254.0.0/16 network. This enables computers on a small network with no DHCP server to communicate without the need for manual configuration.

DNS NAME RESOLUTION

All TCP/IP communication is based on IP addresses, and in TCP/IP parlance, each network interface in a computer is called a host. In addition to IP addresses, hosts can also have names, and the host names are grouped together in units called domains. When users access a Web site on the Internet, they do so by specifying or selecting a DNS name, which consists of a host name and two or more domain names (such as www.adatum.com), not an IP address. This is because names are far easier to remember and use than IP addresses.

For TCP/IP systems to use these friendly host names, they must have some way to discover the IP address associated with a specific name. This discovery process is called *name resolution*, and the application that resolves names into IP addresses is the Domain Name System (DNS).

DNS is a client/server application that is essentially a distributed database. Information about the names and addresses of Internet computers is distributed among thousands of DNS servers all over the world. Virtually all operating systems have a DNS client, called a resolver, that enables them to send a host name to a DNS server and receive the IP address associated with that name in return.

In its most basic form, the DNS name resolution process consists of a resolver submitting a name resolution request to the DNS server specified in its TCP/IP configuration settings. When the server does not possess information about the requested name, it forwards the request to another DNS server on the network. The second server generates a response containing the IP address of the requested name and returns it to the first server, which relays the information in turn to the resolver. In actual practice, the DNS name resolution process can be considerably more complex, but the basic message exchanges are essentially the same.

IPv6 ADDRESSING

When the IP protocol was first developed, in the late 1970s, the Internet was an experimental network used only by a few hundred engineers and scientists. At that time, the 32-bit address space defined in the IPv4 standard seemed enormous. No one could have foreseen the explosive growth of the Internet that began in the 1990s, and which soon threatened to deplete the existing IP address space.

To address this situation, work began in the 1990s on a new revision of the IP protocol, known as Internet Protocol Version 6, or IPv6. IPv6 expands the address space from 32 to 128 bits, which is large enough to provide more than 6.7×10^{23} addresses for each square meter of the Earth's surface.

Because this address space is so huge, IPv6 supports multiple subnet levels, not just one as in IPv4. Individual hosts can also have multiple IPv6 addresses for various purposes, with little chance of the address space being depleted in the near future. IPv6 supports automatic assignment of addresses, in both stateful and stateless configurations.

IPv6 also simplifies the packet header format by moving some of the IPv4 header information to optional fields. This reduces the size of routing tables and decreases the processing burden on routers throughout the IPv6 universe.

IPv6 Address Format

Unlike IPv4 addresses, which use decimal notation, IPv6 addresses use hexadecimal notation, in the form of eight two-byte values, separated by colons, as follows:

XX:XX:XX:XX:XX:XX:XX:XX

Each X is a hexadecimal value for one byte, resulting in a total of 16 bytes, or 128 bits. An example of an IPv6 address would be as follows:

FDC0:0000:0000:02BD:00FF:BECB:FEF4:961D

To simplify the address somewhat, you can remove the leading zeroes, leaving you with the following:

```
FDC0:0:0:02BD:FF:BECB:FEF4:961D
```

> **TAKE NOTE ***
>
> In hexadecimal (or base 16) notation, each digit can have a value from 0 to 9 or A to F, for a total of 16 possible values. Remember, an eight-bit (one-byte) number can have 256 possible values. If each hexadecimal digit can have 16 values, two digits are required to express the 256 possible values for each byte of the address ($16^2 = 256$). This is why some of the two-byte values in the sample IPv6 address require four digits.

To simplify the notation further, you can eliminate the zero blocks from an address and replace them with a double colon, as follows:

```
FDC0::02BD:FF:BECB:FEF4:961D
```

Subnetting IPv6

To identify the network bits of an address, IPv6 uses the same type of notation as CIDR, a prefix followed by a slash, as in the following example:

```
FDC0::02BD/64
```

Subnet prefixes are the only way to identify subnets in IPv6; there are no subnet masks.

Understanding IPv6 Address Types

Much as IPv4 supports unicast, broadcast, and multicast addresses, IPv6 also has three address types:

- **Unicast:** Identifies a single network interface in a computer or other device. Packets addressed to a unicast address are delivered to one node only.
- **Anycast:** Identifies a set of network interfaces. Packets addressed to an anycast address are delivered only to the interface closest to the source (by number of hops).
- **Multicast:** Identifies a group of multiple network interfaces. Packets addressed to a multicast address are delivered to all of the interfaces designated as members of the group. One standard multicast address, known as the "all nodes" multicast group, performs the role of the IPv4 broadcast address, so there is no need for an explicit broadcast address type in IPv6.

IPv6 addresses each have a scope, which defines the area within which the address is unique. The scopes defined in the IPv6 standards are as follows:

- **Node-local:** Limited to an individual interface. This is the equivalent of the loopback address in IPv4.
- **Link-local:** Limited to systems on the directly attached network.
- **Site-local:** Limited to interfaces at a single site. Once intended to be the equivalent of private IPv4 addresses, this scope is now deprecated.
- **Organization-local:** Designed to span multiple sites belonging to an individual organization.
- **Global:** Unique throughout the IPv6 universe.

IPv6 Name Resolution

Name resolution for computers with global IPv6 addresses is provided by the Domain Name System (DNS), just as it is in IPv4. For computers with link-local addresses, which might not have access to a DNS server, the system uses the ***Link Local Multicast Name Resolution (LLMNR)*** protocol.

To use LLMNR, systems transmit name query request messages as multicasts to the local net-work. The request contains the name the computer is trying to resolve. The other computers on the local network, on receiving the messages, compare the requested name with their own names. The computer with the requested name then replies with a message containing its IP address, which it transmits as a unicast to the original requestor.

IPv6 Address Autoconfiguration

At the time IPv4 was conceived, there were some data-link layer implementations that required network administrators to manually assign addresses to the network interface hard-ware for media access control purposes. The designers of IPv4 therefore decided to design an addressing system that was completely independent from the underlying protocol at the data-link layer.

Today, all network interface adapters have factory-assigned hardware addresses, so IPv6 derives its host identifiers from those hardware addresses. There is therefore no need for APIPA or NAT or DHCP host address assignments.

IPv6 address assignment is much more of an automatic process than in IPv4. A technique called *stateless address autoconfiguration* enables computers to configure their own addresses after transmitting router solicitation multicasts to the routers on the network and receiving router advertisement messages in return. For situations where stateless autoconfiguration is not appropriate, Windows 7 workstations can use DHCP for stateful address autoconfigura-tion instead.

IPv6 Transition

More than ten years after the initial publication of the IPv6 standard, and despite its almost universal operating system and router support, the vast majority of the systems on the Internet still rely on IPv4. However, the inclusion of IPv6 support in Windows 7 and Windows Server 2008 R2 makes the operating systems ready for the transition when it occurs. Windows 7, by default, installs support for both IPv4 and IPv6 addressing when it detects a network interface adapter in the computer, as shown in Figure 5-3. Microsoft refers to this as Windows 7's *dual IP stack*.

Figure 5-3

Windows 7 support for IPv4 and IPv6

In addition, the DHCP server application in Windows Server 2008 R2 supports both addressing standards, so when a Windows 7 computer requests an IP address, the DHCP server supplies both IPv4 and IPv6 information. Windows 7 applications that are capable of using IPv6 do so by default; otherwise, applications revert to IPv4.

As the transition from IPv4 to IPv6 proceeds, there are times when it is necessary for computers running IPv6-only applications to exchange messages over an IPv4-only network. Windows 7 (and Windows Server 2008 R2) supports a number of transition mechanisms that make this possible, including the following:

- **IPv4-compatible addresses:** A hybrid IPv6/IPv4 address that enables an IPv6 system to communicate using an IPv4 infrastructure. The address format consists of 96 bits of zeroes, followed by an IPv4 address in its standard dotted decimal notation, as in the following example:
  ::192.168.1.99.

- **IPv4-mapped addresses:** A hybrid IPv6/IPv4 address that enables an IPv6 system to recognize an IPv4-only system. The address format consists of 80 bits of zeroes, followed by 16 bits of ones, followed by an IPv4 address in its standard dotted decimal notation, as in the following example:
  ::ffff:192.168.1.99.

- **6to4:** A tunneling technology that enables computers to transmit IPv6 packets over an IPv4 network. The 6to4 address that an IPv6 system uses when connecting to the IPv6 Internet through an intermediate IPv4 network takes the following format: 2002:<first 156 bits of the IPv4 address>:<second 16 bits of the IPv4 address>::/16. For example, the IPv4 address 192.168.1.99 would appear as follows:
  2002:C0A8:0163::/16.

- **Teredo:** A tunneling protocol that enables computers to transmit IPv6 packets through NAT routers that do not support IPv6. A Teredo address consists of a 32-bit prefix: 2001:0000, followed by the IPv4 address of the Teredo server, 16 flag bits, and the UDP port number and public IPv4 address of the NAT router. These last 48 bits are obfuscated by reversing their bit values.

TAKE NOTE*

Tunneling is a networking technique that enables systems to encapsulate packets within other packets, for security or compatibility purposes. In the case of 6to4, for example, a computer encapsulates IPv6 packets within IPv4 packets using UDP, so that the system can transmit them over an IPv4 network.

DATA ENCAPSULATION

Earlier in this lesson, you learned how data-link layer protocols encapsulate data for transmission, much as an envelope encapsulates a letter for mailing. IP encapsulates data as well, so that it can provide the address of the system that is the packet's final destination. In fact, IP performs its encapsulation first, by adding a header to the data it receives from the transport layer protocol. This header includes the packet's source and destination IP addresses, as well as other information that facilitates the transmission of the packet.

After IP adds its header, it sends the packet down to the data-link layer, where Ethernet adds its own header and footer to the packet. Thus, the data-link layer packet that gets transmitted over the network consists of transport layer data, encapsulated within an IP packet, which is called a *datagram*, which is in turn encapsulated within an Ethernet frame, as shown in Figure 5-4.

Figure 5-4

IP data encapsulation

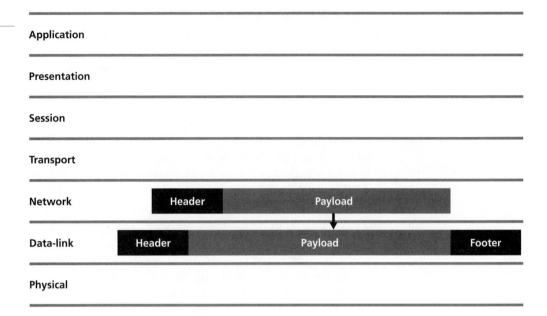

Application

Presentation

Session

Transport

Network

Data-link

Physical

As with Ethernet, one of the functions of the IP header is to identify the protocol that generated the data in the datagram. The Protocol field in the IP header uses codes standardized by the IANA to specify the transport layer protocol that created the packet.

The Transport Layer

> The OSI reference model calls for the network and transport layers to provide a flexible quality of service, so that applications can operate at peak efficiency.

There are two types of protocols that operate at the network and transport layers:

- A *connection-oriented protocol* is one in which two communicating systems establish a connection before they transmit any data. Once the connection is established, the computers exchange packets with complex headers designed to provide error detection and correction. A connection-oriented protocol ensures bit-perfect data transmissions, but at the price of greatly increased overhead.

- A *connectionless protocol* does not require the establishment of a connection, nor does it perform error detection or correction. Systems simply transmit their packets to the destination, without knowing if the destination system is ready to accept data, or if it even exists. Connectionless protocols do not guarantee delivery of their data, but they operate with a very low overhead that conserves network bandwidth.

IP, at the network layer, is a connectionless protocol, and there is no connection-oriented alternative at that layer. At the transport layer, TCP is the connection-oriented protocol, and the connectionless alternative is the User Datagram Protocol (UDP).

CONNECTION-ORIENTED PROTOCOLS

Applications that use TCP require every bit of data they transmit to be received properly at the destination. For example, if you download a service pack from the Microsoft Web site, a single garbled bit could render the package useless. Using the combination of TCP and IP guarantees that every packet arrives intact. If a packet is damaged or lost, the system retransmits it. However, to use TCP, the systems must exchange extra packets to establish a connection and append a 20-byte header to each packet. This adds up to a lot of extra data that has to be transmitted over the network.

CONNECTIONLESS PROTOCOLS

Applications that use UDP are not terribly concerned if a packet goes astray for two reasons. Either the messages are so small that the systems can easily retransmit them if they do not receive a response, or the data transmitted by the application is of a type that can tolerate the loss of an occasional packet.

An example of the former reason is the Domain Name System (DNS) communications that are a part of every Internet transaction. When you type a URL into your web browser, the first thing the system does is send a UDP message to a DNS server requesting the IP address corresponding to the domain name in the URL. This is a tiny message that fits in a single packet, so it's not worth transmitting several additional packets to establish a TCP connection. It's more economical just to retransmit the DNS request if no response is forthcoming.

A good example of the latter reason is streaming video. A video stream consists of large amounts of data, but unlike a file transfer, a few missing bits will not cause a catastrophic failure. A few packets lost from a video stream due to damaged UDP packets might mean a few lost frames, but that would hardly be noticeable to the viewer. The alternative, using TCP to transmit all of the packets, would provide a perfect viewing experience for the user, but at the cost of vastly increased bandwidth.

PORTS AND SOCKETS

Just like the network and data-link layers, transport layer protocols encapsulate the data they receive from the layer above by appending a header to each packet, as shown in Figure 5-5. Unlike the lower layers, however, transport layer protocols are not concerned with addressing packets to the correct system. IP and Ethernet performed the addressing, so there is no need for it here. However, transport layer protocols are concerned with identifying the applications that created the packet and to which the packet will ultimately be delivered.

Figure 5-5

Transport layer data encapsulation

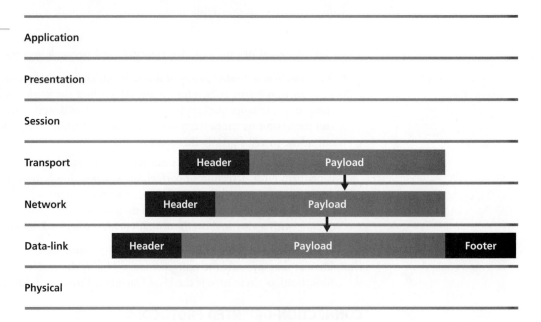

As with the protocol codes included in IP headers, the TCP and UDP headers both contain codes that identify specific applications running on the system. The codes, called *ports*, are again published by the IANA, and the combination of an IP address and a port number is called a *socket*. For example, the standard port number for the Hypertext Transfer Protocol (HTTP), the application layer protocol used for web communications, is 80. If your web browser is sending an HTTP request to a web server with the IP address

192.168.87.33, the web server application on that computer can be identified by the socket 192.168.87.33:80.

There are two basic types of port numbers: *well-known port numbers*, which are numbers permanently assigned to specific applications, and *ephemeral port numbers*, which are created automatically by client applications. In the previous example, the web browser is using the well-known HTTP port 80 as the destination for its packets, but the source port would be an ephemeral port number created by the system running the browser.

This system works because the client is initiating contact with the server. The client has to know the port number to use in its messages to the server, so it uses a well-known port. There is no need for the client to have a well-known port number because the server will be able to discover the client's ephemeral port number from its incoming messages.

Some of the most common well-known port numbers are listed in Table 5-3.

Table 5-3

Well-Known Port Numbers Used by TCP and UDP

SERVICE NAME	PORT NUMBER	PROTOCOL	FUNCTION
ftp-data	20	TCP	FTP data channel; used for transmitting files between systems
ftp	21	TCP	FTP control channel; used by FTP-connected systems for exchanging commands and responses
Ssh	22	TCP and UDP	SSH (Secure Shell) Remote Login Protocol; used to securely log on to a computer from another computer on the same network and execute commands
telnet	23	TCP	Telnet; used to execute commands on network-connected systems
Smtp	25	TCP	Simple Mail Transport Protocol (SMTP); used to send e-mail messages
Domain	53	TCP and UDP	DNS; used to receive host name resolution requests from clients
Bootps	67	TCP and UDP	Bootstrap Protocol (BOOTP) and DHCP servers; used to receive TCP/IP configuration requests from clients
Bootpc	68	TCP and UDP	BOOTP and DHCP clients; used to send TCP/IP configuration requests to servers
http	80	TCP	HTTP; used by web servers to receive requests from client browsers
pop3	110	TCP	Post Office Protocol 3 (POP3); used to retrieve e-mail requests from clients
nntp	119	TCP and UDP	Network News Transfer Protocol; used to post and distribute messages to, and retrieve them from, Usenet servers on the Internet
ntp	123	TCP and UDP	Network Time Protocol; used to exchange time signals for the purpose of synchronizing the clocks in network computers
imap	143	TCP and UDP	Internet Message Access Protocol version 4; used by e-mail client programs to retrieve messages from a mail server
snmp	161	TCP and UDP	Simple Network Management Protocol (SNMP); used by SNMP agents to transmit status information to a network management console
https	443	TCP and UDP	Hypertext Transfer Protocol over TLS/SSL; used by web servers to receive encrypted requests from client browsers

DATA ENCAPSULATION

The headers that the TCP and UDP protocols add to the data they receive from the application layer are vastly different in size and complexity. The headers for both protocols contain source and destination port numbers. The UDP header includes little else, except for a checksum used to check for errors in the header. The TCP header, on the other hand, includes a multitude of fields that implement additional services, including the following:

- **Packet acknowledgment:** Informs the sender which packets have been delivered successfully.
- **Error correction:** Informs the sender which packets must be retransmitted.
- **Flow control:** Regulates the rate at which the sending system transmits its data.

The Upper Layers

> The application layer is the top of the networking stack, and as such, it provides the entrance point for programs running on a computer.

TAKE NOTE *

The session and presentation layers typically do not have individual protocols dedicated to them. In most cases, application layer protocols include functions attributed to all three top layers.

Windows applications themselves have no networking capabilities. They simply make function calls to application layer protocols, which in turn initiate the entire network communications process.

For example, a mail client is a program that enables you to send messages to users on other computers, but the mail program knows nothing about the nature of your network. When you send an e-mail message to someone, the client takes the message and the address of the intended recipient and packages it using an application layer protocol called Simple Mail Transfer Protocol (SMTP). SMTP creates a properly formatted e-mail message and passes it down to the proper protocol at the next lower layer in the networking stack, the transport layer, which for this application is TCP.

TCP then adds its header, passes the packet down to IP at the network layer, which encapsulates it and passes it down to Ethernet at the data-link layer, which adds its frame and transmits it over the network. Thus, by the time the e-mail message reaches the network, it has been encapsulated four times by SMTP, TCP, IP, and Ethernet, as shown in Figure 5-6.

Figure 5-6

Application layer data encapsulation

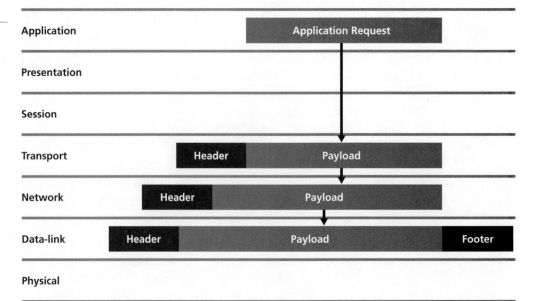

When the packet arrives at its final destination, the networking stack on the receiving computer performs the same steps in reverse. The system passes the incoming packets up through the layers, with each one removing its header and using the header information to pass the contents to the correct protocol at the next higher layer. Finally, the packet arrives at its final terminus, which is an application running on the destination computer, in this case, an e-mail server.

Connecting to a Network

↓
THE BOTTOM LINE

The networking capabilities in Windows 7 have been designed to minimize the threat of intrusion from outside intruders, while providing users with a simple and reliable networking experience. The following sections examine some of the networking tools and concepts in Windows 7.

Networking provides Windows 7 with an open door to a virtually unlimited array of resources, but an open door can let things in as easily as it lets things out. This makes security a primary concern for Windows 7 technical specialists. Windows 7 includes a variety of tools and features that enable users and administrators to manage the operating system's networking capabilities and help protect it against unauthorized access. Many of these features lie "under the hood," and operate invisibly to both users and administrators.

Some of the tools that desktop technicians must use regularly, and the concepts they support, are discussed in the following sections.

Installing Network Support

Windows 7 is usually able to detect a network interface adapter in a computer and automatically install and configure the networking client.

The installation of Windows 7's networking support is usually automatic. When Windows 7 detects a network interface adapter in the computer, either during the operating system installation or afterward, it installs a device driver for the adapter, as well as the components of the default networking stack listed here:

- **Client for Microsoft Networks:** Provides application layer services that enable programs to access shared files and printers on the network.
- **QoS Packet Scheduler:** Enables the network client to prioritize network traffic based on bandwidth availability and changing network conditions.
- **File and Printer Sharing for Microsoft Networks:** Enables the computer to share its files and printers with other users on the network.
- **Internet Protocol Version 6 (TCP/IPv6):** Provides support for the IPv6 network layer protocol, including 128-bit IP addresses.
- **Internet Protocol Version 4 (TCP/IPv4):** Provides support for the IPv4 network layer protocol, including 32-bit IP addresses.
- **Link Layer Topology Discovery Mapper I/O Driver and Link Layer Topology Discovery Responder:** Implement the protocol that enables Windows 7 to compile a map of the computers on the network.

The first time that the computer connects to a network, Windows 7 presents the user with a selection of three network locations. These selections are actually combinations of network discovery and file sharing settings, which determine how much access the workstation user will have to the network and how much access network users will have to the workstation.

These three network location options are as follows:

- **Home:** Indicates that the computer is connected to a private workgroup or HomeGroup network and not directly connected to the Internet. This means that it is safe for the computer to share its files and discover other computers.

TAKE NOTE*

When a Windows 7 computer is set to use the Home, Work, or Public network location, the user can modify the settings manually from the Network and Sharing Center. When the network location is set to Domain, the setting is controlled by domain policy and is not manually configurable. See "Changing the Network Location," later in this lesson for more information.

- **Work:** Indicates that the computer is connected to a small office workgroup network. This means that it is safe for the computer to share its files and discover other computers, but the system cannot create or join a HomeGroup.
- **Public:** Indicates that the computer is connected to a network in a public place, such as an airport or coffee shop "hot spot" for wireless computers, or is connected directly to the Internet without an intervening router. This means that the computer and its shares cannot be seen or accessed from the network, nor can the system create or join a HomeGroup network. In addition, some applications might not be able to access the network.

There is also a fourth option, Domain, which indicates that the computer is connected to an Active Directory Domain Services (AD DS) domain. This option is set automatically when you join the computer to the domain.

Using the Network and Sharing Center

The Network and Sharing Center is a centralized console that provides technical specialists and system administrators with access to most of the major networking tools included with Windows 7.

The Windows 7 Network and Sharing Center provides a central access point for all of the network connections on the computer. Many of the common network configuration and administration tasks that technicians perform on Windows 7 computers start by opening the Network and Sharing Center. As with many Windows tools, there are several ways to open the Network and Sharing Center, two of which are as follows:

- Click Start > Control Panel > Network and Internet > Network and Sharing Center
- Click Start > Search for "Network" > Network and Sharing Center

When the Network and Sharing Center appears, you see a window like the one shown in Figure 5-7.

Figure 5-7

The Network and Sharing Center

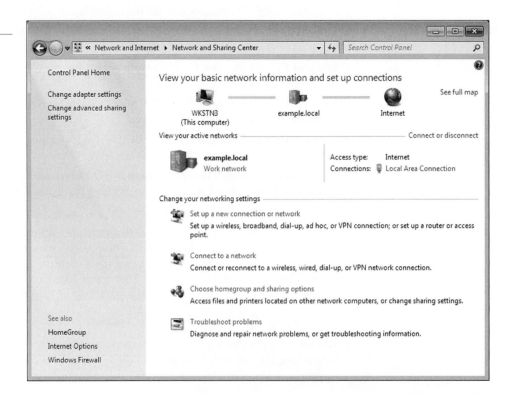

The Network and Sharing Center main window consists of the following elements:

- **Task list (left pane):** Contains links that enable you to manage network adapter settings and configure sharing parameters.
- **Summary network map (top right):** Provides a graphical representation of the computers and networks (represented by icons) in the immediate vicinity of the workstation and their connections (represented by lines). A link also provides access to a complete map of the entire network.
- **View your active networks (middle right):** Displays the name of the network and other information, such as the network location (private, domain, or public), whether the workstation is connected to a local network, the Internet, or both, and the name of the local area connection the system is using to access the network. There are also links that enable you to connect to or disconnect from the network and view the current status of the local area connection.
- **Change your networking settings (bottom right):** Contains switches that enable you to control the sharing and discovery behavior of the network.

UNDERSTANDING NETWORK DISCOVERY

Network Discovery is an important security concept first introduced in Windows Vista. It enables users to control critical network firewall controls with a single switch. Windows Firewall is a feature that was first introduced in the Windows XP Service Pack 2 release, which is now included in Windows 7 as well.

A *firewall* is a software routine that acts as a virtual barrier between a computer and the network to which it is attached. A firewall is essentially a filter that enables certain types of incoming and outgoing traffic to pass through the barrier, while blocking other types.

Firewalls typically base their filtering on the TCP/IP characteristics at the network, transport, and application layers, as follows:

- **IP addresses:** Represent specific computers on the network.
- **Protocol numbers:** Identify the transport layer protocol being used by the packets.
- **Port numbers:** Identify specific applications running on the computer.

If, for example, you want to prevent all computers on the network from accessing your system using the Telnet protocol, you would configure the firewall to block the traffic from all IP addresses using TCP port number 23, the well-known port number associated with Telnet.

Configuring a firewall manually can be an extremely complex task, however. You must be conscious of all the protocols and port numbers used by specific operating system functions and applications. Network Discovery is a Windows 7 feature that simplifies the task of firewall configuration by enabling you to block or allow the protocols and ports needed for the computer to browse and access the network.

Modifying the Network Discovery setting in the Network and Sharing Center controls two functions:

- Whether the computer can see and be seen by the other systems on the network.
- Whether the computer can share its resources and access shared resources on the network.

It is critical to understand that this setting works in both directions. When a Windows 7 computer has Network Discovery turned off, it cannot browse the other computers on the network or access their shares. At the same time, the other computers on the network cannot browse to the Windows 7 computer or access its shares.

The default state of the Network Discovery setting is dependent on the network location, as set manually by the user or automatically by the computer. Computers configured with the Home and Work locations have Network Discovery turned on, and Public computers have it turned off.

CHANGING THE NETWORK LOCATION

After you select the initial network location during the network interface adapter installation, Windows 7 attempts to detect the type of location whenever you connect to a different network. If, for example, you selected Home when you installed Windows 7 on your laptop computer, and you later take the computer to a coffee shop with a wireless network, Windows 7 will most likely detect the change and alter the network location to Public. This turns the Network Discovery and file sharing options off for greater security.

If, for any reason, the computer fails to detect a network change and you want to manually alter the location setting, you can do so by performing the following procedure.

CHANGE THE NETWORK LOCATION

GET READY. Log on to Windows 7 using an account with administrative capabilities.

1. Open the Network and Sharing Center. The Network and Sharing Center window appears.
2. In the View your active networks section, click the current network location. The *Set Network Location* page appears, as shown in Figure 5-8.

Figure 5-8

The Set Network Location page

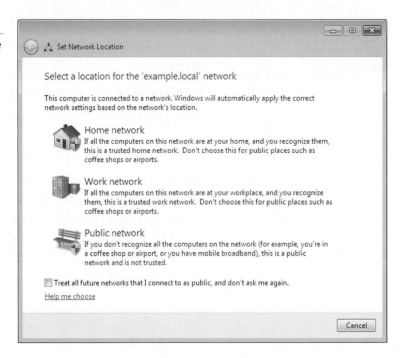

3. Select one of the following network locations. The system connects to the network, reconfigures the Network Discovery settings, and a screen appears, specifying the new network location:
   - Home network
   - Work network
   - Public network
4. Click Close.
5. Close the Network and Sharing Center window.

X REF

For more information on HomeGroup networking, see Lesson 9, "Working with Domains, Workgroups, and HomeGroups."

When you select the Home network location for the first time, the system creates a new HomeGroup network and supplies you with a password for it.

CONFIGURING ADVANCED SHARING SETTINGS

When you are using the Home, Work, or Public network location setting, you can manually change the Network Discovery and other sharing settings by using the following procedure.

 ### CONFIGURE ADVANCED SHARING

GET READY. Log on to Windows 7 using an account with administrative capabilities.

1. Open the Network and Sharing Center. The Network and Sharing Center window appears.
2. In the left pane, click Change advanced sharing settings. The Change sharing options for different network profiles dialog box appears.
3. Click the down arrow for the location whose settings you want to modify, to produce the display shown in Figure 5-9.

Figure 5-9

The Change sharing options for different network profiles dialog box

4. Configure the following settings by selecting one of the options provided:
   - **Network Discovery:** Enables the computer to see other devices on the network and renders it visible from the network.
   - **File and printer sharing:** Enables network users to access the files and printers shared on the computer.
   - **Public folder sharing:** Enables network users to access the Public folders on the computer.
   - **Media streaming:** Enables network users to access media files on the computer and enables the computer to locate media files on the network.
   - **File sharing connections:** Specifies whether clients accessing the computer's shares must use 128-bit encryption.
   - **Password-protected sharing:** Specifies whether network users accessing the computer's shares must have local user accounts with passwords.
   - **HomeGroup connections:** Specifies whether Windows 7 should manage HomeGroup connections automatically.
5. Click Save Changes. The Network and Sharing Center window reappears.

Managing Network Connections

Windows 7 creates and configures local area connections automatically, but you can also manage and modify the properties of the connections manually.

When Windows 7 detects a network interface adapter, it creates a network connection automatically, installs the TCP/IP networking components, and configures it to use DHCP to obtain IP addresses and other network configuration settings. To view and modify the local area connection properties, use the procedures in the following sections.

VIEWING A CONNECTION'S STATUS

Each local area connection on a Windows 7 system has a status dialog box that displays real-time information about the connection. To view the status of a connection, use the following procedure.

 VIEW CONNECTION STATUS

GET READY. Log on to Windows 7 using an account with administrative capabilities.

1. Open the Network and Sharing Center. The Network and Sharing Center window appears.
2. In the View your active networks section, click Local Area Connection or the name of the connection whose status you want to view. The Local Area Connection Status dialog box appears, as shown in Figure 5-10.

Figure 5-10

The Local Area Connection Status dialog box

3. Click Details. The Network Connection Details dialog box appears, as shown in Figure 5-11.
4. Click Close to close the Network Connection Details dialog box.
5. Click Close to close the Local Area Connection Status dialog box.

Figure 5-11

The Network Connection
Details dialog box

The Local Area Connection Status dialog box displays basic information about the connection, such as its speed, which version(s) of IP it is using, and how long the computer has been connected. In the Activity area, you can see the number of bytes that the computer has sent and received in a real-time display, so you can tell if the network connection is currently functional.

At the bottom of the dialog box are buttons that enable you to perform the following tasks:

- **Properties:** Open the Properties sheet for the network connection.
- **Disable/Enable:** Toggle the operational status of the network connection.
- **Diagnose:** Start Windows Network Diagnostics and attempt to detect any problems affecting the network connection.

TAKE NOTE *

Disabling a network connection does not affect its configuration settings in any way. The networking hardware is still installed and configured and the TCP/IP settings remain intact. The connection is simply turned off until you turn it back on again, which renders it immediately operational.

The Network Connection Details page displays the configuration settings for the network connection, including the TCP/IP settings obtained using DHCP.

CONFIGURING IPv4 SETTINGS

Most networks today use DHCP to configure the TCP/IP configuration settings of their workstations. DHCP automates the configuration process and prevents the duplication of IP addresses. However, there are still some situations in which it is desirable or necessary to configure the Windows 7 TCP/IP client manually. To do this, use the following procedure.

CERTIFICATION READY?
Configure IPv4 network
settings.
4.1

CONFIGURE IPv4 SETTINGS

GET READY. Log on to Windows 7 using an account with administrative capabilities.

1. Open the Network and Sharing Center. The Network and Sharing Center window appears.

2. Click Change adapter settings. The Network Connections window appears, as shown in Figure 5-12.

Figure 5-12

The Network Connections window

3. Right click the connection you want to manage and, from the context menu, select Properties. The connection's Properties sheet appears.

> **TAKE NOTE** ✱ You can click the Configure button on the connection's Properties sheet to open the Properties sheet for the network interface adapter hardware. From this sheet, you can configure advanced networking settings, as well as the adapter's hardware resource settings.

4. Select Internet Protocol Version 4 (TCP/IPv4) and click Properties. The Internet Protocol Version 4 (TCP/IPv4) Properties sheet appears, as shown in Figure 5-13.

Figure 5-13

The Internet Protocol Version 4 (TCP/IPv4) Properties sheet

5. Select the Use The Following IP Address option and enter appropriate values for the following parameters:
   - **IP address:** A 32-bit IPv4 address, in dotted decimal notation.
   - **Subnet Mask:** An appropriate mask indicating which part of the IP address is the network identifier and which part the host identifier.
   - **Default Gateway:** The IP address of the router on the local network that the computer should use to access other networks and/or the Internet.

6. Select the Use The Following DNS Server Addresses option and enter appropriate values for the following parameters:
   - **Preferred DNS Server:** The IP address of the DNS server the computer should use to resolve host and domain names into IP addresses.
   - **Alternate DNS Server:** The IP address of a DNS server that the computer should use if the preferred DNS server is unavailable.

+ MORE INFORMATION

Clicking the Advanced button opens the Advanced TCP/IP Settings dialog box, in which you can configure multiple IP addresses, subnet masks, default gateways, DNS servers, and WINS servers for client computers with special requirements.

7. Click OK to close the Internet Protocol Version 4 (TCP/IPv4) Properties sheet.
8. Click OK to close the connection's Properties sheet.

The command-line alternative to this graphical interface is a program called Netsh.exe. Netsh.exe is a powerful tool that you can use interactively or with command-line parameters to configure virtually any Windows 7 networking setting. To configure the basic IPv4 parameters for a network connection, you use the following syntax:

```
netsh interface ipv4 set address connection_name static ip_address
subnet_mask default_gateway
```

An example of an actual command would be as follows:

```
netsh interface ipv4 set address "Local Area Connection" static
192.168.1.23 255.255.255.0 192.168.1.1
```

Then, to configure the DNS server address, you would use the following command syntax:

```
netsh interface ipv4 set dnsservers connection_name static ip_address
```

An example of an actual command would be as follows:

```
netsh interface ipv4 set dnsservers "Local Area Connection" static
192.168.1.99
```

To configure a connection to obtain its settings from a DHCP server, use the following commands:

```
netsh interface ipv4 set address name="Local Area Connection"
source=dhcp
```

```
netsh interface ipv4 set dnsservers name="Local Area Connection"
source=dhcp
```

CONFIGURING IPv6 SETTINGS

Because most computers use IPv6 autoconfiguration or DHCP, manual configuration of the Windows 7 IPv6 implementation is rarely necessary, but it is possible.

The procedure for configuring IPv6 using the graphical interface is the same as that for IPv4, except that, in the Local Area Connection Properties sheet, you select Internet Protocol

CERTIFICATION READY?
Configure IPv6 network settings.
4.2

Version 6 (TCP/IPv6) and click Properties. The Internet Protocol Version 6 (TCP/IPv6) Properties sheet appears, as shown in Figure 5-14.

Figure 5-14

The Internet Protocol Version 6 (TCP/IPv6) Properties sheet

To configure IPv6 from the command prompt, you use Netsh.exe in the same way you would for IPv4, substituting the IPv6 parameter for IPv4 and an IPv6 address for the IPv4 address and subnet mask, as in the following example:

```
netsh interface ipv6 set address "Local Area Connection" static
FE80::7166:22E6:1D18:BDAA
```

To configure DNS server addresses, use a command like this:

```
netsh interface ipv6 set dnsservers "Local Area Connection" static
FE80::7166:22E6:1D18:BD01
```

CREATING A NEW NETWORK CONNECTION

Windows 7 creates local area network connections automatically, but desktop technicians frequently have to create other types of connections manually, such as dial-up Internet connections. To do this, use the following procedure.

 CREATE A NEW NETWORK CONNECTION

GET READY. Log on to Windows 7 using an account with administrative capabilities. If Windows 7 has not detected and installed your modem, you must install it yourself using the Add New Hardware Wizard, accessible from the Device Manager snap-in.

1. Open the Network and Sharing Center. The Network and Sharing Center window appears.
2. Click Set up a new connection or network. The Setup a Connection or Network Wizard appears, displaying the *Choose a connection option* page, as shown in Figure 5-15.

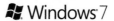

Figure 5-15

The Choose a connection
option page

3. Click Set up a dial-up connection and then click Next. The *Type the information from your Internet service provider (ISP)* page appears, as shown in Figure 5-16.

Figure 5-16

The Type the information from
your Internet service provider
(ISP) page appears

4. Enter the Dial-up phone number, User name, and Password supplied by your ISP. Click the Remember this password check box if you want to avoid typing the password each time you connect to the ISP.

5. Click Connect. The system activates the modem, dials the number you supplied, and attempts to connect to the ISP. If the attempt succeeds, the connection is established and communication with the ISP commences. If the connection attempt does not succeed, a *The Internet Connectivity Test Was Unsuccessful* page appears.

6. To create the dial-up connection without actually connecting to the ISP, click set up the connection anyway. A *The connection to the Internet is ready to use* page appears, as shown in Figure 5-17.

7. Click Close.

Figure 5-17

The Connection to the Internet is ready to use page

Once you have created the dial-up connection, you can open its Properties sheet, just as you did earlier with the local area connection. However, a dial-up connection's Properties sheet, as shown in Figure 5-18, has additional controls for dialing behavior and sharing, as well as the standard network configuration controls.

Figure 5-18

A dial-up connection's Properties sheet

Using Network Map

Network Map is an administration and diagnostics tool that displays a graphical map of the computers on the network and the connections between them.

Network Map is a tool that first appeared in Windows Vista, and is now included in all of the Windows operating systems. Network Map automatically compiles a graphical representation of the network, including icons representing the computers, printers, and other devices attached to it, and lines representing the connections between these elements.

Network Map uses a protocol called Link-Layer Topology Discovery (LLTD) to discover information about the network and the devices attached to it. LLTD devices called *enumerators* transmit requests for information over the network; and other computers, called *responders*, reply with the requested information. This protocol not only enables the computer to discover the existence of other systems on the network, it also tests the connections between them.

DISPLAYING A NETWORK MAP

The Network and Sharing Center displays a summary map on its main window, but to display a complete map of the network, you must click the See full map link, to open the window shown in Figure 5-19. For Windows 7 to display a full map of the network, the following conditions must be met:

- Network Discovery must be turned on.
- If the computer is a member of a Windows domain, group policy must be configured to permit network mapping.
- Any Windows XP computers on the network must have the LLTD Responder software installed.

Figure 5-19

The Network Map page

From a security standpoint, it is not a good idea to allow just anyone to access a map of your network. As a result, when a Windows 7 computer is a member of a Windows domain, network mapping is disabled by the default group policy settings. To control network mapping with group policy, you must use the Group Policy Management Console to open an appropriate group policy object (GPO) and navigate to the Computer Configuration > Administrative Templates > Network > Link-Layer Topology Discovery container. There, you will find the following two policies:

- **Turn on Mapper I/O (LLTDIO) driver:** Enables a computer to map other systems on the network.
- **Turn on Responder (RSPNDR) driver:** Enables a computer to be mapped by other systems on the network.

Enabling these policies, as shown in Figure 5-20, allows you to control whether mapping can occur on domain, public, and private networks.

Figure 5-20

Controlling Network Map
with Group Policy

RUNNING NETWORK DIAGNOSTICS

The Network Map display shows not only the existence of the devices on the network, but their status, and that of the connections between them. Improperly configured computers have yellow warning signs on their icons and non-functioning connections have red Xs on them.

When a problem exists, clicking a warning icon launches Windows Network diagnostics. This utility attempts to automatically discover the cause of the problem and displays possible solutions, as shown in Figure 5-21.

Figure 5-21

Running Windows Network
Diagnostics

You can also launch Windows Network Diagnostics by opening the Network Connections window, right clicking one of the network connections, and selecting Diagnose from the context menu.

Unlike previous troubleshooting tools, Network Diagnostics does not just display error messages, it tells you in clear language what might be wrong and what you have to do to repair the problem. The Network Diagnostics Framework (NDF) includes troubleshooting routines for wireless as well as wired networks. Problems that the system can diagnose include:

- Broken or detached cable connections
- IP address and subnet mask problems
- Default gateway problems
- DNS and DHCP configuration problems
- Networking hardware configuration problems
- Internet server addresses and service settings

If, after identifying a networking problem, the system can repair it automatically, it provides a link that you can select to have it do so. Otherwise, it displays a list of manual fixes that you can perform to address the problem.

Using TCP/IP Tools

Virtually all network operating systems today include support for TCP/IP protocols, and TCP/IP traditionally includes some basic tools that you can use to troubleshoot network connectivity problems yourself.

The traditional TCP/IP troubleshooting tools originated on UNIX systems, and as a result, they are command-line tools that you run in Windows 7 by opening a Command Prompt window first. The Windows implementations of these utilities generally use the same syntax that they did on UNIX.

This section examines some of the most common TCP/IP utilities and their purposes.

USING IPCONFIG.EXE

UNIX and Linux systems have a program called ifconfig (the name is derived from the words *interface configuration*) that you use to manually configure the properties of network interface adapters, including TCP/IP configuration parameters such as IP addresses. Running ifconfig on a UNIX system with just the name of an interface displays the current configuration information for that interface.

All Windows operating systems, including Windows 7, have a graphical interface for configuring network connections, but the configuration display capabilities of ifconfig have been retained in a command-line tool called Ipconfig.exe.

When you run Ipconfig.exe with the /all parameter at the Windows 7 command prompt, you see a display like the one shown in Figure 5-22.

Figure 5-22

The Ipconfig.exe display

```
Administrator: Command Prompt

Microsoft Windows [Version 6.1.7600]
Copyright (c) 2009 Microsoft Corporation.  All rights reserved.

C:\Users\Administrator>ipconfig /all

Windows IP Configuration

        Host Name . . . . . . . . . . . . : Wkstn2
        Primary Dns Suffix  . . . . . . . : example.local
        Node Type . . . . . . . . . . . . : Broadcast
        IP Routing Enabled. . . . . . . . : No
        WINS Proxy Enabled. . . . . . . . : No
        DNS Suffix Search List. . . . . . : example.local

Ethernet adapter Local Area Connection:

        Connection-specific DNS Suffix  . : example.local
        Description . . . . . . . . . . . : Intel(R) PRO/1000 MT Network Connection
        Physical Address. . . . . . . . . : 00-0C-29-13-BC-20
        DHCP Enabled. . . . . . . . . . . : Yes
        Autoconfiguration Enabled . . . . : Yes
        Link-local IPv6 Address . . . . . : fe80::7166:22e6:1d18:b4aa%11(Preferred)
        IPv4 Address. . . . . . . . . . . : 10.0.0.11(Preferred)
        Subnet Mask . . . . . . . . . . . : 255.255.255.0
        Lease Obtained. . . . . . . . . . : Sunday, December 20, 2009 2:48:43 AM
        Lease Expires . . . . . . . . . . : Monday, December 28, 2009 2:48:46 AM
        Default Gateway . . . . . . . . . : 10.0.0.1
        DHCP Server . . . . . . . . . . . : 10.0.0.2
        DHCPv6 IAID . . . . . . . . . . . : 234884137
        DHCPv6 Client DUID. . . . . . . . : 00-01-00-01-12-6D-E4-81-00-0C-29-13-BC-20

        DNS Servers . . . . . . . . . . . : 10.0.0.2
        NetBIOS over Tcpip. . . . . . . . : Enabled

Tunnel adapter isatap.example.local:

        Media State . . . . . . . . . . . : Media disconnected
        Connection-specific DNS Suffix  . : example.local
        Description . . . . . . . . . . . : Microsoft ISATAP Adapter
        Physical Address. . . . . . . . . : 00-00-00-00-00-00-00-E0
        DHCP Enabled. . . . . . . . . . . : No
        Autoconfiguration Enabled . . . . : Yes

C:\Users\Administrator>
```

The value of Ipconfig.exe is particularly apparent when a Windows 7 computer autoconfigures its TCP/IP client or uses DHCP to obtain its IP address and other TCP/IP configuration parameters. A DHCP-configured computer does not display any configuration information in the Local Area Connection Properties sheet; it just shows that the DHCP client is activated. One of the few ways to see what settings the DHCP server has assigned to the computer (without examining the DHCP server itself) is to use Ipconfig.exe.

In addition to displaying the DHCP-obtained configuration settings, Ipconfig.exe also enables you to manually release the IP address the system obtained from the DHCP server and renew existing address leases. By running Ipconfig.exe with the /release and /renew command-line parameters, you can release or renew the IP address assignment of one of the network interfaces in the computer or for all of the interfaces at once.

USING PING.EXE

Ping (Ping.exe) is the most basic of TCP/IP utilities, and it is included in some form with every TCP/IP implementation. On Windows 7 systems, the program is called Ping.exe.

Ping.exe can tell you if the TCP/IP stack of another system on the network is functioning normally. The Ping.exe program generates a series of Echo Request messages using the Internet Control Message Protocol (ICMP) and transmits them to the computer whose name or IP address you specify on the command line. The basic syntax of the Ping program is as follows:

```
ping target
```

The *target* variable contains the IPv4 or IPv6 address or name of any computer on the network. Because Ping.exe is a TCP/IP utility, the target computer can be running any operating system, not just Windows. You can use DNS host and domain names or Windows NetBIOS names in Ping commands. Ping resolves the name into an IP address before sending the Echo Request messages, and it then displays the address in its output.

TCP/IP computers respond to any Echo Request messages they receive that are addressed to them by generating Echo Reply messages and transmitting them back to the sender. When the pinging computer receives the Echo Reply messages, it produces a display like the one shown in Figure 5-23.

Figure 5-23

The Ping.exe display

```
Administrator: Command Prompt

C:\Users\Administrator>ping servera

Pinging servera.example.local [10.0.0.2] with 32 bytes of data:
Reply from 10.0.0.2: bytes=32 time<1ms TTL=128
Reply from 10.0.0.2: bytes=32 time<1ms TTL=128
Reply from 10.0.0.2: bytes=32 time<1ms TTL=128
Reply from 10.0.0.2: bytes=32 time<1ms TTL=128

Ping statistics for 10.0.0.2:
    Packets: Sent = 4, Received = 4, Lost = 0 (0% loss),
Approximate round trip times in milli-seconds:
    Minimum = 0ms, Maximum = 0ms, Average = 0ms

C:\Users\Administrator>
```

In Windows 7's Ping.exe implementation, the display shows the IP address of the computer receiving the Echo Requests, the number of bytes of data included with each request, the elapsed time between the transmission of each request and the receipt of each reply, and the value of the Time To Live (TTL) field in the IP header.

In this example, the target computer was on the same local area network (LAN), so the time measurement is very short—less than 1 millisecond. When pinging a computer on the Internet, the interval is likely to be longer. A successful Ping result like this one indicates that the target computer's networking hardware is functioning properly, as are its TCP/IP protocols, at least as high as the network layer of the OSI model. If a Ping test fails, there might be a firewall blocking the ICMP traffic between the two systems. If there is no firewall, then the Ping test failure indicates that there is a problem in one or both of the computers or in the network medium connecting them.

Ping.exe also has a series of command-line switches that you can use to modify the operational parameters of the program, such as the number of Echo Request messages it generates and the amount of data in each message. To display the syntax of the program, type *ping /?* At the command prompt.

USING TRACERT.EXE

Traceroute is another UNIX program that was designed to display the path that TCP/IP packets take to their final destination. Called traceroute in UNIX, in Windows 7 it is implemented as Tracert.exe. Because of the nature of IP routing, the path from a packet's source to its destination on another network can change from minute to minute, especially on the Internet. Tracert.exe displays a list of the routers that are currently forwarding packets to a particular destination.

Tracert.exe is a variation on Ping.exe. The program uses ICMP Echo Request and Echo Reply messages just like Ping, but it modifies the messages by changing the value of the TTL field in the IP header. The values in the TTL field prevent packets from getting caught in router loops that keep them circulating endlessly around the network. On a Windows 7 computer, the default value for the TTL field is relatively high, 128. Each time a packet passes from one network to another, the router connecting the networks reduces the TTL value by one. If the TTL value ever reaches zero, the router processing the packet discards it and transmits an ICMP error message back to the original sender.

Tracert.exe works by modifying the TTL values in the successive Ping.exe packets that it transmits to a target computer. When you run Tracert.exe from the command prompt with a *target* parameter, the program generates its first set of Echo Request messages with TTL values of 1. When the messages arrive at the first router on their path to the destination, the router decrements the TTL values to 0, discards the packets, and reports the errors to the sender. The error messages contain the router's address, which Tracert.exe displays as the first hop in the path to the destination.

Tracert.exe's second set of Echo Request messages use a TTL value of 2, causing the second router on the path to discard the packets and generate error messages. The Echo Request messages in the third set have a TTL value of 3, and so on. Each set of packets travels one hop farther than the previous set before causing a router to return error messages to the source. The list of routers displayed by the program as the path to the destination is the result of these error messages.

The following is an example of a Tracert.exe display:

```
Tracing route to www.fineartschool.co.uk [173.146.1.1] over a maximum of 30 hops:

1    <10   ms   1     ms   <10   ms    192.168.2.99
2    105   ms   92    ms   98    ms    qrvl-67terminal01.cpandl.com [131.107.24.67.3]
3    101   ms   110   ms   98    ms    qrvl.cpandl.com [131.107.67.1]
4    123   ms   109   ms   118   ms    svcr03-7b.cpandl.com [131.107.103.125]
5    123   ms   112   ms   114   ms    clsm02-2.cpandl.com [131.107.88.26]
6    136   ms   130   ms   133   ms    sl-gw19-pen-6-1-0-T3.fabrikam.com [157.54.116.5]
7    143   ms   126   ms   138   ms    sl-bb10-pen-4-3.fabrikam.com [157.54.5.117]
8    146   ms   129   ms   133   ms    sl-bb20-pen-12-0.fabrikam.com [157.54.5.1]
9    131   ms   128   ms   139   ms    sl-bb20-nyc-13-0.fabrikam.com [157.54.18.38]
10   130   ms   134   ms   134   ms    sl-gw9-nyc-8-0.fabrikam.com [157.54.7.94]
11   147   ms   149   ms   152   ms    sl-demon-1-0.fabrikam.com [157.54.173.10]
12   154   ms   146   ms   145   ms    ny2-backbone-1-ge021.router.fabrikam.com [157.54.173.121]
13   230   ms   225   ms   226   ms    tele-backbone-1-ge023.router.adatum.co.uk [157.60.173.12]
14   233   ms   220   ms   226   ms    tele-core-3-fxp1.router.adatum.co.uk [157.60.252.56]
15   223   ms   224   ms   224   ms    tele-access-1-14.router.adatum.co.uk [157.60.254.245]
16   236   ms   221   ms   226   ms    tele-service-2-165.router.adatum.co.uk [157.60.36.149]
17   220   ms   224   ms   210   ms    www.fineartschool.co.uk [206.73.118.65]

Trace complete.
```

In this example, Tracert.exe displays the path between a computer in Pennsylvania and one in the United Kingdom. Each of the hops contains the elapsed times between the transmission and reception of three sets of Echo Request and Echo Reply packets. In this trace, you can clearly see the point at which the packets begin traveling across the Atlantic Ocean. At hop 13, the elapsed times increase from approximately 150 to 230 milliseconds (ms) and stay in that range for the subsequent hops. This additional delay of only 80 ms is the time it takes the packets to travel the thousands of miles across the Atlantic Ocean.

Ping.exe simply tells you whether two TCP/IP systems are having trouble communicating. It can't pinpoint the location of the problem. A failure to contact a remote computer could be due to a problem in your workstation, in the remote computer, or in any of the routers in between. Tracert.exe can tell you how far your packets are going before they run into the problem.

TAKE NOTE*

Because the configuration of the Internet is constantly changing, there is no guarantee that the route displayed by Tracert.exe is completely accurate. The ICMP messages that execute each step of the Tracert.exe process could conceivably be taking different routes to the same destination, resulting in the display of a composite route between two points that does not actually exist. There is also no way of knowing what path the packets are taking as they return to the source. In addition, routers typically deprioritize ICMP processing in favor of packet forwarding and other more critical router tasks. When a router is busy, it might delay the processing of an Echo Request or Echo Reply packet. The resulting latency numbers will be higher than the delay experienced by actual data packets crossing the network.

USING NSLOOKUP.EXE

The Nslookup.exe command-line utility enables you to generate DNS request messages and transmit them to specific DNS servers on the network. The advantage of Nslookup.exe is that you can test the functionality and the quality of the information on a specific DNS server by specifying it on the command line.

The basic command-line syntax of Nslookup.exe is as follows:

nslookup *DNSname DNSserver*

- *DNSname:* Specifies the DNS name that you want to resolve.
- *DNSserver:* Specifies the DNS name or IP address of the DNS server that you want to query for the name specified in the *DNSname* variable.

There are also many additional parameters that you can include on the command line to control the server query process. The output generated by Nslookup.exe in Windows 7 resembles that shown in Figure 5-24.

Figure 5-24

The Nslookup.exe display

```
C:\Users\Administrator>nslookup microsoft.com 71.242.0.12
Server:  nsphil01.verizon.net
Address:  71.242.0.12

Non-authoritative answer:
Name:    microsoft.com
Addresses:  207.46.197.32
          207.46.232.182

C:\Users\Administrator>_
```

The Nslookup.exe utility has two operational modes: command line and interactive. When you run Nslookup.exe with no command-line parameters, the program displays its own prompt from which you can issue commands to specify the default DNS server to query, resolve multiple names, and configure many other aspects of the program's functionality.

USING NETSTAT.EXE

Netstat.exe is a command-line program that displays status information about the current network connections on a computer running Windows 7 and about the traffic generated by the various TCP/IP protocols. In UNIX, the program is called netstat, and in Windows 7, it is called Netstat.exe.

The syntax for the Windows 7 version of Netstat.exe is as follows:

NETSTAT [*interval*][-a][-b][-e][-f][-n][-o][-p *protocol*][-r][-s][-t]

- *interval:* Specifies the time interval (in seconds) between display refreshes.
- -a: Displays the current network connections and the ports that are currently listening for incoming network connections.
- -b: Displays the executable associated with each active connection and listening port.

- **-e:** Displays Ethernet traffic statistics for the network interface, broken down into bytes, unicast packets, nonunicast packets, discards, errors, and unknown protocols.
- **-f:** When combined with other parameters, causes the program to display foreign addresses as fully qualified domain names.
- **-n:** When combined with other parameters, causes the program to display addresses and port numbers in numerical, rather than alphabetical, form.
- **-o:** Displays the process ID associated with each active connection and listening port.
- **-p *protocol*:** Displays the current active connections for the protocol specified by the *protocol* variable.
- **-r:** Displays the computer's IPv4 and IPv6 routing tables.
- **-s:** Displays detailed network traffic statistics for the IP, ICMP, TCP, and UDP protocols, in both v4 and v6 versions.
- **-t:** Displays the offload state of the current connection.

Part of the default network connection listing displayed by Netstat.exe on a computer running Windows 7 appears in Figure 5-25.

Figure 5-25

The network connection listing in Netstat.exe

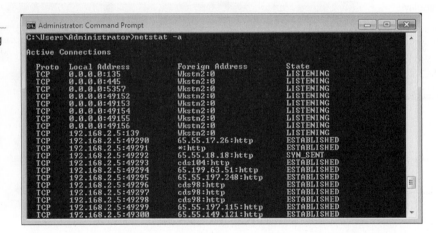

The Ethernet interface statistics, as displayed by netstat.exe, are shown in Figure 5-26.

Figure 5-26

The Ethernet interface statistics in Netstat.exe

The routing tables for a computer running Windows 7 appear as shown in Figure 5-27.

Figure 5-27

The IPv4 and IPv6 routing
tables in Netstat.exe

```
Administrator: Command Prompt

C:\Users\Administrator>netstat -r

Interface List
 11...00 0c 29 13 bc 20 ......Intel(R) PRO/1000 MT Network Connection
  1...........................Software Loopback Interface 1
 13...00 00 00 00 00 00 00 e0 Microsoft ISATAP Adapter #2
===========================================================================

IPv4 Route Table
===========================================================================
Active Routes:
Network Destination        Netmask          Gateway       Interface  Metric
          0.0.0.0          0.0.0.0      192.168.2.99     192.168.2.5     10
        127.0.0.0        255.0.0.0         On-link         127.0.0.1    306
        127.0.0.1  255.255.255.255         On-link         127.0.0.1    306
  127.255.255.255  255.255.255.255         On-link         127.0.0.1    306
      192.168.2.0    255.255.255.0         On-link       192.168.2.5    266
      192.168.2.5  255.255.255.255         On-link       192.168.2.5    266
    192.168.2.255  255.255.255.255         On-link       192.168.2.5    266
        224.0.0.0        240.0.0.0         On-link         127.0.0.1    306
        224.0.0.0        240.0.0.0         On-link       192.168.2.5    266
  255.255.255.255  255.255.255.255         On-link         127.0.0.1    306
  255.255.255.255  255.255.255.255         On-link       192.168.2.5    266
===========================================================================
Persistent Routes:
  None

IPv6 Route Table
===========================================================================
Active Routes:
 If Metric Network Destination      Gateway
  1    306 ::1/128                  On-link
 11    266 fe80::/64                On-link
 11    266 fe80::7166:22e6:1d18:b4aa/128
                                    On-link
  1    306 ff00::/8                 On-link
 11    266 ff00::/8                 On-link
===========================================================================
Persistent Routes:
  None

C:\Users\Administrator>
```

SKILL SUMMARY

IN THIS LESSON YOU LEARNED:

- The networking stack used on Windows 7 computers corresponds roughly to the seven-layer OSI reference model.

- The OSI (Open Systems Interconnection) reference model consists of seven layers: physical, data-link, network, transport, session, presentation, and application.

- Ethernet, the data-link layer protocol used on most LANs, consists of physical layer specifications, a frame format, and a MAC mechanism.

- The network and transport layer protocols work together to provide an end-to-end communication service that achieves the quality of service required by the application requesting network services.

- The functions of the session, presentation, and application layers are often combined into a single application layer protocol.

- Windows 7 includes support for both the IPv4 and IPv6 protocols. IPv6 increases the IP address space from 32 to 128 bits, simplifies the routing process, and improves address autoconfiguration.

- Network Discovery is a Windows 7 feature that simplifies the task of firewall configuration by enabling you to block or allow the protocols and ports needed for the computer to browse and access the network.

- The Network Map utility uses the Link Layer Discovery Protocol (LLTD) to detect network devices and connections.

- Most networks use DHCP to configure their TCP/IP clients, but it is still possible to configure them manually, using a graphical interface or the Netsh.exe command-line utility.

- Windows 7 includes a variety of command-line TCP/IP tools, including Ipconfig.exe, Ping.exe, Tracert.exe, Nslookup.exe, and Netstat.exe.

▪ Knowledge Assessment

Fill in the Blank

Complete the following sentences by writing the correct word or words in the blanks provided.

1. A software routine, which also acts as a filter that blocks certain type of incoming and outgoing traffic, while enabling other types is called a _____.

2. The _____ tool provides a central access point for all of the network controls and connections on a computer running Windows 7.

3. A device that connects one network to another is called a _____.

4. The most common method for illustrating the operations of a networking stack is the _____, which consists of _____ layers.

5. Protocols that do not guarantee delivery of their data, but do operate with a very low overhead that conserve network bandwidth are called _____.

6. The Windows 7 command-line utility that can tell you if the TCP/IP stack of another system on the network is functioning normally is called _____.

7. The Windows 7 command-line utility that enables you to generate DNS request messages and then transmit them to specific DNS servers on the network is called _____.

8. Most networks use _____ to dynamically assign addresses and configure computers to use them.

9. The Windows 7 utility that displays a list of the routers currently forwarding packets to a particular destination is called _____.

10. The top and bottom layers of the OSI model are called the _____ and _____ layers.

True / False

Circle T if the statement is true or F if the statement is false.

T | F 1. The purpose of Network Diagnostics is to display error messages only.

T | F 2. Transport layer protocols are not concerned with addressing packets to the correct system.

T | F 3. The Network Map utility uses a new protocol called Link Layer Topology Discovery (LLTD) to discover information about the network and the devices attached to it.

T | F 4. The protocols that Windows uses by default at the network and transport layers are collectively called TCP/IP.

T | F 5. Home and work computers have Network Discovery turned on, and public computers have it turned off.

T | F 6. There are two basic types of port numbers: ephemeral port numbers and well-known port numbers.

T | F 7. A Windows 7 computer that is connected to a LAN has a hardware address and a computer that is connected to the Internet has an IP address.

T | F 8. The only two layers of the OSI reference model that do not have individual protocols associated with them are the transport layer and the session layer.

T | F 9. Because the configuration of the Internet is constantly changing, the only way you can know for certain what route packets are taking to a specific destination is to use Tracert.exe.

T | F 10. The IPv6 addresses Windows 7 computers use at the network layer are six-byte hexadecimal sequences, hard coded into each network interface adapter by the manufacturer.

Review Questions

1. What is the difference between a hardware address and an IPv4 address?
2. Explain how the process of data encapsulation works on a TCP/IP network when an application sends a message to another computer on the Internet.

■ Case Scenarios

Scenario 5-1: Using Port Numbers

While you are installing an Internet web server on your company network, the owner of the company tells you that he also wants to build a web server for internal use by the company's employees. This intranet web server will not contain confidential information, but it should not be accessible from the company's Internet Web site. To do this, you create a second site on the web server. The Internet site uses the well-known port number for web servers, which is 80. For the intranet site, you select the port number 283. Assuming that the web server's IP address on the internal network is 10.54.3.145, what should the users on the company network do to access the intranet Web site with Microsoft Internet Explorer?

Scenario 5-2: Configuring TCP/IP Clients

Mark is setting up a small Ethernet network in his home by installing network adapters in three computers running Windows 7 and connecting them to a switch. Mark only uses one of the computers to access the Internet with a dial-up modem, but he wants to be able to access files and his printer from any one of the three systems. After he installs the network interface adapters, he notes that the default networking components have been installed on all three systems, and he sets about configuring their TCP/IP configuration parameters manually. Of the settings on the Internet Protocol Version 4 (TCP/IPv4) Properties sheet, which must Mark configure to provide the network connectivity he desires, and which can he leave blank?

9 LESSON

Working with Workgroups and Domains

OBJECTIVE DOMAIN MATRIX

TECHNOLOGY SKILL	OBJECTIVE DOMAIN	OBJECTIVE NUMBER
Introducing User Account Control	Configure user account control (UAC).	5.3

KEY TERMS

Active Directory	domain	secure desktop
Admin Approval Mode	domain controller	special identity
authentication	elevation prompt	User Account Control (UAC)
authorization	group	user profile
credential prompt	mandatory user profile	user rights
directory service	roaming user profile	workgroup

■ Working with Users and Groups

THE BOTTOM LINE

The user account is the fundamental unit of identity in Windows operating systems. In computer terminology, the term *user* has two meanings; it can refer to the human being operating the computer, or it can be an operating system element that represents a single human user.

From a programming perspective, a user account is a relatively simple construct, no more than a collection of properties that apply to the human being or other entity that the user account represents. These properties can include information about the user, such as names and contact information, and identifying characteristics, such as passwords.

➕ MORE INFORMATION

Most user accounts represent humans, but Windows also employs user accounts to provide system processes and applications with access to secured resources. These accounts are no different from standard user accounts structurally; the only difference is that they are created and managed automatically by the operating system or an application.

As an operating system element, the user account and its properties are vital components in two of the most important Windows functions:

- ***Authentication:*** The process of verifying that the identity of the person operating the computer matches that of the user account the person is using to gain access. Typically, to be authenticated, the human user must supply some piece of information associated with the user account, such as a password; demonstrate some personal characteristic, such as a fingerprint; or prove access to an identifying possession, such as a smart card.

- ***Authorization:*** The process of granting an authenticated user a specific degree of access to a specific computer or data resources. In Windows, a user account provides access to permissions that grant the human user access to files and folders, printers, and other resources.

The first thing a human user does with a Windows system is authenticate him- or herself—a process typically referred to as logging on. The human user specifies the name of a user account and supplies a password or other identifying token. Once the authentication is successful, the person is known by that username throughout the Windows session, and the operating system grants access to specific resources using that name.

As the authenticated user begins working with the operating system, the authorization process occurs whenever the user attempts to access certain resources or perform specific tasks. All of the Windows permission systems, including NTFS, share, registry, and ***Active Directory*** permissions, are user based. The access control list (ACL) for each permission-protected resource contains a list of users and the degree of access each user is granted to that resource.

Another user-based Windows element, completely separate from the permission systems, is called ***user rights***. User rights are specific operating system tasks, such as Shut Down the System or Allow Log On Through Terminal Services, which can only be performed by certain users designated by a system administrator.

A ***group*** is another type of entity that Windows uses to represent a collection of users. System administrators can create groups for any reason and with any name, and then use them just as they would a user account. Any permissions or user rights that an administrator assigns to a group are automatically inherited by all of the members of the group.

+ MORE INFORMATION

The concept of group inheritance is one of the fundamental principles of network administration. On all but the smallest networks, administrators typically assign permissions to groups, rather than individual users, and then control access by adjusting group memberships. For example, if a person performing a particular job needs access to a variety of different network resources, it might take an administrator some time to assign all of the rights and permissions that person needs to an individual user account. Later, if that job should be taken over by another person, the administrator has to go through the entire process again twice, once to remove the rights and permissions from the old user's account and once to grant the same rights and permissions to the new user. By creating a group to represent the job, the administrator only has to grant the rights and permissions to the group once. When someone new takes over the job, the administrator only has to remove the departed user from the group and add the new user.

Understanding Local and Domain Users

The concept of users and groups is complicated in Windows because there are two completely separate user account systems: local users and domain users. Which user account system a Windows computer uses depends on whether it is a member of a workgroup or an Active Directory domain.

Windows 7 supports three types of networks: homegroups, workgroups, and domains, as described in the following sections.

INTRODUCING THE HOMEGROUP

New in Windows 7, a homegroup is a simplified networking paradigm that enables users connected to a home network to share the contents of their libraries without the need for creating user accounts and permissions. For more information on creating and using homegroups, see "Sharing with Homegroups" in Chapter 6, "Sharing Resources."

INTRODUCING THE WORKGROUP

A *workgroup* is a collection of computers that are all peers. A peer network is one in which every computer can function as both a server by sharing its resources with other computers, and a client by accessing the shared resources on other computers.

On a workgroup network, each computer has its own set of users and groups that it uses to control access to its own resources. For example, if you want to use one computer to access resources on all four of the other computers on a five-node workgroup network, you must have a user account on each of those four computers. As you connect to each computer, you are authenticated and authorized by each one. If effect, you are logging on to each computer individually.

TAKE NOTE *

Although it is technically a separate authentication process every time a workgroup computer accesses another computer, this does not necessarily mean that users have to supply account names and passwords each time they connect to another computer. If a user has accounts with the same name and password on multiple workgroup computers, then the authentications occur automatically, with no user intervention. This is called *passthrough authentication*. If the passwords for the accounts are different, however, a manual authentication is necessary for each one.

INTRODUCING THE DOMAIN

A *domain* is a collection of computers that all utilize a central directory service for authentication and authorization. A *directory service* is a collection of logical objects that represent various types of network resources, such as computers, applications, users, and groups. Each object consists of attributes that contain information about the object.

TAKE NOTE *

Do not confuse an Active Directory Domain Services (AD DS) domain with a Domain Name System (DNS) domain. An AD DS domain is a collection of Windows computers that are all joined to the Windows directory service. A DNS domain is a collection of Internet host names used by computers that can be running any operating system.

To create a domain, you must have at least one Windows server with the Active Directory Domain Services (AD DS) directory service installed. This server is called a *domain controller*. Each of the computers then joins the domain and is represented by a computer object. In the same way, administrators create user objects that represent human users. In Windows networking, the main difference between a domain and a workgroup is that users log on to the domain once, rather than each computer individually. When users attempt to access network resources, the individual computers hosting the resources send authorization requests to the domain controller, rather than handling the authorizations themselves.

DIFFERENTIATING LOCAL AND DOMAIN USERS

The primary advantage of a domain over a workgroup is that administrators only have to create one user account for each person, while workgroups can require many different user accounts for one person. If, on a workgroup network, a user's password is lost or compromised, someone must change that password on every computer where that user has an account. On a domain, there is only one user account for each person, so only one password change is needed.

Windows 7 computers always have a need for local user accounts, for administrative access to the system, if for no other reason. For networking purposes, though, it is typical to use local user accounts or domain user accounts, but not both. Workgroup networks are typically small and informal, with users administering their own computers. Domain networks are usually larger and have dedicated network administrators responsible for managing user accounts and controlling access to network resources.

Local and domain users are different in several important ways. You use different tools to create and manage the two types of users, and the user accounts themselves are different in composition. As mentioned earlier, a user account consists of attributes, which contain information about the user. Domain users have many more attributes than local users.

As a demonstration of this, Figures 9-1 and 9-2 contain the Properties sheets of a local user account and a domain user account. Notice that the Properties sheet for the local user has

Figure 9-1

The Properties sheet for a local user

Figure 9-2

The Properties sheet for a domain user

only 3 tabs, while the domain user's sheet has 15. This means that the domain user account can store a great deal more information about the user and can access many more different kinds of network resources.

Table 9-1 lists some of the other differences between local and domain users.

Table 9-1

Frequently Asked Questions About Local and Domain Users

Question	Local Users	Domain Users
What tools do you use to manage the user accounts?	The User Accounts control panel or the Local Users and Groups snap-in for Microsoft Management Console (MMC)	The Active Directory Users and Computers MMC snap-in
Where are the user accounts stored?	In the Security Account Manager (SAM) on the local computer	On the Active Directory Domain Services domain controllers
What can you access with the user account?	Local computer resources only	All domain and network resources
What restrictions are there on the user name?	Each username must be unique on the computer	Each username must be unique in the directory

As a technical specialist, the type of user accounts you work with depends on the nature of the networks you manage and their security requirements. Small businesses are more likely to use workgroup networking, in which case you will be working with local user accounts. Depending on the capabilities of the users, you might have to set up all of the user accounts for all of the computers on the network, or you might be able to show the users how to create accounts on their own computers. Local users are relatively simple to create and manage, and a workgroup network is often treated casually.

If your client is a medium or large business, it is more likely to be running an AD DS domain, in which case you will be working primarily with domain user accounts. The question of whether to host a Windows domain is a major decision that an organization usually makes when they are designing and installing the network. Hosting a Windows domain is a costly undertaking, both in terms of the additional hardware and software required and in terms of the time and effort needed for planning and deployment.

INTRODUCING BUILT-IN LOCAL USERS

As mentioned earlier, Windows 7 (like the other Windows workstation operating systems) always has a need for local user accounts. When you perform a standard interactive installation of Windows 7, you are required to create one user account. In addition, the Setup program automatically creates a number of other user accounts.

The following user accounts are built-in on Windows 7:

- **Administrator:** During a typical Windows 7 installation, the Setup program creates an Administrator account and makes it a member of the Administrators group, giving it complete access to all areas of the operating system. However, the Setup program leaves the account in a disabled state and does not assign it a password.

- **New User Account:** During the operating system installation process, the installer must specify the name for a new user account, which the Setup program creates and adds to the Administrators group. This grants the new account full access to the operating system. The installer decides whether to assign a password to this account. Windows 7 uses this account for its initial logons.

- **Guest:** This account is designed for users who require only temporary access to the computer and who do not need high levels of access. The Guest account is disabled, by default, and is a member only of the Guests group, which provides it with only the most rudimentary access to the system.

In addition to these accounts, Windows 7 also creates a number of system and service accounts, none of which you have to manipulate directly.

TAKE NOTE *

After the Windows 7 installation is completed, you might want to consider enabling the Administrator account and assigning it a strong password. This will provide you with administrative access to the system, even if your main user account becomes compromised.

Understanding Local and Domain Groups

Just as there are local and domain users, there are local and domain groups as well. Whether local or domain, a group is essentially just a collection of users and, in some cases, other groups. As mentioned earlier, by assigning rights and permissions to a group, you assign those rights and permissions to all of its members.

USING LOCAL GROUPS

When compared to domain groups, local groups are quite simple and are defined more by what they cannot do than what they can do. Local groups are subject to the following restrictions:

- You can only use local groups on the computer where you create them.
- Only local users from the same computer can be members of local groups.
- When the computer is a member of an AD DS domain, local groups can have domain users and domain global groups as members.
- Local groups cannot have other local groups as members. However, they can have domain groups as members.
- You can only assign permissions to local groups when you are controlling access to resources on the local computer.
- You cannot create local groups on a Windows server computer that is functioning as a domain controller.

INTRODUCING BUILT-IN LOCAL GROUPS

Windows 7 includes a number of built-in local groups that are already equipped with the permissions and rights needed to perform certain tasks. You can enable users to perform these tasks simply by adding them to the appropriate group. Table 9-2 lists the Windows 7 built-in local groups and the capabilities they provide to their members.

TAKE NOTE *

Some of the built-in local groups in Windows 7, such as Administrators, Backup Operators, and Remote Desktop Users, are created for the convenience of system administrators so that they can easily grant certain privileges to users. Other groups, such as IIS_USRS and Replicator, are designed to support automated functions that create their own system user accounts. There is no need to manually add users to these groups.

Table 9-2

Windows 7 Built-in Local Groups and Their Capabilities

BUILT-IN LOCAL GROUP	FUNCTION
Administrators	Members have full administrative access to the entire operating system. By default, the Administrator user and the user account created during the operating system installation are both members of this group.
Backup Operators	Members have user rights enabling them to override permissions for the sole purpose of backing up and restoring files, folders, and other operating system elements.
Cryptographic Operators	Members are capable of performing cryptographic operations.
Distributed COM Users	Members are capable of launching, activating, and using distributed COM objects.
Event Log Readers	Members can read the computer's event logs.
Guests	Members have no default user rights. By default, the Guest user account is a member of this group.
IIS_IUSRS	Group used to provide privileges to dedicated Internet Information Services users.
Network Configuration Operators	Members have privileges that enable them to modify the computer's network configuration settings.
Performance Log Users	Members have privileges that enable them to schedule the logging of performance counters, enable trace providers, and collect event traces on this computer, both locally and from remote locations.
Performance Monitor Users	Members have privileges that enable them to monitor performance counter data on the computer, both locally and from remote locations.
Power Users	Members possess no additional capabilities in Windows 7. In previous Windows versions, the Power Users group provided privileges for a limited number of administrative functions, but in Windows 7, the group is included solely for reasons of backwards compatibility.
Remote Desktop Users	Members can log on to the computer from remote locations using Terminal Services or Remote Desktop.
Replicator	When the computer is joined to a domain, this group provides the access needed for file replication functions. The only member should be a user account dedicated solely to the replication process.
Users	Members can perform most common tasks, such as running applications, using local and network printers, and locking the server. However, members are prevented from making many system-wide configuration changes, whether they do so accidentally or deliberately.
Offer Remote Assistance Helpers	Members can offer remote assistance to other users of the computer.

The built-in local groups in Windows 7, although created by the operating system, are groups like any other. You can modify their properties, change their names, and assign new rights and permissions to them. However, it's a better idea to create your own groups and assign whatever additional rights and permissions you need to them. You can make a single user a member of multiple groups, and the permissions from all of the groups will be combined according to the rules specified in Lesson 6.

INTRODUCING SPECIAL IDENTITIES

Another type of element in Windows 7 (and all other Windows operating systems) is a special identity, which functions like a group. A **special identity** is essentially a placeholder for a collection of users with similar characteristics. For example, the Authenticated Users special identity represents all of the users that are logged on to the computer at a given instant. You can assign rights and permissions to a special identity just as you would to a group.

When the access control list (ACL) for a system resource contains a special identity in one of its access control entries (ACEs), the system substitutes the users that conform to the special identity at the moment the ACL is processed.

TAKE NOTE ★

It's important to understand that the set of computers represented by a special identity can change from minute to minute. The Authenticated Users special identity changes every time a user logs on or off, for example. When you assign rights and permissions to a special identity, the users who receive those rights and permissions are not those who conform to the special identity at the time you make the assignment, but rather those who conform to the special identity at the time the special identity is read from the ACL.

Table 9-3 lists the special identities included in Windows 7.

Table 9-3

Windows 7 Special Identities and Their Constituents

SPECIAL IDENTITY	FUNCTION
Anonymous Logon	Includes all users who have connected to the computer without authenticating.
Authenticated Users	Includes all users with a valid local user account whose identities have been authenticated. The Guest user is not included in the Authenticated Users special identity, even if it has a password.
Batch	Includes all users who are currently logged on through a batch facility such as a task scheduler job.
Console Logon	Includes all users that are logged on to the computer's physical console.
Creator Group	Includes the primary group of the user who created or most recently took ownership of the resource.
Creator Owner	Includes only the user who created or most recently took ownership of a resource.
Dialup	Includes all users who are currently logged on through a dial-up connection.
Everyone	Includes all members of the Authenticated Users special identity plus the Guest user account.
Interactive	Includes all users who are currently logged on locally or through a Remote Desktop connection.
IUSR	Account used to provide anonymous access to web pages through Internet Information Services (IIS).
Local Service	Provides all services configured to run as a local service with the same privileges as the Users group.
Network	Includes all users who are currently logged on through a network connection.
Network Service	Provides all services configured to run as a network service with the same privileges as the Users group.
Owner Rights	Represents the current owner of an object.
Remote Interactive Logon	Includes all users who are currently logged on through a Remote Desktop connection.
Service	Includes all security principals who have logged on as a service.
System	Provides the operating system with all of the privileges it needs to function.
Terminal Server User	Includes all users who are currently logged on to a Terminal Services server that is in Terminal Services version 4.0 application compatibility mode.
The Organization Certificate	Account used by the default IIS user.

■ Creating and Managing Local Users and Groups

THE BOTTOM LINE

Windows 7 provides two separate interfaces for creating and managing local user accounts: the User Accounts control panel and the Local Users and Groups snap-in for the Microsoft Management Console (MMC). Both of these interfaces provide access to the same Security Account Manager (SAM) where the user and group information is stored, so any changes you make using one interface will appear in the other.

Microsoft designed the User Accounts control panel and the Local Users and Groups snap-in for computer users with different levels of expertise, and they provide different degrees of access to the Security Account Manager, as follows:

- **User Accounts:** Microsoft designed the User Accounts control panel for relatively inexperienced end users; it provides a simplified interface with extremely limited access to user accounts. With this interface, it is possible to create local user accounts and modify their basic attributes, but you cannot create groups or manage group memberships (except for the Administrators group).

- **Local Users and Groups:** Microsoft includes this MMC snap-in as part of the Computer Management console; it provides full access to local users and groups, as well as all of their attributes. Designed more for the technical specialist or system administrator, this interface is not difficult to use, but it does provide access to controls that beginning users generally do not need.

TAKE NOTE ✱

Both the User Accounts control panel and the Local Users and Groups snap-in are capable of working with local users and local groups only. You cannot create and manage domain users and groups using these tools. To work with domain users and groups, you must use a domain tool, such as Active Directory Users and Groups, which is supplied with the server operating system that is hosting the Active Directory domain.

Using the User Accounts Control Panel

As described earlier, the first local user account on a Windows 7 computer is the one created during the operating system installation process. The Setup program prompts the installer for an account name, and creates a new user account with administrative privileges. The program also creates the Administrator and Guest accounts, both of which are disabled by default.

When the Windows 7 installation process is completed, the system restarts. Because only one user account is available, the computer automatically logs on using that account. This account has administrative privileges, so at this point you can create additional user accounts or modify the existing ones.

CREATING A NEW USER ACCOUNT

To create a new user account with the User Accounts control panel, use the following procedure.

 CREATE A NEW USER ACCOUNT

GET READY. Log on to Windows 7 using an account with administrator privileges.

TAKE NOTE ✱

This procedure is valid only on Windows 7 computers that are part of a workgroup. When you join a computer to an AD DS domain, you can only create new local user accounts with the Local Users and Groups snap-in.

1. Click Start, and then click Control Panel. The Control Panel window appears.
2. Click User Accounts and Family Safety. The User Accounts and Family Safety window appears, as shown in Figure 9-3.

Figure 9-3

The User Accounts and Family Safety window

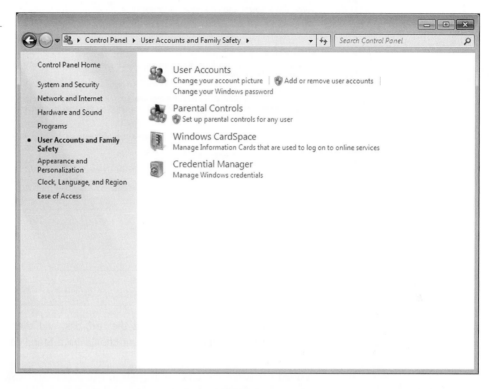

3. Click Add or remove user accounts. The *Choose the account you would like to change* page appears, as shown in Figure 9-4.

Figure 9-4

The Choose the account you would like to change page

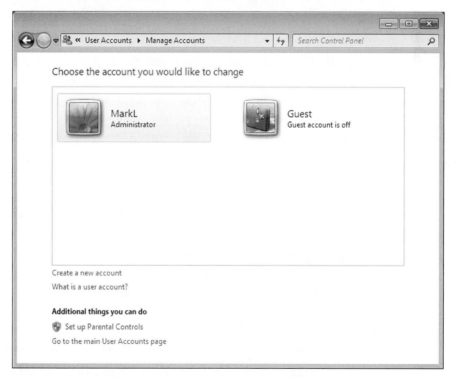

4. Click Create a new account. The *Name the account and choose the account type* page appears, as shown in Figure 9-5.

Figure 9-5

The Name the account and choose the account type page

5. Type a name for the new account in the text box, and then choose the appropriate radio button to specify whether the account should be a Standard user or an Administrator.

TAKE NOTE✱
Recommended network practices call for administrators to use a standardized system for creating user account names. For example, smaller networks often use the first name followed by the first letter of the surname, such as JohnD. For larger networks with a greater chance of name duplication, use of the first initial plus the surname is common, such as JDoe. The purpose of standardizing usernames in this way is to enable any administrator to determine the account name for any user.

6. Click Create Account. The *Choose the account you would like to change* page reappears, with the new account added.

WARNING Following this procedure creates an account that is capable of logging on to the system without supplying a password. For security purposes, in all but the most informal circumstances, you should assign a password to all user accounts immediately after creating them.

This procedure provides only the most rudimentary access to the user account attributes. Apart from supplying a name for the account, all you can do is specify the account type.

What the User Accounts control panel refers to as an account type is actually a group membership. Selecting the Standard user option adds the user account to the local Users group, while selecting the Administrator option adds the account to the Administrators group.

Most critically, when you create a new user account with this procedure, the account is not protected by a password. You must modify the account after creating it to specify a password or change any of its other attributes.

MANAGING A USER ACCOUNT

To see the modifications you can make to an existing local user account with the User Accounts control panel, use the following procedure:

➔ MANAGE USER ACCOUNTS

GET READY. Log on to Windows 7 using an account with Administrator privileges.

1. Click Start, and then click Control Panel. The Control Panel window appears.
2. Click User Accounts and Family Safety. The User Accounts and Family Safety window appears.

3. Click Add or remove user accounts. The *Choose the account you would like to change* page appears.

4. Click one of the existing accounts. The *Make changes to [user's] account* page appears, as shown in Figure 9-6.

Figure 9-6

The Make changes to [user's] account page

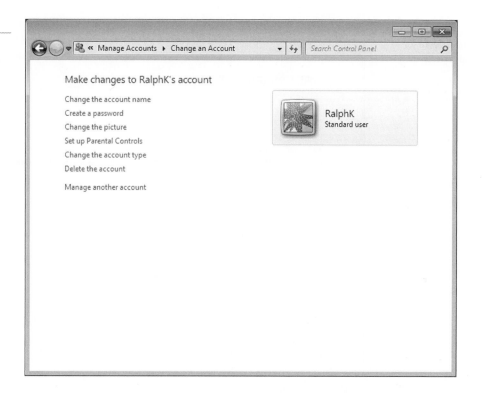

5. Click Change the account name. The *Type a new account name for [user] account* page appears, as shown in Figure 9-7.

Figure 9-7

The Type a new account name for [user's] account page

6. Type a new name for the account in the text box, and then click Change Name. The *Make changes to [user's] account* page reappears.

7. Click Create a password. The *Create a password for [user's] account* page appears, as shown in Figure 9-8.

Figure 9-8

The Create a password for [user's] account page

8. Type a password in the *New password* and *Confirm new password* text boxes and, if desired, supply a password hint.

> **TAKE NOTE**✱ Although Windows 7 does not require them by default in workgroup mode, Microsoft recommends that you use complex passwords for all user accounts. By the Windows definition, a complex password is one that is at least six characters long, does not contain any part of the user account name, and contains characters from three of the following four categories: uppercase letters, lowercase letters, numbers, and symbols. You can configure Windows 7 to require complex passwords by enabling the Password Must Meet Complexity Requirements policy in the Local System Policies snap-in. When you join a computer to an AD DS domain, the system enables the password length and complexity policies by default. For more information, see "Working with Password Policies" later in this lesson.

9. Click Create password. The *Make changes to [user's] account* page reappears, now with a *Remove the password* option added.

10. Click Remove the password. The *Remove a password* page appears, as shown in Figure 9-9.

> **TAKE NOTE**✱ When an administrator adds, modifies, or removes a user account password, the user loses access to all existing Encrypting File System (EFS) files, personal certificates, and cached Internet and network passwords. Therefore, if you are going to use passwords on your network, administrators should always create them (or have users create them) before they perform any cryptographic activities with the account.

Figure 9-9

The Remove a password page

11. Click Remove Password. The *Make changes to [user's] account* page reappears.

12. Click Change the picture. The *Choose a new picture for [user's] account* page appears, as shown in Figure 9-10.

Figure 9-10

The Choose a new picture for [user's] account page

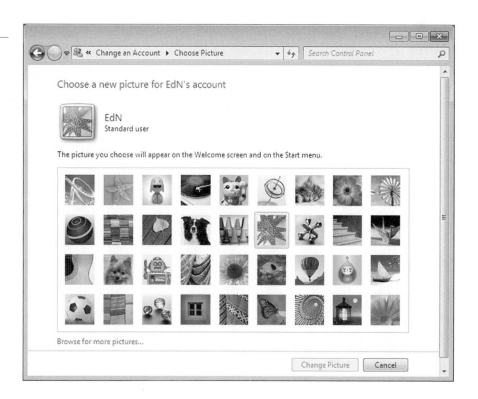

13. Select a new picture for the account, or click Browse for more pictures, and then click Change Picture. The *Make changes to [user's] account* page reappears.

14. Click Change the account type. The *Choose a new account type for [user]* page appears, as shown in Figure 9-11.

Figure 9-11

The Choose a new account type for [user] page

15. Select the Standard user or Administrator radio button, and then click Change Account Type. The *Make changes to [user's] account* page reappears.

16. Click Delete the account. The *Do you want to keep [user's] files?* page appears, as shown in Figure 9-12.

Figure 9-12

The Do you want to keep [user's] files? page

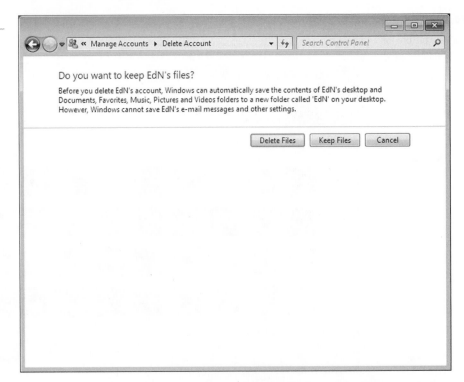

17. Click Delete Files to delete the user profile, or click Keep Files to save it to the desktop. The *Are you sure you want to delete [user's] account?* page appears, as shown in Figure 9-13.

Figure 9-13

The Are you sure you want to delete [user's] account? page

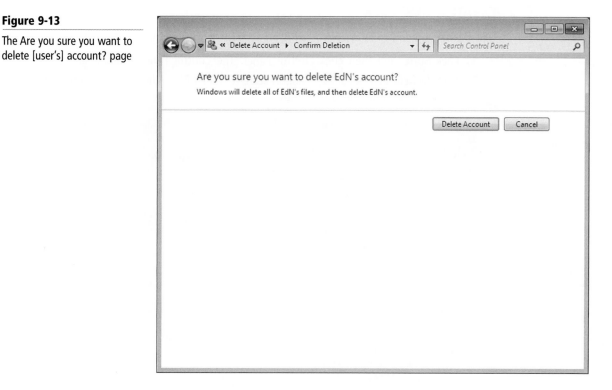

18. Click Delete Account. The *Choose the account you would like to change* page reappears.

19. Close the User Accounts control panel window.

Using the Local Users and Groups Snap-In

As you might have noticed in the previous sections, the User Accounts control panel provides only partial access to local user accounts, and no access to groups other than the Users and Administrators groups. The Local Users and Groups snap-in, on the other hand, provides full access to all of the local user and group accounts on the computer.

By default, the Local Users and Groups snap-in is part of the Computer Management console. However, you can also load the snap-in by itself, or create your own MMC console with any combination of snap-ins you wish.

OPENING THE LOCAL USERS AND GROUPS SNAP-IN

You can open the Local Users and Groups snap-in in one of three basic ways:

- Open the Control Panel from the Start menu and select System and Security > Administrative Tools > Computer Management
- Launch Microsoft Management Console (Mmc.exe), choose File > Add/Remove Snap-In, and then select the Local Users and Groups snap-in.
- Open the Start menu and type Lusrmgr.msc in the search box.

Each of these three methods provides access to the same snap-in and the same controls for creating, managing, and deleting local users and groups.

CREATING A LOCAL USER

To create a local user account with the Local Users and Groups snap-in, use the following procedure.

 CREATE A NEW USER

GET READY. Log on to Windows 7 using an account with Administrator privileges.

1. Click Start, and then click Control Panel. The Control Panel window appears.
2. Click System and Security > Administrative Tools. The Administrative Tools window appears, as shown in Figure 9-14.

Figure 9-14

The Administrative Tools window

3. Double click Computer Management. The Computer Management window appears, as shown in Figure 9-15.

Figure 9-15

The Computer Management window

4. In the scope (left) pane of the console, expand the Local Users and Groups node and click Users. A list of the current local users appears in the details (middle) pane, as shown in Figure 9-16.

Figure 9-16

The Local Users and Groups snap-in

5. Right click the Users folder and, from the context menu, select New User. The New User dialog box appears, as shown in Figure 9-17.

Figure 9-17

The New User dialog box

6. In the User name text box, type the name you want to assign to the user account. This is the only required field in the dialog box.

7. Specify a Full name and a Description for the account, if desired.

8. In the Password and Confirm password text boxes, type a password for the account, if desired.

9. Select or clear the four check boxes to control the following functions:

- **User must change password at next logon:** Forces the new user to change the password after logging on for the first time. Select this option if you want to assign an initial password and have users control their own passwords after the first logon. You cannot select this option if you have selected the *Password never* *expires* check box. Selecting this option automatically clears the *User cannot change password* check box.

- **User cannot change password:** Prevents the user from changing the account password. Select this option if you want to retain control over the account password, such as when multiple users are logging on with the same user account. This option is also commonly used to manage service account passwords. You cannot select this option if you have selected the *User must change password at next logon* check box.

- **Password never expires:** Prevents the existing password from ever expiring. This option automatically clears the *User must change password at next logon* check box. This option is also commonly used to manage service account passwords.

- **Account is disabled:** Disables the user account, preventing anyone from using it to log on.

10. Click Create. The new account is added to the detail pane and the console clears the dialog box, leaving it ready for the creation of another user account.

11. Click Close.

12. Close the Computer Management console.

MANAGING LOCAL USERS

Local user accounts on a Windows 7 computer are not nearly as complex as domain users, but the Local Users and Groups snap-in provides full access to all of the attributes they do possess. To modify a user's attributes, use the following procedure.

 MANAGE A USER

GET READY. Log on to Windows 7 using an account with administrator privileges.

1. Open the Computer Management console.

2. In the console's scope pane, expand the Local Users and Groups subheading, and then click Users. A list of the current local users appears in the details pane.

3. Double click one of the existing user accounts. The Properties sheet for the user account appears, as shown in Figure 9-18.

4. If desired, modify the contents of the Full name and Description text boxes.

Figure 9-18

A user's Properties sheet

5. Select or clear any of the following check boxes:

- **User must change password at next logon:** Forces the new user to change the password after logging on for the first time. Select this option if you want to assign an initial password and have users control their own passwords after the first logon. You cannot select this option if you have selected the *Password never expires* check box. Selecting this option automatically clears the *User cannot change password* check box.

- **User cannot change password:** Prevents the user from changing the account password. Select this option if you want to retain control over the account password, such as when multiple users are logging on with the same user account. This option is also commonly used to manage service account passwords. You cannot select this option if you have selected the *User must change password at next logon* check box.

- **Password never expires:** Prevents the existing password from ever expiring. This option automatically clears the *User must change password at next logon* check box. This option is also commonly used to manage service account passwords.

- **Account is disabled:** Disables the user account, preventing anyone from using it to log on.

- **Account is locked out:** When selected, indicates that the account has been disabled because the number of unsuccessful logon attempts specified in the local system policies has been exceeded. Clear the check box to unlock the account.

6. Click the Member Of tab. The interface shown in Figure 9-19 appears.

Figure 9-19

The Member Of tab of a user's Properties sheet

7. To add the user to a group, click the Add button. The Select Groups dialog box appears, as shown in Figure 9-20.

Figure 9-20

The Select Groups dialog box

8. Type the name of the local group to which you want to add the user in the text box, and then click OK. The group is added to the Member Of list. You can also type part of the group name and click Check Names to complete the name or click Advanced to search for groups.

9. Click the Profile tab. The interface shown in Figure 9-21 appears.

Figure 9-21

The Profile tab of a user's Properties sheet

10. Type a path or filename into any of the following four text boxes as needed:

   • **Profile path:** To assign a roaming or mandatory user profile to the account, type the path to the profile stored on a network share using Universal Naming Convention (UNC) notation, as in the example *server**share**folder*.

   • **Logon script:** Type the name of a script that you want to execute whenever the user logs on.

   • **Local path:** To create a home folder for the user on a local drive, specify the path in this text box.

   • **Connect:** To create a home folder for the user on a network drive, select an unused drive letter and type the path to a folder on a network share using Universal Naming Convention (UNC) notation.

11. Click OK to save your changes and close the Properties sheet.

12. Close the Computer Management console.

For more information on roaming and mandatory user profiles, see "Understanding User Profiles" later in this lesson.

CREATING A LOCAL GROUP

To create a local group with the Local Users and Groups snap-in, use the following procedure.

 CREATE A LOCAL GROUP

GET READY. Log on to Windows 7 using an account with administrator privileges.

1. Open the Computer Management console.

2. In the console's scope pane, expand the Local Users and Groups node and click Groups. A list of the current local groups appears in the details pane.

3. Right click the Groups folder and then, from the context menu, select New Group. The New Group dialog box appears, as shown in Figure 9-22.

Figure 9-22

The New Group dialog box

4. In the Group name text box, type the name you want to assign to the group. This is the only required field in the dialog box.

5. If desired, specify a Description for the group.

6. Click the Add button. The Select Users dialog box appears, as shown in Figure 9-23.

Figure 9-23

The Select Users dialog box

7. Type the names of the users that you want to add to the group, separated by semi-colons, in the text box, and then click OK. The users are added to the Members list. You can also type part of a username and click Check Names to complete the name or click Advanced to search for users.

8. Click Create to create the group and populate it with the user(s) you specified. The console then clears the dialog box, leaving it ready for the creation of another group.

9. Click Close.

10. Close the Computer Management console.

Local groups have no attributes other than a member's list, so the only modifications you can make when you open an existing group are to add or remove members. As noted earlier in this lesson, local groups cannot have other local groups as members, but if the computer is a member of a Windows domain, a local group can have domain users and domain groups as members.

TAKE NOTE*

To add domain objects to a local group, you click the Add button on the group's Properties sheet and, when the Select Users dialog box appears, change the Object Types and Location settings to those of the domain. Then, you can select domain users and groups just as you did local users in the previous procedure.

Working with Domain Users and Groups

> To create and manage AD DS domain users and groups on a Windows 7 workstation, you must install the Remote Server Administration Tools for Windows 7 package.

Creating and managing AD DS domain users and groups is beyond the scope of the 70-680 exam, but suffice it to say that you cannot use any of the tools discussed so far in this lesson to work with domain objects. To create domain users and groups, you use the Active Directory Users and Computers console, which is included with the Windows Server operating systems.

To manage domain objects on a Windows 7 workstation, you must download and install Remote Server Administration Tools for Windows 7, which is available from the Microsoft Download Center at http://www.microsoft.com/Downloads/details.aspx?familyid=7D2F6AD7-656B-4313-A005-4E344E43997D&displaylang=en. Once you have installed the appropriate package for your processor platform, the Remote Server Administration Tools are available for activation in the Windows Features dialog box, which is accessible from the Programs control panel.

Understanding User Profiles

> As discussed in Lesson 2, "Installing Windows 7," a *user profile* is a series of folders, associated with a specific user account, that contain personal documents, user-specific registry settings, Internet favorites, and other personalized information—everything that provides a user's familiar working environment. On a Windows 7 computer, user profiles are stored in the Users folder, in subfolders named for the user accounts.

On computers running Windows 7, user profiles automatically create and maintain the desktop settings for each user's work environment on the local computer. The system creates a new user profile for each user logging on to the computer for the first time.

RECOGNIZING USER PROFILE TYPES
The three main types of user profiles are as follows:

- **Local user profile:** A profile that Windows 7 automatically creates when each user logs on at the computer for the first time. The local user profile is stored on the computer's local hard disk.
- **Roaming user profile:** A copy of a local user profile that is stored on a shared server drive, making it accessible from anywhere on the network.
- **Mandatory user profile:** A roaming profile that users cannot change. Administrators use mandatory user profiles to enforce particular desktop settings for individuals or for a group of users. A fourth variation, called a super-mandatory profile, requires the user to access the server-based profile, or the logon fails.

USING ROAMING PROFILES
To support users who work at multiple computers on the same network, administrators can create roaming user profiles. A *roaming user profile* is simply a copy of a local user profile that is stored on a network share (to which the user has appropriate permissions), so that the user can access it from any computer on the network. No matter which computer a user logs on from, he or she always receives the files and desktop settings from the profile stored on the server.

To enable a user to access a roaming user profile, rather than a local profile, you must open the user's Properties sheet to the Profile tab and specify the location of the roaming profile in the Profile Path field. Then, the next time the user logs on, Windows 7 accesses the roaming user profile in the following manner:

1. During the user's first logon, the computer copies the entire contents of the roaming profile to the appropriate subfolder in the Users folder on the local drive. Having the roaming user profile contents stored on the local drive enables the user access to the profile during later logons, even if the server containing the roaming profile is unavailable.

2. The computer applies the roaming user profile settings to the computer, making it the active profile.

3. As the user works, the system saves any changes he or she makes to the user profile to the copy on the local drive.

4. When the user logs off, the computer replicates any changes made to the local copy of the user profile back to the server where the roaming profile is stored.

5. The next time the user logs on at the same computer, the system compares the contents of the locally stored profile with the roaming profile stored on the server. The computer copies only the roaming profile components that have changed to the copy on the local drive, which makes the logon process shorter and more efficient.

You should create roaming user profiles on a file server that you back up frequently, so that you always have copies of your users' most recent profiles. To improve logon performance for a busy network, place the users' roaming profiles folder on a member server instead of a domain controller.

USING MANDATORY PROFILES

A *mandatory user profile* is simply a read-only roaming user profile. Users receive files and desktop settings from a server-based profile, just as they would with any roaming profile, and they can modify their desktop environments while they are logged on. However, because the profile is read-only, the system cannot save any profile changes back to the server when the users log off. The next time the user logs on, the server-based profile will be the same as during the previous logon.

Windows 7 downloads the mandatory profile settings to the local computer each time the user logs on. You can assign one mandatory profile to multiple users who require the same desktop settings, such as a group of users who all do the same job. Because the profile never changes, you do not have to worry about one user making changes that affect all of the other users. Also, a mandatory profile makes it possible to modify the desktop environment for multiple users by changing only one profile.

To create a mandatory user profile, you rename the Ntuser.dat file in the folder containing the roaming profile to Ntuser.man. The Ntuser.dat file consists of the Windows 7 system registry settings that apply to the individual user account and contains the user environment settings, such as those controlling the appearance of the desktop. Renaming this file with a .man extension makes it read-only, preventing the client computers from saving changes to the profile when a user logs off.

> **WARNING** When you create roaming profiles, you must be conscious of the Windows version running on your various network workstations. Windows 7 user profiles are not compatible with earlier versions of Windows; and in the same way, profiles from DOS-based Windows versions (such as Windows Me) are not compatible with Windows XP and other NT-based Windows versions.

■ Introducing User Account Control

↓
THE BOTTOM LINE

One of the most common Windows security problems arises from the fact that many users perform their everyday computing tasks with more system access than they actually need. Logging on as Administrator or as a user that is a member of the Administrators group grants the user full access to all areas of the operating system. This degree of system access is not necessary to run many of the applications and perform many of the tasks users require every day; it is needed only for certain administrative functions, such as installing system-wide software or configuring system parameters.

For most users, logging on with administrative privileges all the time is simply a matter of convenience. Microsoft recommends logging on as a standard user, and using administrative privileges only when you need them. However, many technical specialists who do this frequently find themselves encountering situations in which they need administrative access. There is a surprisingly large number of common, and even mundane, Windows tasks that require administrative access, and the inability to perform those tasks can negatively affect a user's productivity.

In the past, the recommended practices when a user account has insufficient access to perform a task are as follows:

- Ask a user with the required access to perform the task.
- Log off the computer and log on again with an administrative account.
- Use the Run As feature to access a particular system function with administrative privileges.

Many users find these solutions too inconvenient, however, and they find themselves adding their standard user accounts to the Administrators group, just to avoid the repeated interruptions.

The two main problems with this practice are:

1. **It grants users the ability to make system-wide configuration changes, install unauthorized software, and potentially compromise the security of the network.** For a corporate installation, this can be a major problem. Allowing end users to configure their own systems makes it extremely difficult for technical specialists to troubleshoot problems. Many organizations prefer to enforce strict control over desktop computers to maintain a standard system configuration throughout the enterprise.

2. **A computer running with administrative privileges is left wide open to exploits by all kinds of malware.** If, for example, a user unknowingly downloads an infected file, the potential for damage to the system is far greater if the user is logged on as an administrator at the time, rather than if the user is logged on as a standard user. The same would be true if a burglar broke into the basement of a three-story building. The potential for loss is far greater if all of the interior doors are unlocked than if the burglar can't leave the basement.

Understanding User Account Control

Microsoft decided to solve these problems by keeping all Windows 7 users from accessing the system using administrative privileges unless those privileges are required to perform the task at hand. The mechanism that does this is called *User Account Control (UAC)*.

When a user logs on to Windows 7, the system issues a token, which indicates the user's access level. Whenever the system authorizes the user to perform a particular activity, it consults the token to see if the user has the required privileges. In previous versions of Windows, standard users received standard user tokens and members of the Administrators group received administrative tokens. Every activity performed by an administrative user was therefore authorized using the administrative token, resulting in the problems described earlier.

On a Windows 7 computer running User Account Control (UAC), a standard user still receives a standard user token, but an administrative user receives two tokens: one for standard user access and one for administrative user access. By default, the standard and administrative users both run using the standard user token most of the time.

UNDERSTANDING RECOMMENDED UAC PRACTICES

Despite the introduction of UAC, Microsoft still recommends that all Windows users log on with a standard user account, except when they are logging on for administrative purposes only. As compared to earlier Windows versions, Windows 7 and UAC simplify the process by which standard users can gain administrative access, making the use of standard user accounts less frustrating, even for system administrators.

PERFORMING ADMINISTRATIVE TASKS WITH A STANDARD USER ACCOUNT

When a standard user attempts to perform a task that requires administrative privileges, the system displays a ***credential prompt***, as shown in Figure 9-24, requesting that the user supply the name and password for an account with administrative privileges.

Figure 9-24

A UAC credential prompt

PERFORMING ADMINISTRATIVE TASKS WITH AN ADMINISTRATIVE ACCOUNT

When an administrator attempts to perform a task that requires administrative access, the system switches the account from the standard user token to the administrative token. This is known as ***Admin Approval Mode***.

> **+ MORE INFORMATION**
>
> The decision to run all users with a standard user token was not one that Microsoft made unilaterally. Part of the process of developing UAC involved working with the software developers both at Microsoft and at third-party companies to minimize the number and type of administrative-level access requests made by applications.

Before the system permits the user to employ the administrative token, it might require the human user to confirm that he or she is actually trying to perform an administrative task. To do this, the system generates an elevation prompt. An ***elevation prompt*** is the message box shown in Figure 9-25. This confirmation prevents unauthorized processes, such as those initiated by malware, from accessing the system using administrative privileges.

Figure 9-25

A UAC elevation prompt

In Windows 7, administrators are faced with elevation prompts far less frequently than they are in Windows Vista. In response to complaints from users, Microsoft has modified the default UAC behavior in Windows 7 so that elevation prompts only appear when an application attempts to perform an administrative task. Operating system administration tasks do not generate elevation prompts.

> **TAKE NOTE***
>
> The system component that is responsible for recognizing the need for elevated privileges and generating elevation prompts is called the Application Information Service (AIS). AIS is a Windows 7 service that has to be running for UAC to function properly. Disabling this service prevents applications that require administrative access from launching, resulting in Access Denied errors.

WARNING It is still possible for a malware program to imitate the secure desktop and create its own artificial elevation or credential prompt, but an artificial prompt cannot provide the program with genuine access to administrative functions. The only possible danger is that a malware program could use an artificial credential prompt to harvest administrative account names and passwords from unsuspecting users.

USING SECURE DESKTOP

By default, whenever Windows 7 displays an elevation prompt or a credential prompt, it does so using the secure desktop. The *secure desktop* is an alternative to the interactive user desktop that Windows normally displays. When Windows 7 generates an elevation or credential prompt, it switches to the secure desktop, suppressing the operation of all other desktop controls and permitting only Windows processes to interact with the prompt. The object of this is to prevent malware from automating a response to the elevation or credential prompt and bypassing the human reply.

Configuring User Account Control

> All versions of Windows 7 enable User Account Control by default, but it is possible to configure several of its properties, or even disable it completely.

When Windows 7 starts, if the AIS service is not running and UAC is disabled, the Windows Security Center warns you of its absence and gives you the opportunity to turn it on.

In Windows 7, there are now four UAC settings available through the Control Panel, as compared to the simple on/off switch in Windows Vista. To configure UAC through the Control Panel, use the following procedure.

 CONFIGURE UAC SETTINGS

GET READY. Log on to Windows 7 using an account with administrator privileges.

1. Click Start, and then click Control Panel. The Control Panel window appears.
2. Click System and Security > Action Center. The Action Center window appears.
3. Click Change User Account Control settings. The User Account Control Settings dialog box appears, as shown in Figure 9-26.

Figure 9-26

The User Account Control
Settings dialog box

4. Adjust the slider to one of the following settings and click OK:

- Always notify me
- Notify me only when programs try to make changes to my computer
- Notify me only when programs try to make changes to my computer (do not dim my desktop)
- Never notify me

5. Close the Action Center window.

While the UAC controls in Windows 7 are improved, the most granular control over UAC properties is still through Local Security Policy or, on an AD DS network, Group Policy.

To configure UAC properties using Local Security Policy, use the following procedure.

 CONFIGURE UAC LOCAL SECURITY POLICIES

GET READY. Log on to Windows 7 using an account with administrator privileges.

1. Click Start, and then click Control Panel. The Control Panel window appears.

2. Click System and Security > Administrative Tools. The Administrative Tools window appears.

3. Double click Local Security Policy. The Local Security Policy console appears, as shown in Figure 9-27.

Figure 9-27

The Local Security Policy console

4. Expand the Local Policies header, and then click Security Options. A list of Security Options policies appears in the details pane, as shown in Figure 9-28.

Figure 9-28

The Security Options list

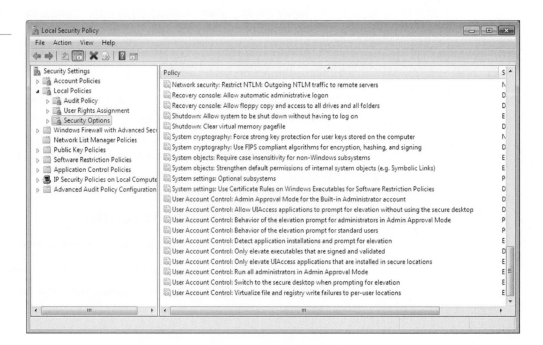

5. Scroll down to the bottom of the policy list until you see the nine policies with the User Account Control prefix, as described in Table 9-4.

Table 9-4

UAC Local Security Policy Settings

POLICY SETTING	VALUES AND FUNCTIONS
User Account Control: Admin Approval Mode for the Built-in Administrator account	When enabled, the built-in Administrator account is issued two tokens during logon and runs in Admin Approval Mode. This is the default setting, except in cases of upgrades from Windows XP systems in which the built-in Administrator account is the only active member of the Administrators group. When disabled, the built-in Administrator account receives only an administrative token and runs with full administrative access at all times.
User Account Control: Allow UIAccess applications to prompt for elevation without using the secure desktop	When enabled, causes User Interface Accessibility programs to disable the secure desktop when displaying elevation prompts. When disabled, elevation prompts use the secure desktop, unless the *User Account Control: Switch to the Secure Desktop when Prompting for Elevation* policy is enabled.
User Account Control: Behavior of the elevation prompt for administrators in Admin Approval Mode	When set to *Elevate without prompting,* administrative users are elevated to the administrative token with no consent or credentials from the human user. This setting, in effect, disables the security provided by UAC and is not recommended. When set to *Prompt for consent on the secure desktop,* administrative users are elevated to the administrative token only after the presentation of an elevation prompt on the secure desktop and the consent of the human user. When set to *Prompt for credentials on the secure desktop,* administrative users are elevated to the administrative token only after the presentation of a credential prompt on the secure desktop, to which the user must supply a valid administrative account name and password, even if he or she is already logged on using such an account. When set to *Prompt for consent,* administrative users are elevated to the administrative token only after the presentation of an elevation prompt and the consent of the human user. This is the default setting. When set to *Prompt for credentials,* administrative users are elevated to the administrative token only after the presentation of a credential prompt, to which the user must supply a valid administrative account name and password, even if he or she is already logged on using such an account.
User Account Control: Behavior of the elevation prompt for standard users	When set to *Automatically deny elevation requests,* suppresses the credential prompt and prevents standard users from being elevated to an administrative token. Standard users can perform administrative tasks only by using the Run As program or by logging on using an administrative account. This is the default setting for the Windows 7 Enterprise edition. When set to *Prompt for credentials on the secure desktop,* standard users attempting to perform an administrative function receive a credential prompt on the secure desktop, to which the user must supply a valid administrative account name and password. When set to *Prompt for credentials,* standard users attempting to perform an administrative function receive a credential prompt, to which the user must supply a valid administrative account name and password. This is the default setting for the Windows 7 Home Basic, Home Premium, Professional, and Ultimate editions.

(*continued*)

Table 9-4 *(continued)*

POLICY SETTING	VALUES AND FUNCTIONS
User Account Control: Detect application installations and prompt for elevation	When enabled, an attempt to install an application causes standard users to receive a credential prompt and administrative users to receive an elevation prompt. The user must supply authentication credentials or consent before the installation can proceed. This is the default setting. When disabled, elevation and credential prompts are suppressed during application installations, and the installations will fail. This setting is for use on enterprise desktops that use an automated installation technology, such as Microsoft System Center Configuration Manager.
User Account Control: Only elevate executables that are signed and validated	When enabled, requires successful public key infrastructure (PKI) signature verifications on all interactive applications that request administrative access. Unsigned applications will not run. When disabled, both signed and unsigned applications will run. This is the default setting.
User Account Control: Only elevate UIAccess applications that are Installed in secure locations	When enabled, Windows 7 will provide access to the protected system user interface only if the executable is located in the Program Files or Windows folder on the system drive. If the executable is not located in one of these folders, access will be denied, despite a positive response to the elevation prompt. This is the default setting. When disabled, the folder location checks are omitted, so any application can be granted access to the protected system user interface upon successful completion of the elevation prompt.
User Account Control: Run all administrators in Admin Approval Mode	When enabled, standard users receive credential prompts and administrative users receive elevation prompts, when either one requests administrative privileges. This policy essentially turns UAC on and off. A change in the value of this policy does not take effect until the system is restarted. This is the default setting. When disabled, the AIS service is disabled and does not automatically start. This turns UAC off and prevents elevation and credential prompts from appearing. When the system starts, the Windows Security Center warns the user that operating system security is reduced and provides the ability to activate UAC.
User Account Control: Switch to the secure desktop when prompting for elevation	When enabled, causes Windows 7 to display all elevation prompts on the secure desktop, which can receive messages only from Windows processes. This is the default setting. When disabled, causes Windows 7 to display all elevation prompts on the interactive user desktop.
User Account Control: Virtualize file and registry write failures to per-user locations	When enabled, allows non-UAC-compliant applications to run by redirecting write requests to protected locations, such as the Program Files and Windows folders or the HKLM\Software registry key, to alternative locations in the registry and file system. This process is called virtualization. This is the default setting. When disabled, virtualization is disabled, and non-UAC-compliant applications attempting to write to protected locations will fail to run. This setting is recommended only when the system is running UAC-compliant applications exclusively.

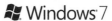

6. Double click one of the User Account Control policies. The Properties sheet for the policy appears, as shown in Figure 9-29.

Figure 9-29

The Properties sheet of a UAC policy

7. Select the radio button (or drop-down list option) for the setting you want the policy to use, and then click OK. The Properties sheet closes.

8. Repeat Steps 6 and 7 to configure other policies, if desired.

9. Close the Local Security Policy console and the Administrative Tools window.

SKILL SUMMARY

IN THIS LESSON YOU LEARNED:

- The user account is the fundamental unit of identity in Windows operating systems.

- A group is an identifying token that Windows uses to represent a collection of users.

- A workgroup is a collection of computers that are all peers. A peer network is one in which every computer can function as both a server by sharing its resources with other computers and as a client by accessing the shared resources on other computers.

- A domain is a collection of computers that all utilize a central directory service for authentication and authorization.

- Windows 7 includes a number of built-in local groups that are already equipped with the permissions and rights needed to perform certain tasks.

- A special identity is essentially a placeholder for a collection of users with a similar characteristic.

- Windows 7 provides two separate interfaces for creating and managing local user accounts: the User Accounts (or user Accounts and Family Safety) control panel and the Local Users and Group snap-in for the Microsoft Management Console (MMC).

(*continued*)

SKILL SUMMARY *(continued)*

- A roaming user profile is simply a copy of a local user profile that is stored on a network share, so that the user can access it from any computer on the network.

- A mandatory user profile is simply a read-only roaming user profile.

- On a Windows 7 computer running User Account Control (UAC), a standard user still receives a standard user token, but an administrative user receives two tokens: one for standard user access and one for administrative user access.

- When a standard user attempts to perform a task that requires administrative privileges, the system displays a credential prompt, requesting that the user supply the name and password for an account with administrative privileges.

- When an administrator attempts to perform a task that requires administrative access, the system switches the account from the standard user token to the administrative token. This is known as Admin Approval Mode.

- Before the system permits the user to employ the administrative token for an application task, it requires the user to confirm that he or she is actually trying to perform the task. To do this, the system generates an elevation prompt.

- The secure desktop is an alternative to the interactive user desktop that Windows normally displays. When Windows 7 generates an elevation or credential prompt, it switches to the secure desktop, suppressing the operation of all other desktop controls and permitting only Windows processes to interact with the prompt.

- User Account Control is enabled by default in all Windows 7 installations, but it is possible to configure its properties, or even disable it completely, using Local Security Policy.

■ Knowledge Assessment

Matching

Complete the following exercise by matching the terms with their corresponding definitions.

    a. switches an account from the standard user token to the administrative token
    b. displayed when a regular user requires administrative access
    c. confirmation of a user's identity
    d. suppresses the operation of all controls except the UAC prompt
    e. enables users to access their desktops from any workstation
    f. grants a user a specific degree of access to a resource
    g. hosts an AD DS domain
    h. displayed when an administrator requires administrative access
    i. placeholder for a collection of users with a similar characteristic
    j. a profile that multiple users can run simultaneously

_____ **1.** credential prompt

_____ **2.** roaming user profile

_____ **3.** Admin Approval Mode

_____ **4.** special identity

_____ **5.** authentication

_____ **6.** elevation prompt

_____ **7.** mandatory user profile

_____ **8.** secure desktop

_____ **9.** authorization

_____ **10.** domain controller

Multiple Choice

Select one or more correct answers for each of the following questions.

1. What is the term used to describe a read-only copy of a user profile stored on a network share?
   a. mandatory profile
   b. super-mandatory profile
   c. roaming profile
   d. search profile

2. When you create a new user account with the User Accounts control panel, you can only add it to which of the following groups? (Choose all that apply.)
   a. Administrators
   b. Users
   c. Power Users
   d. Guests

3. When you log on to a newly installed Windows 7 computer for the first time, why can you not use the Administrator account?
   a. Local Security Policy prevents its use.
   b. The Administrator account has no password.
   c. There is no Administrator account.
   d. The Administrator account is disabled.

4. Which of the following statements is true?
   a. The User Accounts control panel can create local users and local groups only.
   b. The User Accounts control panel can create local and domain users.
   c. The User Accounts control panel can create local users only.
   d. The User Accounts control panel can create local users, local groups, domain users, and domain groups.

5. Which of the following actions can you NOT perform from the Control Panel?
   a. Disable UAC
   b. Disable secure desktop
   c. Disable elevation prompts for operating system tasks only
   d. Disable elevation prompts for application tasks only

6. Which of the following can be members of local groups? (Choose all that apply.)
   a. Local users
   b. Domain users
   c. Other local groups
   d. Domain groups

7. Which of the following built-in Windows 7 accounts are special identities? (Choose all that apply.)
   a. Administrators
   b. Everyone
   c. Authenticated Users
   d. IIS_IUSRS

8. Under which of the following conditions are Windows 7 local user accounts required to use complex passwords?
   a. When the computer is joined to a domain
   b. When one of the Account Lockout Policy settings is enabled in Local Security Policy
   c. When the accounts are members of the Administrators group
   d. When UAC is disabled

9. Which of the following Windows 7 built-in local groups does not provide members with any additional privileges?
   a. Backup Operators
   b. Cryptographic Operators
   c. Power Users
   d. Remote Desktop Users

10. Which of the following is the default UAC setting for a computer that is not joined to an AD DS domain?
    a. Always notify me
    b. Notify me only when programs try to make changes to my computer
    c. Notify me only when programs try to make changes to my computer (do not dim my desktop)
    d. Never notify me

Review Questions

1. Explain why it is recommended that administrators not disable the *User Account Control: Switch to the secure desktop when prompting for elevation* policy.

2. Explain how a special identity differs from a local group.

■ Case Scenario

Scenario 9-1: Configuring UAC

You are a system administrator for a company network running all Windows 7 workstations, and you rely on User Account Control to minimize the possibility of system infiltration by unauthorized software. Many of the department employees spend most of their time performing administrative tasks for the network and therefore require administrative access to their systems. The IS department for the company headquarters also uses an "open office" design, meaning that employees are constantly wandering around to each others' work areas, often leaving their workstations logged on.

You are concerned about the danger of unattended workstations being used to gain administrative access to the systems. What changes can you make to the UAC configuration to minimize this possibility? Explain how these changes would enhance the security of the systems.

Securing Windows 7

OBJECTIVE DOMAIN MATRIX

TECHNOLOGY SKILL	OBJECTIVE DOMAIN	OBJECTIVE NUMBER
Introducing Windows Firewall	Configure Windows Firewall.	4.4
Using the Encrypting File System	Configure file and folder access.	5.2
Authenticating and Authorizing Users	Configure authentication and authorization.	5.4

KEY TERMS

authenticated exception

brute force

filter

firewall

malware

multifactor authentication

Personal Identity Verification (PIV)

private key

public key

rules

spyware

user rights

Windows Biometric Framework

■ Authenticating and Authorizing Users

THE BOTTOM LINE

As mentioned in Lesson 9, "Working with Workgroups and Domains," authentication and authorization are two of the most important functions of Windows 7. Authentication confirms the identification of a user accessing computer or network resources, and authorization specifies which resources the user is permitted to access.

Network resources require varying levels of security, and technical specialists are often responsible for seeing to it that users have access only to the information they need to do their jobs, and no more. Authentication is crucial to this process, because before you can provide access to protected resources, you must confirm the identity of those to whom you are providing access.

The user authentication process is typically based on one or more of the following:

- **Something the user knows:** A secret shared between the user and management—usually in the form of a password—is the simplest and most common form of authentication. However, users can forget, share, or otherwise compromise passwords, often without knowing it.

- **Something the user has:** A token of some kind, carried by the user, such as a smart card, can serve as proof of identity. While tokens can easily be lost or stolen, users are typically aware of the loss, and the time during which the system is compromised is brief.

- **Something the user is:** Biometric identification is the use of physical characteristics to confirm a user's identity. Fingerprints are the most commonly used biometric identifier, but there are also technologies that are based on ocular scans, facial recognition, and other characteristics.

Because each of these identification methods has inherent weaknesses, networks requiring high security often use more than one. For example, a network that issues smart cards to users nearly always requires some sort of password as well. This technique is known as ***multifactor authentication***.

Authentication is nearly always a balance between security and convenience, and nowhere is this truer than in user authentication. As a technical specialist responsible for network security, you could conceivably demand that your users log on each day by typing 72-character passwords, scanning security bracelets permanently fastened to their wrists, and having their identities confirmed with a blood sample. There are, however, likely to be objections to this treatment from users.

Working with Passwords

Passwords are the most common user identifier on Windows networks, primarily because they do not require any additional hardware or software. Passwords can provide excellent security as well, as long as they are used properly.

When left to their own devices, users tend to employ password policies that can compromise their effectiveness as a security mechanism. Potential intruders can obtain passwords in two possible ways: by cracking them or by discovering them.

Cracking is the process of repeatedly guessing passwords until you find the right one. Cracking is a mathematical process in which a software program tries all of the possible passwords until it finds the right one. This is sometimes known as a ***brute force*** process.

Password discovery is a process in which the intruder tries to guess a password based on the user's personal information, or tries to dupe the user into supplying the password. This is also known as social engineering.

These methods are possible only when users compromise their passwords in some way. Some of the ways in which users can weaken the security of their passwords are as follows:

- **Short passwords:** Shorter passwords are mathematically easier to guess. A three-character alphabetical password has 26^3 or 17,576 possible values. Increasing the password to seven characters increases the number of possible values to 26^7 or over eight billion password combinations.

- **Simple passwords:** Passwords that use only lowercase characters are also mathematically easier to guess than those that use mixed lowercase and uppercase characters. A seven-character password using upper and lowercase characters would have 52^7 or over one trillion possible values. Passwords that use numerical characters and symbols as well increase their strength even further.

- **Unchanging passwords:** A brute force attack takes time to try every possible password combination, so changing passwords forces an attacker to start all over. The fewer the possible password combinations an attacker has to try, the more frequently you should change the password.

- **Predictable passwords:** Users often select passwords based on predicable values, such as birthdays, social security numbers, or names of children and pets. Attackers that have access to this type of information can make more educated password guesses.

Windows 7 includes features that can provide users with a more convenient password experience, and also compel them to obey network password selection and maintenance policies that minimize these potential weaknesses. Some of these features are discussed in the following sections.

CONFIGURING PASSWORD POLICIES

Windows 7 supports a number of Group Policy settings that administrators can use to enforce password security practices on individual computers or on Active Directory Domain Services (AD DS) networks. By enforcing these password practices, you can ensure that your systems remain secure, even though the end users are responsible for their own passwords.

To configure password policies using Local Security Policy, use the following procedure.

 CONFIGURE PASSWORD POLICIES

GET READY. Log on to Windows 7 using an account with administrator privileges.

1. Click Start, and then click Control Panel. The Control Panel window appears.
2. Click System and Security > Administrative Tools. The Administrative Tools window appears.
3. Double click Local Security Policy. The Local Security Policy console appears, as shown in Figure 10-1.

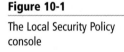
Figure 10-1

The Local Security Policy console

4. Expand the Account Policies header, and then click Password Policy. A list of password policies appears in the details pane, as shown in Figure 10-2.

Figure 10-2

Password Policies in the Local
Security Policy console

5. Double click one of the password policies described in Table 10-1. The Properties
   sheet for the policy appears, as shown in Figure 10-3.

Table 10-1

Windows Password Policy
Settings

PASSWORD POLICY SETTINGS	VALUES AND FUNCTION
Enforce password history	Specifies the number of unique passwords that users have to supply before Windows 7 permits them to reuse an old password. Possible values range from 0 to 24. The default value is 0.
Maximum password age	Specifies how long a single password can be used before Windows 7 forces the user to change it. Possible values range from 0 to 999. A value of 0 causes the password never to expire. The default value is 42 days.
Minimum password age	Specifies how long a single password must be used before Windows 7 permits the user to change it. Possible values range from 0 to 998. The default value is 0 days, which enables the user to change the password immediately.
Minimum password length	Specifies the minimum number of characters Windows 7 permits in user-supplied passwords. Possible values range from 0 to 14. The default value is 0, which means that no password is required.
Password must meet complexity requirements	When enabled, indicates that passwords supplied by users must be at least six characters long, with no duplication of any part of the user's account name; and must include characters from at least three of the following four categories: uppercase letters, lowercase letters, numbers, and symbols. By default, this policy is disabled.
Store passwords using reversible encryption	When enabled, causes Windows 7 to store user account passwords using a less effective encryption algorithm. This policy is designed to support authentication protocols that require access to the user's password, such as the Challenge Handshake Authentication Protocol (CHAP). From a security perspective, this policy is functionally equivalent to using plaintext passwords. The default value is disabled.

Figure 10-3

The Properties sheet of a
password policy

6. Configure the policy by setting a value using the spin box, radio button, or other control, and then click OK. The Properties sheet closes.

7. Repeat Steps 5 and 6 to configure other policies, if desired.

8. Close the Local Security Policy console and the Administrative Tools window.

In an enterprise network environment, technical specialists generally prefer to configure these settings using AD DS Group Policy, so they can distribute them to large numbers of workstations simultaneously. To configure password policies on an AD DS network, you must run the Group Policy Management Editor console and create a Group Policy object, which you then link to a domain, site, or organizational unit object in your AD DS tree. The password policies in a GPO are located in the Computer Configuration\Policies\Windows Settings\ Security Settings\Account Policies\Password Policies node, as shown in Figure 10-4. The policy settings themselves are exactly the same.

TAKE NOTE*

The Group Policy Management Editor console is supplied with the Windows Server operating systems and installed automatically on AD DS domain controllers. To manage AD DS Group Policy settings on a Windows 7 workstation, you must download and install the Remote Server Administration Tools for Windows 7 package. For more information, see "Working with Domain Users and Groups" in Lesson 9, "Working with Workgroups and Domains."

Figure 10-4

Password Policies in an AD DS Group Policy object

CONFIGURING ACCOUNT LOCKOUT POLICIES

It is possible to penetrate any password-protected resource, given enough time and an unlimited number of access attempts. The brute force approach to password penetration is supported by programs designed to try thousands of different character combinations in an attempt to find the one that matches the password.

Windows 7 can protect against brute force password penetration techniques by limiting the number of unsuccessful logon attempts allowed by each user account. When a potential infiltrator exceeds the number of allowed attempts, the system locks the account for a set period of time. To impose these limits, you can use Local Security Policy for stand-alone computers or Group Policy for AD DS networks.

To set account lockout parameters using Local Security Policy, use the following procedure.

 CONFIGURE ACCOUNT LOCKOUT POLICIES

GET READY. Log on to Windows 7 using an account with administrator privileges.

1. Click Start, and then click Control Panel. The Control Panel window appears.
2. Click System and Security > Administrative Tools. The Administrative Tools window appears.
3. Double click Local Security Policy. The Local Security Policy console appears.
4. Expand the Account Policies header, and then click Account Lockout Policy. A list of policies appears in the details pane, as shown in Figure 10-5.

Figure 10-5

Account Lockout Policies in the
Local Security Policy console

5. Double click one of the policies described in Table 10-2. The Properties sheet for the policy appears, as shown in Figure 10-6.
6. Configure the policy by setting a value using the spin box, radio button, or other control, and then click OK. The Properties sheet closes.
7. Repeat Steps 5 and 6 to configure other policies, if desired.
8. Close the Local Security Policy console and the Administrative Tools window.

Table 10-2

Windows Account Lockout
Policy Settings

ACCOUNT LOCKOUT POLICY SETTING	VALUES AND FUNCTION
Account lockout duration	Determines the period of time that must pass after a lockout before Windows 7 automatically unlocks a user's account. The policy is not set by default, as it is viable only in conjunction with the Account Lockout Threshold policy. Possible values range from 0 to 99999 minutes (about 10 weeks). A low setting (5 to 15 minutes) is usually sufficient to reduce attacks significantly without unreasonably affecting legitimate users who are mistakenly locked out. A value of 0 requires an administrator to unlock the account manually. When the Account Lockout Threshold policy is activated, this policy is activated as well and set to a default value of 30 minutes.
Account lockout threshold	Specifies the number of invalid logon attempts that will trigger an account lockout. Possible values range from 0 to 999. A value that is too low (as few as three, for example) may cause lockouts due to normal user error during logon. A value of 0 prevents accounts from ever being locked out. The default value is 0.
Reset account lockout counter after	Specifies the period of time that must pass after an invalid logon attempt before the lockout counter resets to zero. Possible values range from 1 to 99999 minutes, and must be less than or equal to the account lockout duration. When the Account lockout threshold policy is activated, this policy is activated as well and set to a default value of 30.

Figure 10-6

The Properties sheet of an
account lockout policy

TAKE NOTE* As with password policies, you can also deploy account lockout policies on an AD DS network using Group Policy.

USING CREDENTIAL MANAGER

Users and administrators alike often become frustrated when forced to re-enter passwords
whenever they have to access a protected resource. This is one reason why Microsoft modified
the default behavior of User Account Control in Windows 7 to eliminate elevation prompts
for administrative operating system tasks.

Credential Manager is a Windows 7 tool that stores the usernames and passwords people supply to servers and Web sites in a protected area called the Windows Vault. When a user selects
the *Remember my credentials* check box while authenticating in Windows Explorer, Internet
Explorer, or Remote Desktop Connection, as shown in Figure 10-7, the system adds the
credentials to the Windows Vault.

Figure 10-7

Credential Manager

From the Credential Manager window in Control Panel, you can see the resources for which the Windows Vault contains credentials, as shown in Figure 10-8, although you cannot view the passwords themselves.

Figure 10-8

Credential Manager

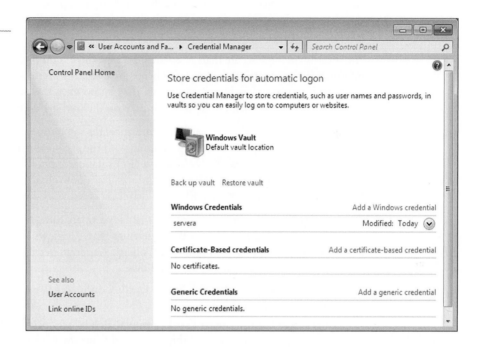

It is also possible to add credentials directly to the vault using Credential Manager, by clicking *Add a Windows credential*, or one of the similar links. The interface shown in Figure 10-9 then appears, in which you can specify the address of a resource and the credentials that go with it. In the same way, you can specify a resource and select a certificate from the computer's store.

Finally, you can back up the contents of the Windows Vault from Credential Manager and restore it to the same or another computer, to protect the credentials or migrate them.

Figure 10-9

The Add a Windows Credential window

Using Smart Cards

> Smart cards provide a high-security alternative to passwords for user authentication.

A smart card is a credit card-like device that contains a chip, on which is stored a digital certificate that serves as an identifier for a particular user. On a computer equipped with a card reader, a user can authenticate him- or herself by specifying a username and inserting the smart card.

Smart cards are more secure than passwords, because there is no practical way to duplicate the information they contain by guessing or brute force attack. It is possible for users to have their smart cards lost or stolen, but in most cases, they know when this occurs and can report the loss. An administrator can then revoke the certificate on the card, rendering it invalid and useless.

Windows has supported smart card authentication for some time, but until Windows 7, you had to install a third-party device driver along with the card reader hardware. By including support for the *Personal Identity Verification (PIV)* standard, published by the National Institute of Standards and Technology (NIST), Windows 7 can now obtain drivers for PIV smart cards from Windows Update, or use a PIV minidriver included with the operating system.

For organizations that are committed to the use of smart cards for authentication, there are two smart card-related Group Policy settings that Windows 7 supports. These settings, located in the Computer Configuration\Policies\Windows Settings\Security Settings\Local Policies\Security Options node, are as follows:

- **Interactive Logon: Require Smart Card:** Configures Windows 7 to allow only smart card user authentications.
- **Interactive Logon: Smart Card Removal Behavior:** Specifies how Windows 7 should behave when a user removes the smart card from the reader while logged on to the computer. The possible values are as follows:
  - **No action:** Enables the user to remove the smart card without affecting the session. This is the default setting.
  - **Lock Workstation:** Disables the workstation while leaving the session open until the user reinserts the smart card. This enables the user to leave the workstation temporarily without leaving the smart card and without having to log off.
  - **Force Logoff:** Causes the workstation to log the user off as soon as the smart card is removed.
  - **Disconnect if a Remote Desktop Services session:** Disconnects the computer from the Remote Desktop Services server without logging the user off from the session. The user can then resume the session by reinserting the smart card at the same or another computer.

Managing Certificates

> Windows 7 uses digital certificates for a variety of authentication tasks, internally, on the local network, and on the Internet. Every user account has a certificate store containing a variety of certificates obtained by various means.

Windows 7 creates some certificates itself, such as the self-signed certificate it uses for the Encrypting File System. Others it downloads from other computers, such as servers on the Internet. In most cases, activities involving certificates are invisible to the user. Windows 7 obtains most of the certificates it needs automatically and stores them for future use.

However, it is possible for users to manage their certificate stores directly, including creating backups of certificates for disaster recovery or migration purposes. Windows 7 includes a Certificates snap-in for MMC that provides access to the certificate store, but the snap-in is not accessible from the Start menu or the Control Panel.

To access the Certificates snap-in, type certmgr.msc in the Start menu's search box. This loads the snap-in and points it at the current user account, as shown in Figure 10-10.

Figure 10-10

The Certificates snap-in

Double clicking one of the certificates in the store displays a Certificate dialog box like the one shown in Figure 10-11. This dialog box contains information about the certificate and the data stored in it.

Figure 10-11

A Certificate dialog box

To back up a certificate to a file, right click it in the snap-in and, in the context menu, select All Tasks > Export, to launch the Certificate Export Wizard. This wizard prompts you to select a format for the file, as shown in Figure 10-12, and the location where you want to save it.

Figure 10-12

The Export File Format page in the Certificate Export Wizard

Using Biometrics

Biometric authentication uses a scan of a physical characteristics to confirm the identity of a user.

Biometric authentication is theoretically more secure than a token-based or secret-based authentication method because the identifying characteristic is difficult or impossible to duplicate. The grisly stories of severed body parts being used to fool biometric scanners are (hopefully) fictitious because the technology exists to confirm that a finger or other appendage is still connected to a living body.

There are a great many third-party biometric authentication solutions available, most of which take the form of fingerprint scanners for laptop computers. Prior to Windows 7, the operating system included no support for biometric devices at all, and required the third-party vendor to supply a complete software solution along with the hardware. However, Windows 7 includes a new component called the ***Windows Biometric Framework***, which provides a core biometric functionality and a Biometric Device control panel.

Even with the Windows Biometric Framework, however, the reliability of these technologies and the security they provide can vary widely. Most biometric solutions include a secondary authentication method, such as a password or a smart card, for when the biometric scan fails. Others are multifactor solutions, requiring both a biometric scan and another form of authentication.

Elevating Privileges

Since the Windows Vista release, Microsoft has made a concerted effort to persuade users not to log on to Windows for their everyday tasks using an administrative account. This practice not only makes accidental configuration changes more possible, it also increases the likelihood of intrusion by malevolent attackers.

The preferred mechanism for performing tasks that require administrative privileges is to use the Run As feature to execute a program using another account. Shortcuts in the Start menu have a *Run as administrator* option in their context menus, which causes standard users to receive a credential prompt and administrators to receive an elevation prompt, according to the system's normal User Account Control (UAC) practices.

It is also possible to use the Runas.exe command-line program to execute an application using any other account. The syntax for the Runas.exe program is as follows:

```
runas [/user:domain\user] [/profile] [/noprofile] [/savecred]
[/smartcard] [/env] [/netonly] [/trustlevel] [/showtrustlevels]
"program.exe /parameter"
```

- **/user:domain\user:** Specifies the account that Runas.exe should use to execute the program. The account can be specified in the form *domain\user* or u*ser@domain*. The domain variable can also be the name of a stand-alone workstation and *user* a local user account.
- **/profile:** Causes the Runas.exe program to load the profile of the account specified by the /user parameter. This is the default value.
- **/noprofile:** Prevents the Runas.exe program from loading the profile of the account specified by the /user parameter. Without the profile, the program cannot access the EFS-encrypted files belonging to the account specified by the /user parameter.
- **/savecred:** Causes the Runas.exe program to save the credentials for the account specified by the /user parameter in the Windows Vault or, in the case of a previously saved account, to use the credentials saved in the vault.
- **/smartcard:** Specifies that the credentials for the account specified by the \user parameter will be supplied using a smart card.
- **/env:** Causes the Runas.exe program to use the current environment, rather than the one of the account specified by the /user parameter.
- **/netonly:** Specifies that the credentials of the account specified by the /user variable are for remote access only.
- **"program.exe /parameter":** Specifies the name of the application that Runas. exe should run with elevated privileges, along with any of the application's necessary command-line parameters.

A typical example of a Runas command line would appear as follows:

```
runas /user:example\administrator "notepad.exe \script.vbs"
```

When you run the command, the program prompts for the password to the Administrator account, loads the user profile for the account, executes Notepad.exe, and then loads the Script.vbs file.

Troubleshooting Authentication Issues

The most common problem related to authentication experienced by Windows 7 users is password loss. There is no way for a user or an administrator to read a password from a user account on a Windows system, whether it is stored in the Security Account Manager (SAM), the Windows Vault, or an AD DS domain controller.

When a user loses a Windows 7 account password, there is no way to reclaim it; the only solution is to reset (i.e., change) the password. There are two ways of doing this: either the user resets his or her own password or an administrator resets it.

To reset your own password, you must supply the old one first. If you cannot do this, because you have lost or forgotten the old password, the only solution is to use a password reset disk. The password reset disk supplies the old password for you, enabling you to reset the password to a new value.

The problem with this solution is that you must have created a password-reset disk before losing your password. In the User Accounts control panel, the *Make changes to your user account* page for each user has a link that enables the user to run the Forgotten Password Wizard and create a password reset disk, using a floppy disk or a USB flash drive, as shown in Figure 10-13.

Figure 10-13

The Create a Password Reset Disk page in the Forgotten Password Wizard

When a user loses his or her password, and does not have a password reset disk, the only alternative is for an administrator to reset the password, using either the Local Users and Groups snap-in or the *Manage Accounts* page of the User Accounts control panel. Administrators can reset passwords without having to supply the old password first.

The problem, however, is that an administrative reset causes the user to lose access to all EFS-encrypted files, all certificates in the user's personal certificate store, and all passwords stored in the Windows Vault. These passwords might be recoverable from a backup of the Windows Vault or the EFS key, but it would be a lot easier if the user had created a password-reset disk in the first place.

Authorizing Users

Authentication confirms a user's identity. Authorization grants the user access to certain resources.

A successful authentication confirms that a user is who he or she purports to be, but logging on successfully does not guarantee access to system resources. Some authenticated users have full access to the system, while others might have almost none. The difference between the two is the resources that they are authorized to access.

USING PERMISSIONS

The most commonly used mechanisms for authorizing users in Windows 7 are the NTFS, share, and registry permission systems. By adjusting permissions in the protected resources, administrators can specify who should have access to them and what degree of access users should receive.

For more information on managing permissions, see Lesson 6, "Sharing Resources."

CONFIGURING USER RIGHTS

Some people confuse the concept of user permissions with that of user rights; in Windows 7, these are two different concepts. In Windows 7, *user rights* are policies that define specific operating system functions. For example, in order to sit down at a Windows 7 computer and log on, users must not only have accounts, they also must possess the *Allow log on locally* user right.

Administrators can assign user rights to individual users, but as with permissions, this is rare. The more practical alternative is to assign user rights to groups and then add individual users to the groups as needed.

In fact, Windows 7 does this for you, by default. The built-in local groups on a computer running Windows 7 receive their special capabilities through default user rights assignments. For example, the Remote Desktop Users group has been assigned the *Allow log on through Remote Desktop Services* user right.

To assign user rights to users or groups, you can open the Local Security Policy snap-in on a Windows 7 workstation and browse to Security Settings\Local Policies\User Rights Assignment, as shown in Figure 10-14. In an AD DS environment, you open a GPO and browse to the Computer Configuration\Policies\Windows Settings\Security Settings\Local Policies\User Rights Assignment node. In both interfaces, there are 44 user rights assignments that you can grant to local or domain users and groups.

Figure 10-14

User Rights Assignments

■ Defending Against Malware

THE BOTTOM LINE

Malware is one of the primary threats to Windows 7 security, and the operating system includes a variety of tools that you can use to combat it. The following sections examine these tools and how to implement and configure them.

Windows 7 holds security as one its primary goals. Beginning with the Windows XP Service Pack 2 release, Windows has monitored the state of the security mechanisms included with the operating system and warns the user if any components are misconfigured, outdated, or not functioning.

Chief among the threats to Windows 7 computers is malicious software created specifically for the purpose of infiltrating or damaging a computer system without the user's knowledge or consent. This type of software includes a variety of technologies, including viruses, Trojan horses, worms, spyware, and adware. The term most commonly used to collectively refer to these malicious software technologies is *malware*.

The types of malware to which Windows 7 is susceptible range from the relatively innocuous to the extremely destructive. The effects it can have on a Windows 7 computer include the following:

- Collect usage information about the computer user and transmit to an Internet server.
- Display advertisements on the user's system.
- Use the system's email address book to send spam.
- Attach code to document files that spreads to other files on any system opening the document.
- Install and run a program that enables a remote user to take control of the system.
- Damage or destroy the files stored on the computer.
- Infiltrate the computer's boot sector and spread to other systems.

Malware is, in most cases, introduced onto a computer by a deliberate action on the part of a user. Someone opens an email attachment, installs an infected program, or accesses a dangerous Web site, and the malicious code is introduced to the system. Windows 7 includes a variety of tools that attempt to prevent users from inadvertently infecting their computers and also attempt to block the activities of malicious software programs once they are present.

Security is a pervasive concern throughout the Windows 7 operating system, and as a result there are some Windows 7 security mechanisms that are discussed elsewhere in this text:

- In Lesson 7, "Working with Applications," you learn about the security features included in Internet Explorer 8.
- In Lesson 9, "Working with Workgroups and Domains," you learn how User Account Control helps to prevent malware from obtaining administrative privileges.
- In Lesson 12, "Working with Mobile Computers," you learn about the security features specifically designed for use on mobile and wireless computers.

Introducing Windows 7 Action Center

The Windows 7 Action Center ensures that your system is protected from malware intrusion by notifying you if any of the Windows 7 security mechanisms are not running properly.

Like the Network and Sharing Center, the Action Center is a centralized console that enables users and administrators to access, monitor, and configure the various Windows 7 security mechanisms. The primary function of the Action Center is to provide an automatic notification system that alerts users when the system is vulnerable.

Action Center is a service that starts automatically and runs continuously on Windows 7 computers, by default. The service constantly monitors the different security mechanisms running on the computer. If Action Center detects a mechanism that is not functioning properly for any of several reasons, it displays an icon in the notification area (formerly known as the taskbar tray) to inform the user of the condition, as shown in Figure 10-15.

Figure 10-15

The Action Center menu in the notification area

ACCESSING ACTION CENTER

When the user clicks the notification area icon to open the Action Center window (or clicks Start > Control Panel > System and Security > Action Center), the system displays information about the problems it has discovered, and links possible solutions.

For example, the Action Center window shown in Figure 10-16 contains a Virus Protection warning. Clicking *Find a program online* opens a web page on Microsoft's site linking to various providers of virus protection software. In the same way, clicking *Change settings* in the Windows Update warning box opens a Choose a Windows Update option dialog box, from which you can activate the Windows Update client.

Figure 10-16

The Action Center window

The Action Center window is divided into two main sections: Security and Maintenance. The Security section, in addition to monitoring the computer's security status, provides users with a single point of access to information about Windows 7 security, in the form of the following indicators:

- Network firewall
- Windows Update
- Virus Protection
- Spyware and unwanted software protection
- Internet security settings
- User Account Control
- Network Access Protection

The Maintenance section contains these indicators:

- Check for solutions to problem reports
- Backup
- Check for updates
- Troubleshooting: System Maintenance

Each of these indicators displays the current status of the security or maintenance feature and, if appropriate, supplies a link to the controls for that feature.

Links to other related features appear on the left side of the window, including a link to the Change Action Center Settings window, as shown in Figure 10-17. From this window, you can control which messages appear in the Action Center interface.

Figure 10-17

The Change Action Center Settings window

Introducing Windows Firewall

> Windows Firewall protects Windows 7 computers by blocking dangerous traffic, both incoming and outgoing.

As discussed in Lesson 5, "Connecting to a Network," a *firewall* is a software program that protects a computer by allowing certain types of network traffic in and out of the system while blocking others. Firewalls are essentially packet filters that examine the contents of packets and the traffic patterns to and from the network to determine which packets should be allowed passage through the filter.

CERTIFICATION READY?
Configure Windows Firewall.
4.4

Network connections are all but ubiquitous in the computing world these days. All business computers are networked, and virtually all home computers have an Internet connection. Many homes have local area networks as well. Network connections provide Windows 7 users with access to virtually unlimited resources, but any door that allows data out can also allow data in. Some of the hazards that firewalls protect against are as follows:

- Trojan horse applications that users inadvertently download and run can open a connection to a computer on the Internet, enabling an attacker on the outside to run programs or store data on the system.
- A mobile computer can be compromised while connected to a public network and then brought onto a private network, compromising the resources there.
- Network scanner applications can probe systems for unguarded ports, which are essentially unlocked doors that attackers can use to gain access to the system.
- Attackers that obtain passwords by illicit means, such as social engineering, can use remote access technologies to log on to a computer from another location and compromise its data and programming.

UNDERSTANDING FIREWALLS

As noted in Lesson 5, firewalls typically base their filtering on the TCP/IP characteristics at the network, transport, and application layers, as follows:

- **IP addresses:** Represent specific computers on the network.
- **Protocol numbers:** Identify the transport layer protocol being used by the packets.
- **Port numbers:** Identify specific applications running on the computer.

To filter traffic, firewalls use *rules* that specify which packets are allowed to pass through the firewall and which are blocked. Firewalls can work in two ways, as follows:

- Admit all traffic, except that which conforms to the applied rules
- Block all traffic, except that which conforms to the applied rules

Generally speaking, blocking all traffic by default is the more secure arrangement. From the firewall administrator's standpoint, you start with a completely blocked system, and then start testing your applications. When an application fails to function properly because network access is blocked, you create a rule that opens up the ports the application needs to communicate.

This is the method that the Windows Firewall service in Windows 7 uses by default for incoming network traffic. The default rules preconfigured into the firewall are designed to admit the traffic used by standard Windows networking functions, such as file and printer sharing. For outgoing network traffic, Windows Firewall uses the other method, allowing all traffic to pass except that which conforms to a rule.

MONITORING WINDOWS FIREWALL

Windows Firewall is one of the programs monitored by the Action Center service. The main Action Center window indicates whether Windows Firewall is running, and also whether any third-party firewall products are running.

When you open the Start menu and click Control Panel > System and Security > Windows Firewall, a Windows Firewall window appears, displaying the firewall's status in greater detail, as shown in Figure 10-18.

Figure 10-18

The Windows Firewall window

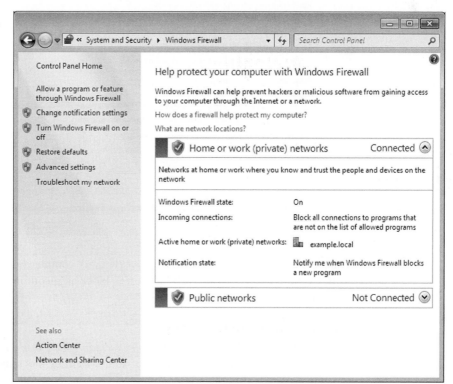

The Windows Firewall window contains expandable headings for the computer's network locations: home or work, public, and domain (if the computer is joined to an AD DS domain). Each of the headings contains the following information:

- Whether the computer is connected to a domain, private, or public network
- Whether the Windows Firewall service is currently turned on or off
- Whether inbound and outbound connections are blocked
- Whether users are notified when a program is blocked

Windows Firewall maintains a separate profile for each of the network locations, so you can have a different firewall configuration for each one. Whenever you are working with Windows Firewall settings, you must be conscious of the profile to which the settings apply.

USING THE WINDOWS FIREWALL CONTROL PANEL

On the left side of the Windows Firewall window is a series of links that enable you to change the firewall notification settings, configure Windows Firewall to allow a specific program through its barrier, turn Windows Firewall on and off, and configure advanced firewall settings.

Clicking *Change notification settings* or *Turn Windows firewall on or off* displays the *Customize settings for each type of network* dialog box, as shown in Figure 10-19. As in the Windows firewall window, controls for the domain profile only appear when the computer is joined to an AD DS domain.

Figure 10-19

The Customize settings for each type of network dialog box

Using this interface, you can turn Windows Firewall completely on or off for each of the network locations and configure each location to block all incoming traffic and notify the user when the firewall blocks a program.

Blocking Incoming Connections

Selecting the *Block all incoming connections, including those in the list of allowed programs* check box enables you to increase the security of your system by blocking all unsolicited attempts to connect to your computer. Note, however, that this does not prevent you from performing common networking tasks, such as accessing Web sites and sending or receiving emails. These activities are not unsolicited connection attempts; they begin with the client contacting the server first. When the firewall detects the outgoing traffic from your web browser to a web server on the Internet, for example, it knows that it should admit the incoming response from the server.

Allowing Programs through the Firewall

Users might want to modify the firewall settings in other ways also, typically because a specific application requires access to a port not anticipated by the firewall's preconfigured rules. Clicking *Allow a program or feature through Windows Firewall* opens the *Allow programs to communicate through Windows Firewall* dialog box, as shown in Figure 10-20. In this dialog box, you can open up a port through the firewall for specific programs and features installed on the computer, simply by selecting the appropriate check boxes.

Figure 10-20

The Allow programs to communicate through Windows Firewall dialog box

Opening a port in your firewall is an inherently dangerous activity. The more holes you make in a wall, the greater the likelihood that intruders will get in. For this reason, the Windows Firewall controls in the Windows 7 Control Panel are quite limited, more so than in Windows Vista. In Windows 7, you cannot open up specific port numbers using Control Panel; you can only select from a list of installed applications and features. For full access to Windows Firewall, you must use the Windows Firewall with Advanced Security console, as discussed in the next section.

USING THE WINDOWS FIREWALL WITH ADVANCED SECURITY CONSOLE

The Windows Firewall with Advanced Security console provides direct access to the rules that control the behavior of Windows Firewall. To access the console, open Control Panel from the Start menu, and then click *System* and *Security* > *Administrative Tools* > *Windows Firewall with Advanced Security*. The Windows Firewall with Advanced Security console appears, as shown in Figure 10-21.

Figure 10-21

The Windows Firewall with
Advanced Security console

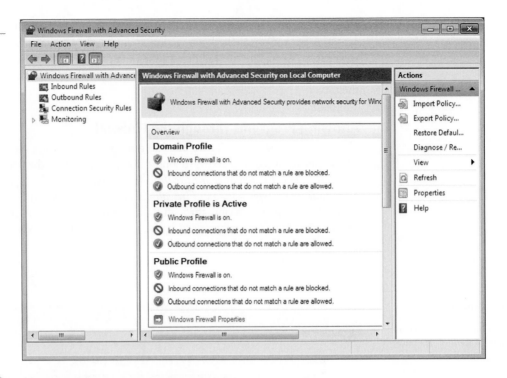

Configuring Profile Settings

At the top of the details pane, in the Overview section, are status displays for the computer's
three possible network locations. Windows Firewall maintains separate profiles for each of the
three possible network locations: domain, private, and public. If you connect the computer
to a different network, as in the case of a laptop computer that you bring to an Internet "hot
spot" in a coffee shop, Windows Firewall loads a different configuration for that profile and a
different set of rules.

As you can tell from the Overview display, the default Windows Firewall settings call for the
same basic configuration for all three profiles: the firewall is turned on, incoming traffic is
blocked unless it matches a rule, and outgoing traffic is allowed unless it matches a rule. You
can change this default behavior by clicking the Windows Firewall Properties link, which displays the Windows Firewall with Advanced Security on Local Computer Properties sheet, as
shown in Figure 10-22.

Figure 10-22

The Windows Firewall with
Advanced Security on Local
Computer Properties sheet

In this Properties sheet, each of the three location profiles has a tab with identical controls that enable you to modify the default profile settings. You can, for example, configure the firewall to shut down completely when it is connected to a domain network, and turn the firewall on with its most protective settings when you connect the computer to a public network. You can also configure the firewall's notification option, which specifies whether the firewall should display a message to the user when it blocks a program, and its logging behavior.

The most important settings in the Properties sheet are those that establish the default behavior for each profile, because these settings determine the nature of the rules that Windows Firewall will use. In the default settings, *Inbound connections* is set to Block, so the rules you create must allow certain types of traffic to pass through the firewall. If you change the default to allow inbound connections, then you must create rules that block certain types of traffic. The setting for *Outbound connections* are the opposite, by default.

Creating Rules

Selecting programs in the Windows Firewall control panel is a relatively friendly method for working with firewall rules. In the Windows Firewall with Advanced Security console, you can work with the rules in their raw form. Selecting either Inbound Rules or Outbound Rules in the scope pane displays a list of all the rules operating in that direction, as shown in Figure 10-23. The rules that are currently operational have a check mark in a green circle, while the rules not in force are grayed out.

> **TAKE NOTE** ✱
>
> It is important to remember that in the Windows Firewall with Advanced Security console, you are always working with a complete list of rules for all of the profiles, while in the Windows Firewall Settings dialog box, you are working only with the rules that apply to the currently active profile.

Figure 10-23

The Inbound Rules list in the Windows Firewall with Advanced Security console

The default rules for three profiles differ, with the public profile providing the most secure environment and the private profile the least. Table 10-3 lists some of the primary networking services in Windows 7 and their default firewall settings for each profile. This is a highly simplified list, as most of these services use a variety of protocols that all require their own rules for incoming and outgoing traffic. When you modify the default networking behavior in Windows 7—such as when you enable Network Discovery in the Advanced Sharing Settings control panel—the controls change the default settings for the Windows Firewall rules.

Table 10-3

Default Windows Firewall Rules Settings

SERVICE	PRIVATE	PUBLIC	DOMAIN
Core Networking	Enabled	Enabled	Enabled
File and Printer Sharing	Enabled	Disabled	Disabled
Homegroup	Disabled	N/A	N/A
Network Discovery	Enabled	Disabled	Disabled
Remote Desktop	Disabled	Disabled	Disabled

TAKE NOTE Whenever a network service fails to function as expected, checking the rules for that service in the Windows Firewall with Advanced Security console should be one your first troubleshooting steps.

Creating new rules with this interface provides a great deal more flexibility than the Windows Firewall control panel. When you right click the *Inbound Rules* or *Outbound Rules* node and select *New Rule* from the context menu, the New Rule Wizard, shown in Figure 10-24, takes you through the process of configuring the following sets of parameters:

- **Rule Type:** Specifies whether you want to create a program rule, a port rule, a variant on one of the predefined rules, or a custom rule. This selection determines which of the following pages the wizard displays.

- **Program:** Specifies whether the rule applies to all programs, to one specific program, or to a specific service.

TAKE NOTE The New Inbound Rule and New Outbound Rule Wizards are adaptive, meaning that you will not see all of the pages listed here each time you run the wizard. The option you select on the Rule Type page determines what additional pages appear next.

Figure 10-24

The New Inbound Rule Wizard

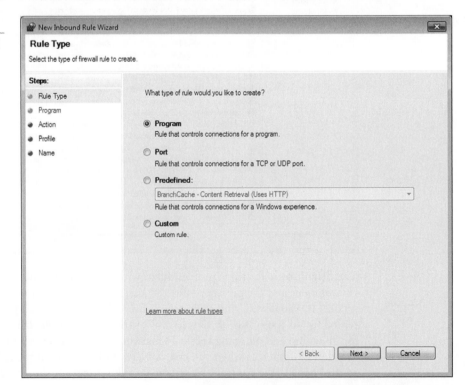

- **Protocol and Ports:** Specifies the protocol and the local and remote ports to which the rule applies. This enables you to specify the exact types of traffic that the rule should block or allow.

- **Scope:** Specifies the IP addresses of the local and remote systems to which the rule applies. This enables you to block or allow traffic between specific computers.

- **Action:** Specifies the action the firewall should take when a packet matches the rule. You configure the rule to allow traffic if it is blocked by default, or block traffic if it is allowed by default. You can also configure the rule to allow traffic only when the connection between the communicating computers is secured using IPsec. This is called an *authenticated exception*.

- **Profile:** Specifies the profile(s) to which the rule should apply: domain, private, and/or public.

- **Name:** Specifies a name and (optionally) a description for the rule.

The rules you can create using the New Rule Wizards range from simple program rules to highly complex and specific rules that block or allow only specific types of traffic between specific computers. The more complicated the rules become, however, the more you have to know about TCP/IP communications in general and the specific behavior of your applications. Modifying the default firewall settings to accommodate some special applications is relatively simple, but creating an entirely new firewall configuration is a formidable task.

Using Filters

Although what a firewall does is sometimes referred to as packet filtering, in the Windows Firewall with Advanced Security console, the term *filter* is used to refer to a feature that enables you to display rules according to the profile they apply to, their current state, or the group to which they belong.

For example, to display only the rules that apply to the public profile, click *Action > Filter By Profile > Filter By Public Profile*. The display changes to show only the rules that apply to the public profile. In the same way, you can apply a filter that causes the console to display only the rules that are currently turned on, or the rules that belong to a particular group. Click *Action > Clear All Filters* to return to the default display showing all of the rules.

Creating Connection Security Rules

Windows 7 includes a feature in Windows Firewall that incorporates IPsec data protection into the Windows Firewall. The IP Security (IPsec) standards are a collection of documents that define a method for securing data while it is in transit over a TCP/IP network. IPsec includes a connection establishment routine, during which computers authenticate each other before transmitting data, and a technique called *tunneling*, in which data packets are encapsulated within other packets for their protection.

+ MORE INFORMATION

Data protection technologies such as the Windows 7 Encrypting File System (EFS) and BitLocker protect data while it is stored on a drive. However, they do nothing to protect data while it is being transmitted over the network, because they both decrypt the data before sending it. IPsec, by contrast, protects data while it is in transit.

In addition to inbound and outbound rules, the Windows Firewall with Advanced Security console enables you to create connection security rules, using the New Connection Security Rule Wizard. Connection security rules define the type of protection you want to apply to the communications that conform to Windows Firewall rules.

When you right click the *Connection Security Rules* node and select *New Rule* from the context menu, the New Connection Security Rule Wizard, shown in Figure 10-25, takes you through the process of configuring the following sets of parameters:

- **Rule Type:** Specifies the basic function of the rule, such as to isolate computers based on authentication criteria, to exempt certain computers (such as infrastructure servers) from authentication, to authenticate two specific computers or groups of computers, or to tunnel communications between two computers. You can also create custom rules combining these functions.

- **Endpoints:** Specifies the IP addresses of the computer that will establish a secured connection before transmitting any data.

- **Requirements:** Specifies whether authentication between two computers should be requested or required in each direction.

- **Authentication Method:** Specifies the type of authentication the computers should use when establishing a connection.

- **Profile:** Specifies the profile(s) to which the rule should apply: domain, private, and/or public.

- **Name:** Specifies a name and (optionally) a description for the rule.

Figure 10-25

The New Connection Security Rule Wizard

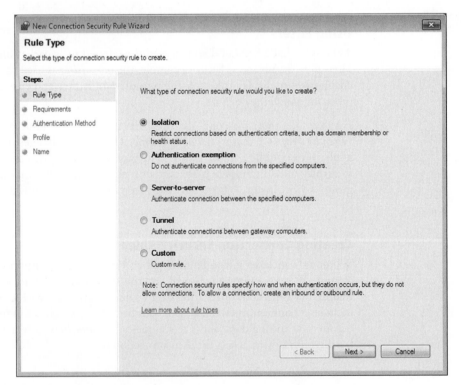

CONFIGURING WINDOWS FIREWALL WITH GROUP POLICY

As with many other Windows 7 features, configuring Windows Firewall on individual computers is not practical in an enterprise network environment. However, it is possible to configure firewall settings on Windows workstations using Group Policy.

When you browse to the Computer Configuration\Policies\Windows Settings\Security Settings\ Windows Firewall with Advanced Security node in a GPO, you see the interface shown in Figure 10-26, which is similar to that of the Windows Firewall with Advanced Security console.

Figure 10-26

The Windows Firewall with Advanced Security node in a GPO

Clicking *Windows Firewall Properties* opens a dialog box with the same controls as the Windows Firewall with Advanced Security on Local Computer Properties sheet and clicking *Inbound Rules and Outbound Rules* launches the same wizards as the console.

Introducing Windows Defender

> Windows Defender is a Windows 7 application that prevents the infiltration of spyware into the system.

Originally, the people who created and disseminated viruses and other types of malware did so purely out of gratuitous vandalism. Today, the primary motive is profit, and this has led to the development of new kinds of malware. *Spyware*, for example, is a type of software that gathers information about computer users and transmits it back to the attacker.

The type of information spyware can gather ranges from the trivial to the critical. Some programs simply collect information about users' web surfing habits, the better to target potential customers with their marketing efforts. Others collect personal and confidential information about the computer's users, including passwords and account numbers, which attackers can use for identity theft and other crimes. In addition to compromising the security of a computer, spyware can also affect its performance by consuming system resources.

Windows 7 includes an application called Windows Defender that helps to defend against spyware by scanning the places where it most commonly infiltrates a computer. Spyware is typically a program that is installed along with other software that the user deliberately downloads and installs. To be effective, spyware has to be running all the time, so the installer typically places the program in one of the standard Windows preloading mechanisms, such as the Startup folder and the Run key in the registry. Windows Defender has a set of predefined definitions that it searches for in these places, which help it to identify specific threats.

Windows Defender also includes real-time monitoring, which attempts to prevent spyware from infiltrating the computer as it is installed. When Defender detects a potentially dangerous installation, it alerts and prompts the user to ignore, quarantine, or remove the program, or add it to an Always Allow list that permits it to run on the computer.

Windows Defender runs by default on Windows 7 computers, and performs a scan every day at 2:00 a.m. Windows Update also supplies Defender with signature updates on a regular basis, to keep the program current. When you open the main Windows Defender window,

WARNING Windows Defender is not a full-featured antivirus program, as it cannot detect or remove true viruses, Trojans, and other types of malware. Windows 7 does not include a comprehensive antivirus solution, and Microsoft recommends that you purchase and install a third-party antivirus product. In fact, Windows Action Center monitors the computer for the presence of antivirus software and warns users when it fails to find it, even when Windows Defender is present and running.

as shown in Figure 10-27, by typing *Windows Defender* on the Start menu's search box, the program displays the results of the most recent scan, as well as information about the current configuration settings.

To perform an additional scan at any time, simply click the *Scan* link at the top of the window, and the program starts running.

Figure 10-27

The Windows Defender window

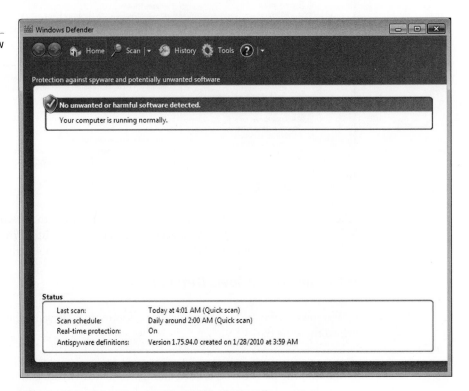

CONFIGURING WINDOWS DEFENDER

You can modify the configuration of Windows Defender by using the following procedure.

 CONFIGURE WINDOWS DEFENDER

GET READY. Log on to Windows 7 using an account with administrative capabilities.

1. Click Start, and then type Defender in the search box. A Windows Defender link appears in the search results.

TAKE NOTE*

Unlike Windows Vista, Windows Defender is difficult to find in Windows 7. There is no shortcut in the Start menu, and it only appears in the Control Panel when you select the *Large icons* or *Small icons* view.

2. Click Windows Defender. The Windows Defender window appears. This window shows the current status of Windows Defender and indicates whether the program has detected any unwanted or harmful software.

3. Click Tools. The *Tools and Settings* page appears, as shown in Figure 10-28.

Figure 10-28

The Windows Defender Tools and Settings page

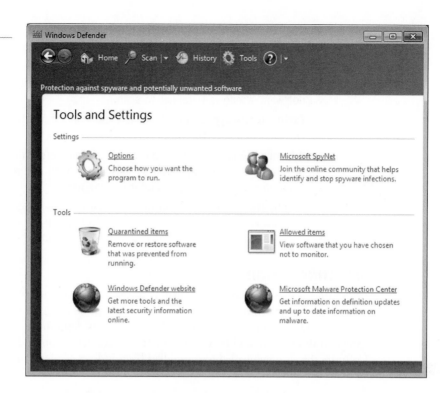

4. Click Options. The *Options* page appears, as shown in Figure 10-29.

Figure 10-29

The Windows Defender Options page

5. Modify the configuration settings for any of the following items and click Save.

• **Automatic scanning:** Specifies if, when, and how often Defender should scan the system. You can also configure the program to download updated definitions before scanning.

• **Default actions:** Specifies what action Defender should take when it detects items at each of the alert levels.

- **Real-time protection:** Specifies whether Defender should provide real-time protection and enables you to specify which types of real-time protection Defender should provide.
- **Excluded files and folders:** Specifies the names of files and folders that you do not want Windows Defender to scan.
- **Excluded file types:** Specifies the extensions of file types that you do not want Windows Defender to scan.
- **Advanced:** Enables you to configure Defender to scan within archives, create a restore point before applying actions, scan email and removable drives, and use heuristics to locate partial signature matches.
- **Administrator:** Enables you to configure Defender to alert all users if it detects spyware and to allow all users to initiate Defender scans.

6. Close the Windows Defender window.

UPDATING DEFINITIONS

Protecting Windows 7 computers against malware is a constant struggle between the attackers who create the malicious software and the people who design protective software. As a result, Windows Defender relies on continual updates to its definitions, which determine what the program should scan and how. Windows Defender definition updates are included in the software that is downloaded and installed by Windows Updates on a regular basis.

Using the Malicious Software Removal Tool

The Malicious Software Removal Tool is a one-time virus scanner program that Microsoft distributes with its monthly updates.

As stated earlier, Windows 7 does not include a full-featured antivirus program, and Microsoft strongly recommends that users obtain and install one. However, Microsoft does provide the Malicious Software Removal Tool, which can serve as a substitute or a backup to third-party antivirus products.

The Malicious Software Removal Tool is a single user virus scanner that Microsoft supplies in each of its monthly operating system updates. The tool scans the system for viruses and other forms of malware immediately after its installation, and removes any potentially damaging software that it finds. Because the tool is designed for a single use only, there are no controls, and it is not permanently installed in the operating system.

For systems with no other antivirus protection, the Malicious Software Removal Tool can function as a substitute until you obtain one. For systems that already have antivirus software, the tool functions as an effective backup. There are types of malware that are capable of disabling well-known virus scanners, and the Malicious Software Removal Tool can provide an effective scan in the event that the main software is not functioning.

■ Protecting Sensitive Data

THE BOTTOM LINE   Windows 7 includes tools like Encrypting File System (EFS) and BitLocker, which make it possible to prevent data theft using cryptography.

Malware is not the only threat to the security of a Windows 7 computer. The primary reason for having security tools such as Windows Firewall and Windows Defender is to protect the data on a computer. However, tools like these can do nothing to prevent simple, old-fashioned

TAKE NOTE*

BitLocker drive encryption is a particularly useful protection mechanism for portable computers, and is therefore covered in Lesson 12, "Using Mobile Computers."

attacks, such as when someone sits down at a computer while the user is at lunch and copies that person's data, or if someone simply steals the entire computer.

Windows 7 includes other tools that you can use to protect your clients' data from more direct attacks, such as those discussed in the following sections.

Using the Encrypting File System

> The Encrypting File System (EFS) protects users' data by encrypting and decrypting it on the fly as the user works.

CERTIFICATION READY?
Configure file and folder access.
5.2

The Encrypting File System (EFS) is a feature of NTFS that encodes the files on a computer so that even if an intruder can obtain a file, he or she will be unable to read it. The entire system is keyed to a specific user account, using the public and private keys that are the basis of the Windows public key infrastructure (PKI). The user who creates a file is the only person who can read it.

As the user works, EFS encrypts the files he or she creates using a key generated from the user's *public key*. Data encrypted with this key can be decrypted only by the user's personal encryption certificate, which is generated using his or her *private key*.

TAKE NOTE*
> Only the Professional, Enterprise, and Ultimate editions of Windows 7 support EFS. The Home Basic and Home Premium editions do not support EFS.

When the user logs on to the computer, the system gains access to the keys that are necessary to encrypt and decrypt the EFS-protected data. To the user, the encryption process is completely invisible, and usually does not have a major impact on system performance. The user creates, accesses, and saves files in the normal manner, unaware that the cryptographic processes are taking place.

If another user logs on to the computer, he or she has no access to the other user's private key, and therefore cannot decrypt the encrypted files. An attacker can conceivably sit down at the computer and try to copy the files off to a flash drive, but he or she will receive an "Access Denied" error message, just as if he or she lacked the appropriate NTFS permissions for the files.

There are two main restrictions when implementing EFS:

- EFS is a feature of the NTFS file system, so you cannot use EFS on FAT drives.
- You cannot use EFS to encrypt files that have already been compressed using NTFS compression.

ENCRYPTING A FOLDER WITH EFS

In Windows 7, you can use Windows Explorer to encrypt or disable EFS on any individual files or folders, as long as they are on an NTFS drive. To encrypt a file or folder, use the following procedure.

 ENCRYPT A FOLDER

GET READY. Log on to Windows 7.

1. Click Start, and then click All Programs > Accessories > Windows Explorer. The Windows Explorer window appears.
2. Right click a file or folder and then, from the context menu, select Properties. The Properties sheet for the file or folder appears, as shown in Figure 10-30.

Figure 10-30

A folder's Properties sheet

3. On the General tab, click Advanced. The Advanced Attributes dialog box appears, as shown in Figure 10-31.

Figure 10-31

The Advanced Attributes dialog box

4. Select the Encrypt contents to secure data check box, and then click OK.

5. Click OK to close the Properties sheet. If you selected a folder that contains files or subfolders, a Confirm Attribute Changes dialog box appears, as shown in Figure 10-32, asking you to choose whether to apply changes to the folder only, or to the folder and all of its subfolders and files.

Figure 10-32

A Confirm Attribute Changes dialog box

TAKE NOTE*

If you elect to apply changes to the selected folder only, EFS does not encrypt any of the files that are currently in the folder. However, any files that you create, copy, or move to the folder after you enable EFS will be encrypted.

6. Select a confirmation option and click OK. Depending on how many files and folders there are to be encrypted, the process could take several minutes.

DETERMINING WHETHER A FILE OR FOLDER IS ENCRYPTED

Technical specialists commonly receive calls from users who are unable to access their files because they have been encrypted using EFS and the user is unaware of this fact. To resolve the problem, you must first determine whether the files are encrypted or not, and whether the user has the proper NTFS permissions.

Windows Explorer displays the names of encrypted files in green, by default, but this setting is easily changed in the Folder Options dialog box. To verify that a folder or file is encrypted, use the following procedure.

 VIEW THE ENCRYPTION ATTRIBUTE

GET READY. Log on to Windows 7.

1. Click Start, and then click All Programs > Accessories > Windows Explorer. The Windows Explorer window appears.
2. Right click a file or folder and then, from the context menu, select Properties. The Properties sheet for the file or folder appears.
3. On the General tab, click Advanced. The Advanced Attributes dialog box appears. If the *Encrypt contents to secure data* check box is selected, the file or folder is encrypted.
4. Click OK to close the Advanced Attributes dialog box.
5. Click OK to close the Properties sheet.

Configuring Parental Controls

Parental control enables parents to limit their children's access to specific Internet sites, games, and applications.

Just as parents often want to control what their children watch on television, they also may want to control their child's computing habits. Windows 7, in its Home Premium edition and above, includes parental controls that you can use to exercise the following restrictions:

- Enforce time limits for computer use.
- Restrict access to games by rating, content, or title.
- Allow or block specific applications.

SETTING UP USERS

Parental controls are based on user accounts, so parents must create accounts for all family members and enforce their use.

Windows 7 Parental Controls are keyed to user accounts, so the first thing parents have to do is create separate accounts for their children and make sure the family becomes accustomed to logging on and off of their accounts whenever they use the computer. In many cases, this is the most difficult part of the process. Many families are accustomed to using a single account, often one with administrative privileges, and leaving it logged on at all times. This obviously poses dangers both to the operating system and to the parents' ideas of what children should and should not be permitted to see.

In addition to creating user accounts for everyone in the family, parents must make sure that all of the accounts on the computer have passwords and that the passwords remain secure. If an account with administrative privileges does not have a password, then a child can simply log on using that account and modify or turn off the parental controls.

X REF

For more information on creating user accounts, see Lesson 9, "Working with Workgroups and Domains."

SETTING UP PARENTAL CONTROLS

After creating user accounts, you can then impose restrictions on those accounts.

Once you have created user accounts for the children whose access you want to restrict, use the following procedure to configure Parental Controls.

 SET UP PARENTAL CONTROLS

GET READY. Log on to Windows 7 using an account with administrative capabilities.

1. Click Start, and then click Control Panel. The Control Panel window appears.
2. Click User Accounts and Family Safety > Parental Controls. The *Choose a user and set up Parental Controls* page appears, as shown in Figure 10-33.

Figure 10-33

The Choose a user and set up Parental Controls page

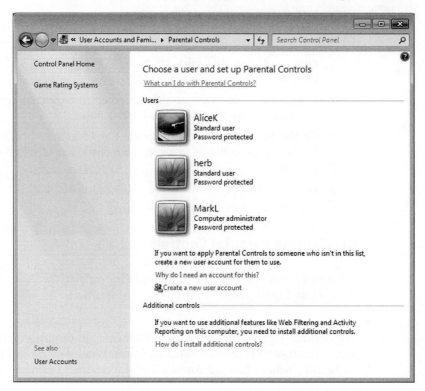

3. Select the account for which you want to configure parental controls. The *User Controls* page appears, as shown in Figure 10-34.

Figure 10-34

The User Controls page

4. Click the On, enforce current settings radio button to enforce the current setting. By default, the Parental Control engine compiles activity reports about the accounts under its protection, but you can turn them off by clicking the Off radio button under Activity Reporting.

5. To impose computer time limits, under Windows Settings, click Time limits. The *Time Restrictions* page appears, as shown in Figure 10-35. Specify in the grid what hours of the day the user is permitted access to the computer.

Figure 10-35

The Time Restrictions page

6. To control access to games, under Windows Settings, click Games. The *Game Controls* page appears, as shown in Figure 10-36, where you can do the following:

- Specify whether the user can play games
- Allow and block games according to ratings
- Create a list of games to be allowed or blocked

Figure 10-36

The Game Controls page

7. To control access to applications, under Windows Settings, click Allow and block specific programs. The *Application Restrictions* page appears, as shown in Figure 10-37, on which you can create a list of the only applications the user is permitted to run.

Figure 10-37

The Application Restrictions page

8. Click OK after configuring each page, and then click OK again to close the User Controls page.

9. Repeat the entire procedure for any other user accounts you want to control.

SKILL SUMMARY

IN THIS LESSON YOU LEARNED:

- Windows 7 supports a number of Group Policy settings that administrators can use to enforce password security practices on individual computers or on Active Directory Domain Services (AD DS) networks.

- Credential Manager is a Windows 7 tool that stores the usernames and passwords people supply to servers and Web sites in a protected area called the Windows Vault.

- The most commonly used mechanisms for authorizing users in Windows 7 are the NTFS, share, and registry permission systems. You can also assign user rights to provide access to operating system activities.

- Malware is malicious software created specifically for the purpose of infiltrating or damaging a computer system without the user's knowledge or consent. This type of software includes a variety of technologies, including viruses, Trojan horses, worms, spyware, and adware.

- Action Center is a centralized console that enables users and administrators to access, monitor, and configure the various Windows 7 security mechanisms.

- Windows Firewall is a software program that protects a computer by allowing certain types of network traffic in and out of the system while blocking others.

- You configure Windows Firewall by creating rules that specify what types of traffic to block and/or allow.

- Windows Defender helps to defend against spyware by scanning the places where it most commonly infiltrates a computer.

- The Malicious Software Removal Tool is a single user virus scanner that Microsoft supplies in each of its monthly operating system updates.

- The Encrypting File System (EFS) is a feature of NTFS that encodes the files on a computer so that even if an intruder can obtain a file, he or she will be unable to read it.

- Windows 7, in its Home Premium and higher editions, includes parental controls that you can use to exercise restrictions over other users' computing habits.

Knowledge Assessment

Matching

Complete the following exercise by matching the terms with their corresponding definitions.

    a. automated password guessing
    b. Windows authorization mechanism
    c. passwords plus smartcards
    d. stored in a digital certificate
    e. standard for smart card support
    f. decrypts data encrypted with a certificate
    g. firewall exceptions
    h. standard for fingerprint scanners and other devices
    i. potentially destructive software
    j. firewall rule requiring IPsec

_____ **1.** multifactor authentication

_____ **2.** malware

_____ **3.** brute force

_____ **4.** Personal Identity Verification (PIV)

_____ **5.** private key

_____ **6.** Windows Biometric Framework

_____ **7.** user rights

_____ **8.** authenticated exception

_____ **9.** public key

_____ **10.** rules

Multiple Choice

Select one or more correct answers for each of the following questions.

1. Which of the following account lockout policy modifications could you make to ensure that user passwords cannot be intercepted by analyzing captured packets?
   a. Increase the Enforce Password History value
   b. Enable the Password Must Meet Complexity Requirements setting
   c. Decrease the Account Lockout Threshold value
   d. Disable the Store Passwords Using Reversible Encryption policy

2. Which of the following mechanisms is most often used in firewall rules to allow traffic on to the network?
   a. hardware addresses
   b. IP addresses
   c. protocol numbers
   d. port numbers

3. Which of the following NTFS features is incompatible with EFS encryption?
   a. compression
   b. IPsec
   c. permissions
   d. parental controls

4. Which of the following command-line parameters will prevent a program executed using Runas.exe from accessing the elevated user's encrypted files?
   a. /env
   b. /noprofile
   c. /showcred
   d. /profile

5. Which of the following actions can you NOT perform from the Windows Firewall control panel? (Choose all that apply.)
   a. Allow a program through the firewall in all three profiles
   b. Manage firewall exceptions for the domain profile
   c. Create firewall exceptions based on port numbers
   d. Turn Windows firewall off for all three profiles

6. Which of the following policy modifications would make it harder for intruders to penetrate user passwords by a brute force attack? (Choose all that apply.)
   a. Increase the value of the Reset Account Logon Counter After policy
   b. Enable the Password Must Meet Complexity Requirements policy
   c. Increase the Account Lockout Threshold value
   d. Reduce the value of the Minimum Password Age policy

7. Connection security rules require that network traffic allowed through the firewall use which of the following security mechanisms?
   a. EFS
   b. IPsec
   c. UAC
   d. PIV

8. Which of the following statements about Windows Defender is true?
   a. Windows Defender uses rules that you create to control its scans.
   b. Windows Defender can detect spyware that is already present on the system, but it cannot prevent the infiltration of new spyware.
   c. Windows Defender eliminates the need for third-party anti-virus software.
   d. Windows Defender requires definition updates that are supplied free with the regularly scheduled Windows Update downloads.

9. Which of the parental controls has been removed from Windows 7?
   a. Application restrictions
   b. User time limits
   c. Restricted access to games
   d. Internet filtering

10. The built-in local groups on a Windows 7 workstation receive their special capabilities through which of the following mechanisms?
    a. parental controls
    b. Windows firewall rules
    c. NTFS permissions
    d. user rights

Review Questions

1. List the basic tasks that a parent must perform to successfully implement Parental Controls on a computer running Windows 7, so that the children all have an equal amount of computer time and are prevented from playing inappropriate games.

2. For each of the following Password Policy and Account Lockout Policy settings, specify whether increasing the policy value increases or decreases the security provided by that setting:
   - Account Lockout Threshold
   - Enforce Password History

- Reset Account Lockout Counter After
- Maximum Password Age
- Account Lockout Duration
- Minimum Password Length

■ Case Scenarios

Scenario 10-1: Using Password and Account Lockout Policies

You are working on a corporate network owned by a company with several government contracts to develop classified technology. You have been assigned the task to create a set of password and account policy settings that meet the following criteria:

- Users must change passwords every four weeks and cannot reuse the same passwords for one year.
- User passwords must be at least 12 characters long, case sensitive, and consist of letters, numbers, and symbols.
- Users are allowed no more than three unsuccessful logon attempts before the account is permanently locked down until released by an administrator.

In the following table, enter the values for the policies that will meet these requirements.

POLICY SETTING	VALUE
Enforce Password History	
Maximum Password Age	
Minimum Password Age	
Minimum Password Length	
Password Must Meet Complexity Requirements	
Store Passwords Using Reversible Encryption	
Account Lockout Threshold	
Account Lockout Duration	
Reset Account Lockout Counter After	

Scenario 10-2: Configuring Windows Firewall

You are a desktop technician in the IT department of a small corporation. Today is the day of the company picnic and, as the junior member of the department, you have been left in charge of the entire corporate network while everyone else is out of the office. Shortly after 2:00 p.m., an email arrives from the company's biggest customer, complaining that they can't access the web server they use to place their orders. After checking the web server logs, it seems clear that the server is undergoing a denial-of-service attack because there are suddenly hundreds of Internet computers repeatedly trying to access it. What temporary modifications could you make to Windows Firewall on the Windows 7 computer that stands between the web server and the Internet that would allow customers to access the web server while blocking the attackers?

11 LESSON

Administering Windows 7

OBJECTIVE DOMAIN MATRIX

Technology Skill	Objective Domain	Objective Number
Using Remote Access Technologies	Configure remote management.	4.5
Using BranchCache	Configure BranchCache.	5.5
Using Backup and Restore	Configure backup.	8.1
Performing a System	Configure system recovery options.	8.2
Restoring Files	Configure file recovery options.	8.3

KEY TERMS

Boot Configuration Data (BCD)

BranchCache

distributed cache mode

hosted cache mode

incremental backup

Power-on self-test (POST)

Remote Assistance

Remote Desktop

Remote Desktop Protocol (RDP)

system image backup

system restore point

volume shadow copies

Windows Recovery
  Environment (Windows RE)

Windows Remote Management

■ Understanding Troubleshooting Practices

THE BOTTOM LINE

Troubleshooting is a primary function of the Windows 7 technical specialist. Users call for help because something doesn't work or they've done something wrong, and it is up to you to determine what the problem is and how to fix it.

Many technical specialists have troubleshooting skills that are largely intuitive, and this is fine. However, when troubleshooting a problem in a professional environment, whether it's a corporate enterprise network, a help desk in a retail store, or a freelance consultancy, it is important to have a set troubleshooting procedure. This will enable you to explain to the client what you've done, share your findings with your colleagues, and account for your time and effort.

Many troubleshooting calls stem from user error, that is, people who are using the software or hardware improperly. These can often be cleared up immediately with some remedial user training. When you are faced with what appears to be a serious problem, however, you should follow a set troubleshooting procedure that consists of steps similar to the following:

1. Establish the symptoms.
2. Identify the affected area.
3. Establish what has changed.
4. Select the most probable cause.
5. Implement a solution.
6. Test the result.
7. Document the solution.

Various desktop technicians might use slightly different steps or perform them in a slightly different order, but the overall process should be similar. The following sections examine each of these steps.

Establishing the Symptoms

> Have the user explain the problem and assign it a priority.

The first step in troubleshooting any problem is to determine exactly what is going wrong. Depending on the situation, you might also have to note the effects of the problem so that you can assign it a priority. In a business environment, the support staff often receives more calls for help than they can handle at one time. In these cases, it is essential to establish a system of priorities that dictates which calls are addressed first. Just as in the emergency department of a hospital, priorities should not necessarily be based on who is first in line. The severity of the problem and its potential for wide-reaching effects should determine who receives attention first. However, it is also not wise to ignore the political reality that senior management problems are often addressed before those of the rank and file.

Some of the guidelines you might use to establish service priorities are as follows:

- **Shared resources take precedence over individual resources:** A problem with a computer that prevents other users from performing their jobs should take precedence over one that affects only a single user.
- **Network-wide problems take precedence over workgroup or departmental problems:** A problem with a computer that provides services to the entire network, such as a file or print server, should take precedence over a problem with a departmental resource.
- **Departmental issues should be rated according to the function of the department:** A problem with a computer belonging to a department that is critical to the organization, such as order entry or a customer service call center, should take precedence over a problem with a computer belonging to a department that can better tolerate a period of downtime, such as research and development.
- **System-wide problems take precedence over application problems:** A problem that puts an entire computer out of commission and prevents a user from getting any work done should take precedence over a problem a user is experiencing with a single device or application.

It sometimes can be difficult to determine the exact nature of a problem from a description supplied by a relatively inexperienced user. Part of the process of narrowing down the cause of a problem involves obtaining accurate information about what has occurred. Users are often vague about what they were doing when they experienced the problem, or even what the indications of the problem were. For example, in many cases, users call for help because they received an error message, but they neglect to write down the exact wording of the message. Training users in the proper procedures for documenting and reporting problems is often part of the desktop technician's job. It might not be any help now, but it can be beneficial the next time a user receives an error.

Begin by asking the user questions like these:

- What exactly were you doing when the problem occurred?
- What were you doing just before the problem occurred?
- Were you ever able to complete the task you were performing successfully? If so, what has changed?
- Have you had any other problems with your computer lately?
- Was the computer behaving normally just before the problem occurred?
- Has any hardware or software been installed, removed, or reconfigured recently?
- Did you or anyone else do anything to try to resolve the problem?

Identifying the Affected Area

Isolate the hardware or software component that is the source of the problem.

The next step in troubleshooting a network problem is to see whether it can be duplicated. Computer problems that can be reproduced are far easier to fix, primarily because you can easily test to see whether a solution was successful. However, many problems are intermittent or might occur for only a short period of time. In these cases, you might have to leave the incident open until the problem occurs again. In some instances, having the user reproduce the problem can lead to a solution. User error is a common cause of problems that might at first seem to be hardware related.

If you can duplicate a problem, you can set about finding the source of the difficulty. For example, if a user has trouble opening a file in a word processing application, the difficulty might lie in the file itself, in the application, or in the disk drive where the file is stored. The process of isolating the location of the problem consists of logically and methodically eliminating elements that are not the cause.

If you can duplicate the problem, you can begin to isolate the cause by reproducing the conditions under which the problem occurred. To do this, use a procedure like the following:

1. Have the user reproduce the problem on the computer repeatedly, to determine whether the user's actions are causing the error.
2. If possible, sit at the computer yourself and perform the same task. If the problem does not occur, the cause might lie in how the user is performing a particular task. Watch the user carefully to see if he or she is doing something wrong. It is possible that you and the user are performing the same task in different ways and that the user's method is exposing a problem that yours does not.
3. If the problem recurs when you perform the task, log off from the user's account, log on using a different account, and repeat the task. If the problem does not recur, the user is probably lacking the rights or permissions needed to perform the task.
4. If the problem recurs, and the computer is connected to a network, try to perform the same task on a similarly equipped computer connected to the same network. If you cannot reproduce the problem on another computer, you know that the cause lies in the user's computer. If the problem occurs on another computer, then there is likely to be a network problem that is affecting both computers.

Establishing What Has Changed

> Ask the user if the computer has recently been upgraded or reconfigured.

When a computer that used to work properly now does not, it stands to reason that some change has occurred. When a user reports a problem, it is important to determine how the computing environment changed immediately before the malfunction. Unfortunately, getting this information from the user can often be difficult. The response to the question "Has anything changed on the computer recently?" is nearly always "No." Only later will the user remember to mention that a major hardware or software upgrade was performed just before the problem occurred. In an organization with properly established maintenance and documentation procedures, you should be able to determine whether the user's computer has been upgraded or modified recently. IT or departmental records are the first place to look for information like this.

Major changes, such as the installation of new hardware or software, are obvious possible sources of the problem, but you must be aware of causes produced by more subtle changes as well. Tracking down the source of a networking problem can often be a form of detective work, and learning to "interrogate" your "suspects" properly can be an important part of the troubleshooting process.

Selecting the Most Probable Cause

> Look for the simplest possible causes of the problem first.

Once you have narrowed down the possible sources of the problem, you can begin to compile a list of possible causes. Almost any computer problem can have many possible causes, and it is up to you to determine which is the most likely culprit.

There's an old medical school axiom that says when you hear hoofbeats, think horses, not zebras. In the context of computer troubleshooting, this means that when you look for the possible causes of a problem, start with the obvious first. For example, if a computer fails to print a document, do not start by checking the drivers and the printer configuration; check the simple things first, such as whether the printer is plugged in and connected to the computer. You also must work methodically and document everything so that you do not duplicate your efforts.

Implementing a Solution

> Try different solutions until the problem is solved.

After you isolate the problem, try to determine whether hardware or software is the culprit. If it is a hardware problem, you might replace the unit that is at fault or use an alternative that you know is functioning properly. Printing problems, for example, might force you to repair or replace the printer itself. If the problem is inside the computer, you might need to start replacing components, such as hard drives, until the defective component is found. If you determine that the problem is caused by software, try reinstalling the application.

In some cases, the process of isolating the source of a problem includes resolving the problem. For example, if you determine that a printer cable is bad by replacing it with a new one, then the replacement resolves the problem. In other cases, however, the resolution might be more involved, such as one that requires reinstalling an application or even the operating system. Because the user may need to use the computer to complete important tasks, you might have to wait to resolve the problem until a later time, when the computer is not in use and after you have had a chance to back up its data. Sometimes you can use an interim solution, such as a substitute computer, until you can definitively resolve the problem.

Testing the Results

Try to recreate the problem to make sure that the solution is effective.

After implementing a resolution to the problem, you should return to the beginning of the process and repeat the task that originally caused the problem. If the problem no longer occurs, you should test any other functions related to the changes you made to ensure that solving one problem has not created another. At this point, the time you have spent documenting the troubleshooting process becomes worthwhile. Repeat the procedures used to duplicate the problem exactly to ensure that the trouble the user originally experienced has been completely eliminated, and not just temporarily masked. If the problem was intermittent to begin with, it might take some time to ascertain whether the solution has been effective. It might be necessary to check with the user several times to make sure that the problem is not recurring.

Documenting the Solution

Keep a complete record of the entire troubleshooting process.

Although it is presented here as a separate step, the process of documenting all of the actions you perform should begin as soon as the user calls for help. A well-organized technical support organization should have a system in place in which each problem call is registered as a trouble ticket that eventually contains a complete record of the problem and the steps taken to isolate and resolve it. In many cases, a technical support organization operates using tiers, which are groups of technicians with different skill levels. Calls come in to the first tier, and if the problem is sufficiently complex or the first-tier technician cannot resolve it, the call is escalated to the second tier, which is composed of senior technicians. As long as all who are involved in the process document their activities, there should be no problem when one technician hands off the trouble ticket to another. In addition, keeping careful notes prevents people from duplicating one another's efforts.

The final phase of the troubleshooting process is to explain to the user what happened and why. Of course, the average computer user is probably not interested in hearing all the technical details, but it is a good idea to let users know whether their actions caused the problem, exacerbated it, or made it more difficult to resolve. Educating users can lead to a quicker resolution next time or can even prevent a problem from occurring altogether.

■ Using Troubleshooting Tools

THE BOTTOM LINE Repairing anything requires the right tools and the ability to use them properly.

Windows 7 includes a variety of tools that can aid in the troubleshooting process, some of which were discussed earlier in this book. Table 11-1 lists these tools, along with the lesson that covered the tool.

Table 11-1

Windows 7 Troubleshooting Tools

TOOL	FUNCTION	LOCATION
Upgrade Advisor	Determines whether a computer can run Windows 7 and identifies components that could be upgraded to provide better performance.	Lesson 1
Windows PE	Provides a pre-installation environment from which you can use command-line tools to work with drivers, disks, and network resources.	Lesson 2
Windows Easy Transfer	Enables you to back up and restore user profile information. In the event of a catastrophic malfunction that requires a reinstallation of the operating system, you can use this tool to preserve the user's personalized working environment.	Lesson 2
Performance Information and Tools	Assigns a numerical score to each of the computer's main components, enabling you to identify bottlenecks that affect system performance.	Lesson 8
Disk Management snap-in	Displays information about the storage devices installed in the computer and provides tools for managing partitions and volumes.	Lesson 4
Properties sheets	Shares, disk drives, and most other components in a Windows computer have a Properties sheet that contains a Security tab, which is where you work with the permissions that control access to the component.	Lessons 4, 6
Windows Backup	Performs backups of selected document files. Before performing any major procedure on a client's computer, you should perform a backup of important files.	Lesson 11
User Accounts control panel	Enables you to create and manage local user accounts.	Lesson 9
Local Users and Groups snap-in	Provides comprehensive control over local users and groups.	Lesson 9
Local Security Policies console	Provides access to granular controls that enable you to set system security policies and regulate access to specific system functions.	Lessons 7, 8, 9
Group Policy Object Editor	Provides access to controls that enable you to configure an extensive collection of local and Active Directory Domain Services policies for specific Windows features and components.	Lessons 7, 8, 9
Device Manager	Enables you to view information about and manage the drivers for all of the hardware devices installed in the computer.	Lesson 4
Network and Sharing Center	Provides a central point of access for most Windows 7 networking components and tools.	Lesson 5
Network Map	Provides a graphical depiction of the network topology.	Lesson 5
Network Diagnostics	Displays networking error messages, and specifies in plain language what might be wrong and how to repair the problem.	Lesson 5
Ipconfig.exe	Displays configuration data for all of the network interfaces in the computer.	Lesson 5
Ping.exe	Tests network connections to other TCP/IP systems.	Lesson 5
Tracert.exe	Displays the names of the routers on the path taken by packets to a specific destination.	Lesson 5
Nslookup.exe	Enables you to send customized DNS requests to a specific DNS server.	Lesson 5

(continued)

Table 11-1 (*continued*)

TOOL	FUNCTION	LOCATION
Windows Action Center	Provides a central point of access for most Windows 7 security and maintenance components and tools.	Lesson 10
Windows Firewall	Enables you to control what types of network traffic are permitted to enter and leave a computer.	Lesson 10
Windows Update	Enables you to configure a computer to automatically download and install operating system updates.	Lesson 8
Windows Defender	Prevents the infiltration of spyware into a Windows 7 system.	Lesson 10
Malicious Software Removal Tool	A single use virus scanner that Microsoft updates monthly.	Lesson 10
Parental Controls	Enables you to limit the system access granted to specific users.	Lesson 10
Event Viewer	Displays log information about operating system components.	Lesson 8
Performance Monitor	Displays continuous real-time information about the performance of specific system hardware and software components.	Lesson 8

Using Remote Access Technologies

Remote access technologies enable a user on one computer to effectively take control of another computer on the network. For desktop technicians, this capability can save many hours of travel time.

A main objective for desktop technicians working on large corporate networks is to minimize the amount of travel from site to site to work on individual computers. Some of the troubleshooting tools included with Windows 7 are capable of managing services on remote computers as well as on the local system. For example, most MMC snap-ins have this capability, enabling technicians to work on systems throughout the enterprise without traveling. However, most snap-ins are specialized tools used only for certain administration tasks. For comprehensive access to a remote computer, Windows 7 includes two tools that are extremely useful to the desktop technician: Remote Assistance and Remote Desktop.

CERTIFICATION READY?
Configure remote management.
4.5

USING MICROSOFT MANAGEMENT CONSOLE

The shortcuts to various Microsoft Management Console (MMC) tools that appear in the Start menu and the Control Panel of a computer running Windows 7 are all configured to manage resources on the local system. However, many of the snap-ins supplied with Windows 7 enable you to manage other Windows computers on the network as well. There are two ways to access a remote computer using an MMC snap-in, as follows:

- Redirect an existing snap-in to another system.
- Create a custom console with snap-ins directed to other systems.

To connect to and manage another system using an MMC snap-in, you must launch the console with an account that has administrative credentials on the remote computer. The exact permissions required depend on the functions performed by the snap-in. If your credentials do not provide the proper permissions on the target computer, you will be able to load the snap-in, but you will not be able to read information from or modify settings on the target computer.

Redirecting a Snap-in

A snap-in that is directed at a specific system typically has a Connect To Another Computer command in its Action menu. Selecting this command opens a Select Computer dialog box, as shown in Figure 11-1, in which you can specify or browse to another computer on the network. Once you select the name of the computer you want to manage and click OK, the snap-in element in the scope pane changes to reflect the name of the computer you selected.

Figure 11-1

The Select Computer dialog box in an MMC console

Not every snap-in has the ability to connect to a remote computer, because some do not need it. For example, the Active Directory Domain Services consoles automatically locate a domain controller for the current domain and access the directory service from there. There is no need to specify a computer name. However, you will find Change Domain and Change Domain Controller commands in the Action menu in these consoles, which enable you to manage a different domain or select a specific domain controller in the present domain.

Creating a Remote Console

Connecting to a remote computer by redirecting an existing console is convenient for impromptu management tasks, but it is limited by the fact that you can access only one computer at a time. You also have to open the console and redirect it every time you want to access the remote system. A more permanent solution is to create a custom console with snap-ins that are already directed at other computers.

When you add a snap-in to a custom console, you select the computer you want to manage with that snap-in. You can also add multiple copies of the same snap-in to a custom console, with each one pointed at a different computer. This adds a whole new dimension to MMC's functionality. Not only can you create custom consoles containing a variety of tools, you can also create consoles containing tools for a variety of computers. For example, you can create a single console containing multiple instances of the Event Viewer snap-in, with each one pointing to a different computer. This enables you to monitor the event logs for computers all over the network from a single console.

USING REMOTE ASSISTANCE

Remote Assistance is a Windows 7 feature that enables an administrator, trainer, or technical specialist at one location to connect to a distant user's computer, chat with the user, and either view all of the user's activities or take complete control of the system. Remote Assistance eliminates the need for administrative personnel to travel to a user's location for any of the following reasons:

- **Technical support:** A desktop technician can use Remote Assistance to connect to a remote computer to modify configuration parameters, install new software, or troubleshoot user problems.

- **Troubleshooting:** By connecting in read-only mode, an expert can observe a remote user's activities and determine whether improper procedures are the source of problems the user is experiencing. The expert can also connect in interactive mode to try to recreate the problem or to modify system settings to resolve it. This is far more efficient than trying to give instructions to inexperienced users over the telephone.

- **Training:** Trainers and help desk personnel can demonstrate procedures to users right on their systems, without having to travel to their locations.

> **TAKE NOTE**＊ In Microsoft interfaces and documentation, the person connecting to a client using Remote Assistance is referred to as an expert or a helper.

To receive remote assistance, the computer running Windows 7 must be configured to use the Remote Assistance feature in one of the following ways:

- **Using Control Panel:** Open the System and Security control panel and click *Allow Remote Access*. In the System Properties sheet, select the *Allow Remote Assistance connections to this computer* check box, as shown in Figure 11-2. By clicking the *Advanced* button, the user can specify whether the expert can take control of the computer or simply view activities on the computer. The user can also specify the amount of time that the invitation for remote assistance remains valid.

Figure 11-2

The Remote tab of the System Properties sheet

- **Using Group Policy:** Use the Group Policy Object Editor console to access the computer's Local Computer Policy settings. Browse to the Computer Configuration > Administrative Templates > System > Remote Assistance container and enable the Solicited Remote Assistance policy, as shown in Figure 11-3. The Solicited Remote Assistance policy also enables you to specify the degree of control the expert receives over the client computer, the duration of the invitation, and the method for sending email invitations. The Offer Remote Assistance policy enables you to specify the names of users or groups that can function as experts, and whether those experts can perform tasks or just observe. You can also configure these same settings in Group Policy object (GPO) linked to an Active Directory Domain Services (AD DS) domain, site, or organizational unit object.

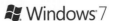
Figure 11-3

The Solicited Remote Assistance policy in the Group Policy Object Editor console

Creating an Invitation

To request a Remote Assistance session, a client must issue an invitation and send it to a particular expert. The client can send the invitation using email, or save it as a file to be sent to the expert in some other manner. To create an invitation, use the following procedure.

 CREATE AN INVITATION

GET READY. Log on to Windows 7.

1. Click Start, and then click All Programs > Maintenance > Windows Remote Assistance. The Windows Remote Assistance Wizard appears, displaying the *Do you want to ask for or offer help?* page, as shown in Figure 11-4.

Figure 11-4

The Do you want to ask for or offer help? page in the Windows Remote Assistance wizard

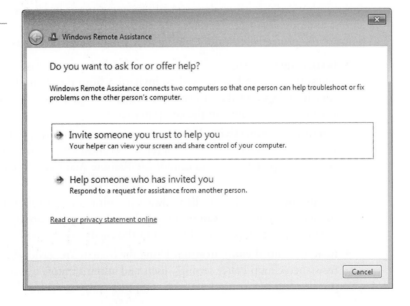

2. Click Invite someone you trust to help you. The *How do you want to invite your trusted helper?* page appears, as shown in Figure 11-5.

Figure 11-5

The How do you want to invite someone to help you? page in the Windows Remote Assistance wizard

3. Select *Save the invitation as a file*. A Save As combo box appears.
4. Specify a name for the invitation file and the location of the folder in which the wizard should create the invitation and click Save.
5. The Windows Remote Assistance window appears, displaying the password you must supply to the helper or expert.

TAKE NOTE*

You can also opt to send an invitation to the helper via email or by using Easy Connect.

Once the expert receives the invitation, invoking it launches the Remote Assistance application, which enables the expert to connect to the remote computer. Using this interface, the user and the expert can talk or type messages to each other and, by default, the expert can see everything that the user is doing on the computer. If the client computer is configured to allow remote control, the expert can also click the Take Control button and operate the client computer interactively.

Securing Remote Assistance

Because an expert offering remote assistance to another user can perform virtually any activity on the remote computer that the local user can, this feature can be a significant security hazard. An unauthorized user who takes control of a computer using Remote Assistance can cause almost unlimited damage. However, Remote Assistance is designed to minimize the dangers. Some of the protective features of Remote Assistance are as follows:

- **Invitations:** No person can connect to another computer using Remote Assistance unless that person has received an invitation from the client. Clients can configure the effective lifespan of their invitations in minutes, hours, or days to prevent experts from attempting to connect to the computer later.

- **Interactive connectivity:** When an expert accepts an invitation from a client and attempts to connect to the computer, a user must be present at the client console to grant the expert access. You cannot use Remote Assistance to connect to an unattended computer.

- **Client-side control:** The client always has ultimate control over a Remote Assistance connection. The client can terminate the connection at any time, by pressing the Esc key or clicking Stop Control (ESC) in the client-side Remote Assistance page.

- **Remote control configuration:** Using the System Properties sheet or the Remote Assistance Group Policy settings, users and administrators can specify whether experts are permitted to take control of client computers. An expert who has read-only access cannot modify the computer's configuration in any way using Remote Assistance. The group policies also enable administrators to expert status to grant specific, so that no one else can use Remote Assistance to connect to a client computer, even with the client's permission.

- **Firewalls:** Remote Assistance uses Transmission Control Protocol (TCP) port number 3389 for all its network communications. For networks that use Remote Assistance internally and are also connected to the Internet, it is recommended that network administrators block this port in their firewalls to prevent users outside the network from taking control of computers that request remote assistance. However, it is also possible to provide remote assistance to clients over the Internet, which would require leaving port 3389 open.

USING REMOTE DESKTOP

While Remote Assistance is intended to enable users to obtain interactive help from other users, *Remote Desktop* is an administrative feature that enables users to access computers from remote locations, with no interaction required at the remote site. Remote Desktop is essentially a remote control program for Windows computers; there are no invitations and no read-only capabilities. When you connect to a computer using Remote Desktop, you can operate the remote computer as though you were sitting at the console and perform most configuration and application tasks.

> **➕ MORE INFORMATION**
>
> One of the most useful applications of Remote Desktop is to connect to servers, such as those in a locked closet or data center, that are not otherwise easily accessible. In fact, some administrators run their servers without monitors or input devices once the initial installation and configuration of the computer is complete, relying solely on Remote Desktop access for everyday monitoring and maintenance.

Remote Desktop is essentially an implementation of the Remote Desktop Services (formerly known as Terminal Services) technology built into the Windows server operating systems. When you use Remote Desktop Services on a server to host a large number of clients, you must purchase licenses for them. However, Windows 7 allows a single Remote Desktop connection for administrative purposes, without the need for a separate license.

The Remote Desktop Connection client communicates with a host computer using the *Remote Desktop Protocol (RDP)*. This protocol essentially transmits screen information, keystrokes, and mouse movements between the two computers. Any applications you launch in the client are still running on the remote computer, using its processor, memory, and storage resources.

When you connect to a computer using Remote Desktop, you must log on, just as you would if you were sitting at the console, meaning that you must have a user account and the appropriate privileges to access the host system. After you log on, the system displays the desktop configuration associated with your user account, and you can then proceed to work as you normally would.

Activating Remote Desktop

By default, the Remote Desktop Services service that powers the server side of Remote Desktop is not started on computers running Windows 7. Before you can connect to a distant computer using Remote Desktop, you must start it using the controls on the Remote tab of the System Properties sheet, which you access from the Control Panel. Select one of the Allow Connections options, depending on your security needs, and click *OK*.

TAKE NOTE * Because Remote Desktop requires the remote user to perform a standard logon, it is inherently more secure than Remote Assistance, and needs no special security measures such as invitations and session passwords. However, you can also click *Select Users* on the Remote tab to display a Remote Desktop Users dialog box, in which you can specify the names of the users or groups that are permitted to access the computer using Remote Desktop. All users with Administrator privileges are granted access by default.

Using the Remote Desktop Connection Client

In addition to the Remote Desktop Services service, Windows 7 includes the Remote Desktop Connection client program needed to connect to a host computer. To connect to a remote computer with the client, use the following procedure.

 RUN THE REMOTE DESKTOP CLIENT

GET READY. Log on to Windows 7.

1. Click Start, and then click All Programs > Accessories > Remote Desktop Connection. The Remote Desktop Connection dialog box appears, as shown in Figure 11-6.

Figure 11-6

The Remote Desktop Connection dialog box

2. Click Options. The dialog box expands to show additional controls, as shown in Figure 11-7.

Figure 11-7

The General tab in the expanded Remote Desktop Connection dialog box

3. On the General tab, type the name of the host computer you want to access in the Computer text box. Then click the Display tab, as shown in Figure 11-8.

Figure 11-8

The Display tab in the Remote Desktop Connection dialog box

4. In the *Remote desktop size* box, use the slider to select the desired size for the image of the host computer's desktop that will appear on the client system. In the Colors box, select the desired color depth using the drop-down list. Then click the Local Resources tab, as shown in Figure 11-9.

Figure 11-9

The Local Resources tab in the Remote Desktop Connection dialog box

5. Using the controls provided, specify which of the resources on the remote computer you want to bring to your local computer, including sound, printers, clipboard, smart cards, serial ports, drives, and other Plug and Play devices. In the Keyboard box, specify how you want the client to handle the Windows key combinations you press on your local computer. Then click the Experience tab, as shown in Figure 11-10.

Figure 11-10

The Experience tab in the Remote Desktop Connection dialog box

6. On the Experience tab, you can enhance the performance of the Remote Desktop Connection client by eliminating nonessential visual effects from the display information transmitted over the network. Select one of the network connection speeds from the drop-down list or choose the items you want to suppress by clearing their check boxes.

7. Click Connect to initiate the connection process. A Windows Security dialog box appears.

8. Supply User Name and Password values to log on to the remote computer, and then click OK. A Remote Desktop window appears containing an image of the remote computer's desktop.

Using Windows Remote Management

Using Windows Remote Management, administrators can execute programs from the command line on remote computers without having to open a Remote Desktop session.

Windows Remote Management is a Windows 7 service that enables administrators to execute commands on remote computers, using Windows PowerShell or the Windows Remote Shell (WinRS.exe) command-line program. However, Windows 7 does not start the service by default or configure the computer to allow remote management communications. To do this, you must complete the following procedure.

➔ CONFIGURE REMOTE MANAGEMENT

GET READY. Log on to Windows 7 using an account with administrative privileges.

1. Click Start, and then click All Programs > Accessories. Right click Command Prompt and, from the context menu, select *Run as administrator*. An Administrator: Command Prompt window appears.

TAKE NOTE*

If you are working on a computer that is a member of a workgroup, a User Account Control message box appears, in which you must click *Yes* to continue.

2. From the command prompt, type the following command and press Enter:

   winrm quickconfig

3. The command prompts you to start the WinRM service, as shown in Figure 11-11. Type y and press Enter to continue.

Figure 11-11

Starting the WinRM service

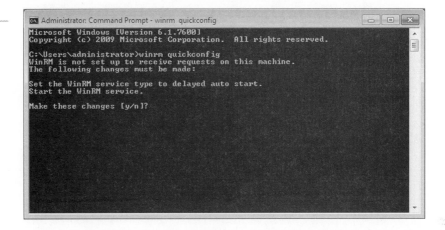

4. The command prompts you to create a listener for incoming remote management requests and configure the required firewall exception. Type y and press Enter to continue, as shown in Figure 11-12.

5. Close the Administrator: Command Prompt window.

Figure 11-12

Configuring a listener and firewall exception

In addition to this manual method, you can also configure Windows Remote Management using the Group Policy settings found in the Computer Configuration\Policies\Administrative Templates\Windows Components\Windows Remote Management (WinRM) container of every Group Policy object (GPO), as shown in Figure 11-13.

Figure 11-13

Windows Remote Management
Group Policy settings

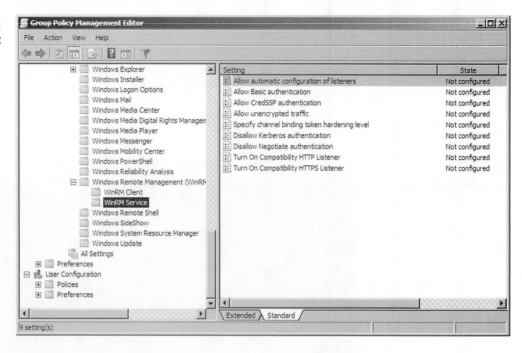

USING WINRS.EXE

Once you have configured the Remote Management service, you can execute commands
on other computers that have been similarly configured. To execute a command from the
Windows 7 command prompt, you must use the WinRS.exe program.

To use WinRS.exe, you frame the command you want to execute on the remote computer as
follows:

winrs –r:*computer* [-u:*user*] [-p:*password*] command

- **–r:*computer*:** Specifies the name of the computer on which you want to execute the
  command, using a NetBIOS name or a fully qualified domain name (FQDN).

- **–u:*user*:** Specifies the account on the remote computer that you want to use to execute the command.

- **–p:*password*:** Specifies the password associated with the account specified in the –u
  parameter. If you do not specify a password on the command line, WinRS.exe prompts
  you for one before executing the command.

- ***command*:** Specifies the command (with arguments) that you want to execute on the
  remote computer.

You can configure the behavior of WinRS.exe using the Group Policy settings found in
the Computer Configuration\Policies\Administrative Templates\Windows Components\
Windows Remote Shell container of every Group Policy object (GPO), as shown in
Figure 11-14.

Figure 11-14

Windows Remote Shell Group
Policy settings

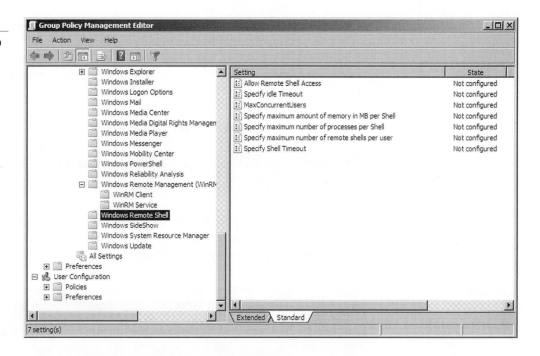

USING POWERSHELL REMOTE COMMANDS

It is also possible to execute commands on remote computers using Windows PowerShell version 2, the version included with Windows 7. Like WinRS.exe, PowerShell requires the Windows Remote Management service to be configured and running on both computers. The configuration parameters are exactly the same.

To execute a PowerShell command on a remote computer, you must open an elevated PowerShell session and use the following syntax:

```
icm computer {command}
```

- **computer:** Specifies the name of the computer on which you want to execute the command.
- **{command}:** Specifies the PowerShell command you want to execute on the remote computer. The command must be enclosed in curly brackets.

+ MORE INFORMATION

The icm command is an alias for the Invoke-Command cmdlet, which you can use in its place if desired. For information on the other parameters supported by the Invoke-Command cmdlet, see the help screens for the cmdlet.

■ Troubleshooting Installation and Startup Issues

THE BOTTOM LINE

Learning the troubleshooting process is better than learning to fix specific problems. However, troubleshooting startup problems can be difficult because the usual tools are unavailable.

This lesson has so far concentrated on general troubleshooting procedures and the troubleshooting tools that Windows 7 provides. This is in keeping with the belief that, to become an efficient troubleshooter, it is better to concentrate on learning the general process than dealing with specific problems. After all, there are an unlimited number of things that can go wrong on a computer and, as the old saying goes, giving a man a fish feeds him for a day, but teaching him to fish feeds him for life.

One of the more difficult types of problem to troubleshoot is one that prevents the computer from starting properly because you don't have access to all of the troubleshooting tools included with Windows 7. To troubleshoot a Windows 7 computer that fails to start, you must have an understanding of the startup procedure and knowledge of the tools that are available to you.

Understanding the Windows 7 Startup Process

Windows 7 uses a startup process that is substantially different from those of Windows XP and previous versions, and technical specialists should be familiar with the changes.

The Windows 7 startup procedure is vastly different from those of Windows XP and other NT-based Windows versions. Table 11-2 lists the new components found in Windows 7, and the Windows XP components they replace.

Table 11-2

Windows XP and Windows 7 Startup Components

WINDOWS 7 COMPONENT	FUNCTION	WINDOWS XP COMPONENT
Windows Boot Manager Windows Boot Loader	Displays the boot menu and loads the kernel	NTLDR
Boot Configuration Data (BCD) registry file	Contains the boot options displayed on the boot menu	Boot.ini
Merged into the kernel, as hardware profiles are no longer needed	Detects hardware and loads the appropriate hardware profile	Ntdetect.com
Windows Recovery Environment (Windows RE)	Provides limited access to operating system tools	Recovery Console

The Windows 7 startup process consists of the following steps:

1. **Power-on self-test (POST) phase:** When you first turn the computer on, it loads the BIOS or Extensible Firmware Interface (EFI) and runs a hardware self-test procedure that detects the devices installed in the system and configures them using settings stored in non-volatile memory. After the main POST, any devices with their own BIOS firmware (such as video display adapters) can run their own self-test procedures.

2. **Initial startup phase:** On BIOS-equipped computers, the system reads the BIOS settings to determine which hardware device it should use to boot the computer. When booting from a hard disk, the system loads the master boot record (MBR) from the disk and locates the active (bootable) partition. The system then loads and runs a stub program called Bootmgr, which switches the processor from real mode to protected mode and loads the Windows Boot Manager application. EFI computers have their own built-in boot manager, which Windows 7 configures to run the same Windows Boot Manager application, eliminating the need for the interim disk location steps.

3. **Windows Boot Manager phase:** The system reads the *Boot Configuration Data (BCD)* registry file, which contains the system's boot menu information, and provides the user with access to the boot menu, as shown in Figure 11-15. If there is only one operating system installed on the computer, the boot menu only appears when the user presses the a key just after the POST, or presses the F8 key to display the Advanced Boot Options menu. If there are multiple operating systems installed, the boot menu appears, providing the user with 30 seconds to select one of the operating systems before it loads the default.

Figure 11-15

The Windows 7 boot menu

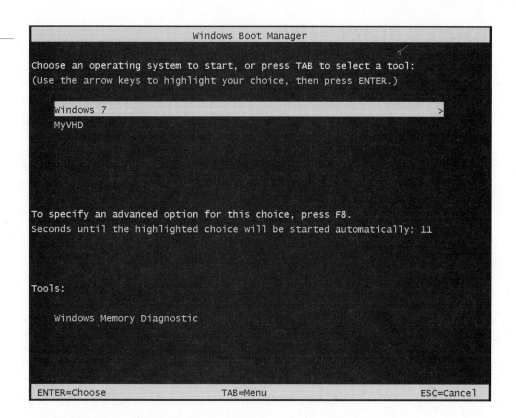

```
                        Windows Boot Manager

Choose an operating system to start, or press TAB to select a tool:
(Use the arrow keys to highlight your choice, then press ENTER.)

    Windows 7                                                          >
    MyVHD




To specify an advanced option for this choice, press F8.
Seconds until the highlighted choice will be started automatically: 11



Tools:

    Windows Memory Diagnostic




ENTER=Choose                    TAB=Menu                    ESC=Cancel
```

4. **Windows Boot Loader phase:** The system initiates the memory paging process and loads various operating system elements into memory, such as the Windows kernel, the hardware abstraction layer (HAL), the system registry hive, and boot class device drivers, but it does not actually run them.

5. **Kernel loading phase:** The system runs the Windows Executive (consisting of the Windows kernel and the HAL), which processes the registry hive and initializes the drivers and services specified there. The kernel then starts the Session Manager, which loads the kernel-mode part of the Win32 subsystem, causing the system to switch from text mode to graphics mode. Then the kernel loads the user-mode portion of Win32, which provides applications with indirect, protected access to the system hardware. At this time, the system also performs delayed rename operations resulting from system updates that must replace files that were in use when the update was installed. Finally, the kernel creates additional virtual memory paging files and starts the Logon Manager.

6. **Logon phase:** The system loads the Service Control Manager (SCM) and the Local Security Authority (LSA), and then presents the logon user interface (LogonUI). The interface passes the credentials supplied by the user to the LSA for authentication, and the SCM loads the Plug and Play services and drivers that are configured for autoloading. If the authentication is successful, the Logon Manager launches Userinit.exe, which is responsible for applying group policy settings and running the programs in the Startup group, and then loads the Windows Explorer shell, which provides the Windows desktop.

Troubleshooting Startup Failures

The first step in troubleshooting a startup failure is determining exactly where in the startup process the failure is occurring.

The symptoms of a startup failure differ depending on where in the process the failure occurs. Therefore, the first step to take when a Windows 7 computer fails to start is to determine exactly where in the startup sequence the problem is occurring.

POST FAILURES

One of the most fundamental questions a troubleshooter can ask is whether a problem is being caused by a hardware or a software failure. If a computer fails to make it through the POST successfully, the problem is unquestionably hardware-related. In most cases, the BIOS will display an error message or produce a series of beeps identifying the exact problem that is causing the failure. Consult the BIOS documentation for more information on its error messages and/or beep codes.

> **+ MORE INFORMATION**
>
> Some BIOS programs enable you to select between a "quick" POST and an extended "diagnostic" sequence. At the first sign of a hardware problem, you should switch to the diagnostic mode to gather as much information as possible about the problem.

INITIAL STARTUP FAILURES

A failure during the initial startup phase typically results in a "Non-system disk or disk error," which means that there is an issue with the BIOS configuration, the storage subsystem, or the file system. Startup failures that occur before the progress bar appears are typically caused by one of the following problems:

- **Incorrect BIOS Settings:** If the boot settings in the BIOS are misconfigured, the system might be attempting to boot from the wrong device. For example, if the BIOS is configured to boot from the CD or DVD drive, and there is no bootable disk in the drive, the computer will be unable to start.

- **Hardware faults:** If anyone has recently worked inside the computer's case, you might want to begin by checking the hard drive's power and data connections. Also, if there is an internal problem with the hard disk, such as corruption of the MBR, the system might not be able to locate the active partition.

- **Missing startup files:** If some of the required startup files are missing or damaged, the computer will fail to boot. This could be due to the installation of another operating system over Windows 7, accidental deletion of system files, or data corruption on the hard disk.

- **Data corruption:** Corrupted data on a disk drive can be the result of a hardware fault, environmental factors (such as magnetic fields), or some form of malware.

Resolving these problems can require the replacement of a hardware component, but in many cases you can repair them using the specialized recovery tools provided with Windows 7, as discussed later in this lesson.

DRIVER AND SERVICE FAILURES

The appearance of the progress bar indicates that the kernel has loaded successfully. When a startup failure occurs after the progress bar appears, but before the logon user interface appears, the problem could be hardware-related, but it is most likely due to an issue with one of the drivers or services that the kernel is attempting to load. Resolving the problem is a matter of determining which of the drivers or services is at fault.

To locate the offending driver or service, you must first attempt to get the computer started by using the Last Known Good Configuration option, Safe Mode, or other means. Then you can examine the event logs, enable the boot log, and run the System Information tool to gather information on what is affecting the startup sequence. Finally, use Device Manager or the Services console to disable the offending drivers or services. Once you are able to get the computer started in normal node, you can begin to examine the problematic driver or service, perhaps replacing them with an updated version or rolling back to a previous one.

LOGON FAILURES

When the startup process fails after the user has supplied logon credentials, the problem is most likely due to one of the applications running from the Startup group. The simplest way to prevent the startup applications from running is to hold down the Shift key when logging on, until the icons appear on the desktop. When you do this, the startup applications do not load, but only for that session.

Once the system is started, you can try loading each of the startup applications in turn to see which one is causing the problem. After isolating the offending application, you can see about reconfiguring, upgrading, or uninstalling it, so that the problem is eliminated.

Using Recovery Tools

Windows 7 includes specialized tools for diagnosing and repairing startup problems.

Windows 7 has many tools that you can use for troubleshooting system and network problems, but if the computer fails to start, these tools are not available. Fortunately, Windows 7 includes a special working environment that you can use when the system fails to start, as well as a selection of tools that you can use in that environment.

USING ALTERNATE BOOT OPTIONS

In many cases, just getting the computer to start can be half of the troubleshooting battle. Once the computer is started, you have access to the configuration interface and the Windows 7 troubleshooting tools that can help you solve the problem. If the problem is hardware-related, you are unlikely to get the system started until you repair or replace the malfunctioning component. However, if the startup problem occurs after the progress bar appears, you can probably get the system started in one of the following ways:

- **To suppress drivers and services:** Press F8 repeatedly, immediately after the POST completes and before the progress bar appears. From the Advanced Boot Options menu, shown in Figure 11-16, select Last Known Good Configuration or, if that does not work, one of the Safe Mode options.

Figure 11-16

The Advanced Boot Options menu

```
                          Advanced Boot Options

Choose Advanced Options for: Windows 7
(Use the arrow keys to highlight your choice.)


    Repair Your Computer

    Safe Mode
    Safe Mode with Networking
    Safe Mode with Command Prompt

    Enable Boot Logging
    Enable low-resolution video (640x480)
    Last Known Good Configuration (advanced)
    Directory Services Restore Mode
    Debugging Mode
    Disable automatic restart on system failure
    Disable Driver Signature Enforcement

    Start Windows Normally

Description: View a list of system recovery tools you can use to repair
            startup problems, run diagnostics, or restore your system.


ENTER=Choose                                              ESC=Cancel
```

• **To suppress startup applications:** Press the Shift key while logging on and hold it down until the icons appear on the desktop.

The Last Known Good Configuration option reverses all of the system configuration, driver, and registry changes you made since the computer last booted successfully. The Safe Mode options start the computer with a minimal set of generic drivers, just those needed to run the system. Once the system is running, you can exercise control over it and gather information about the startup process using the tools covered in the following sections.

USING THE STARTUP AND RECOVERY DIALOG BOX

The Startup and Recovery dialog box provides basic controls that enable you to configure the Windows 7 startup process by modifying the BCD registry file. To open the Startup and Recovery dialog box, use the following procedure.

 OPEN THE STARTUP AND RECOVERY DIALOG BOX

GET READY. Log on to Windows 7.

1. Click Start, and then click Control Panel > System and Security > System. The System control panel appears.

2. Click Advanced System Settings. After confirming your action, the System Properties sheet appears.

3. Click the Advanced tab, as shown in Figure 11-17.

Figure 11-17

The Advanced tab of the System Properties sheet

4. In the Startup and Recovery box, click Settings. The Startup and Recovery dialog box appears, as shown in Figure 11-18.

Figure 11-18

The Startup and Recovery
dialog box

In this dialog box, you can specify which operating system to load on a dual boot computer, and also specify how long the boot menu and recovery options menu appear by default. You can also exercise control over the computer's logging behavior during system startup.

USING THE SYSTEM CONFIGURATION TOOL

If you can get Windows 7 to start in Safe Mode, the System Configuration tool enables you to exercise a great deal of control over the startup process. You can select the type of startup to perform, configure a variety of BCD registry file settings, and specify individual applications and services to be omitted from the startup sequence.

> **➕ MORE INFORMATION**
>
> While the System Configuration tool provides more access to the BCD registry settings than the Startup and Recovery dialog box, it is not the most comprehensive BCD editing tool available. To exercise complete control over the BCD, you must use the BCDEdit.exe tool from the command line in Windows 7 or Windows RE.

X REF

For more information on using the General and Startup tabs to address system performance issues, see "Using the System Configuration Tool," in Lesson 8, "Managing and Monitoring Windows 7 Performance."

To start the System Configuration tool, click Start, type *msconfig* in the search box, and press Enter. The System Configuration dialog box appears. The dialog box contains the following tabs:

- **General:** Provides controls that enable you to perform a normal, diagnostic, or selective startup sequence. You can use these options to suppress specific parts of the startup process in the hope of bypassing the component causing the problem.
- **Boot:** Controls BCD registry settings that enable you to select the operating system to install and configure a limited boot sequence, as shown in Figure 11-19. Clicking *Advanced options* displays a BOOT Advanced Options dialog box, which you can use to control the system hardware used during the startup sequence.

Figure 11-19

The Boot tab in the System
Configuration dialog box

• **Services:** Enables you to select the services that will run during the startup sequence, as shown in Figure 11-20. By disabling all of the services and then enabling them one at a time as you repeatedly restart the computer, you can determine which service is causing a startup failure.

Figure 11-20

The Services tab in the System
Configuration dialog box

• **Startup:** Enables you to select the startup applications that will run during the startup sequence. By disabling all of the startup applications and then enabling them one at a time as you repeatedly restart the computer, you can determine which application is causing a startup failure.

• **Tools:** Enables you to launch a variety of Windows 7 configuration and troubleshooting tools, as shown in Figure 11-21.

TAKE NOTE* When you make changes to the system startup configuration using the System Configuration tool, Windows 7 displays a message when users log on, reminding them of the changes, so they do not forget to restore the original configuration.

Figure 11-21

The Tools tab in the System Configuration dialog box

ENABLING BOOT LOGGING

Boot logging gathers information about the most recent startup process and saves it to a text file for later examination. However, boot logging is not enabled by default. To enable boot logging, use the following procedure.

 ENABLE BOOT LOGGING

1. Turn the computer on.
2. When the POST completes, press the F8 key repeatedly until the Advanced Boot Options menu appears.
3. Select Enable Boot Logging. The system creates a log file in the \Windows folder called Ntblog.txt.
4. The startup procedure continues, adding information to the log file as it proceeds.

The boot log contains a list of all the files that Windows 7 attempts to load during the startup process, along with a status indicator specifying whether each file loaded successfully. If you enable boot logging during a normal startup, and then perform a Safe Mode startup, the system will append the Safe Mode startup information to the existing log. This enables you to compare the two startup sequences and determine which files are required for a successful, normal startup that are not required for a Safe Mode startup. If the Safe Mode startup is successful and a normal one is not, then one of those files must be causing the problem.

USING WINDOWS RE

As you learned in Lesson 2, "Installing Windows 7," the Windows 7 installation process uses the Windows Preinstallation Environment (Windows PE) to boot the system for the first time and initiate the Setup program. Windows PE is a stripped-down operating system that, unlike the DOS environment used in previous Windows versions, supports the same drivers used in a complete Windows 7 installation, as well as a subset of the Win32 application programming interface (API).

For computers that already have the operating system installed, Windows 7 includes the **_Windows Recovery Environment (Windows RE)_**, which is essentially the same as Windows PE. By booting into Windows RE, you bypass all of the drivers, applications, and services that can be the source of a startup problem. Windows RE also provides access to a collection of recovery tools that can identify and even repair many of the problems that can prevent the system from starting.

To run Windows RE, use the following procedure:

1. Insert a Windows 7 installation DVD into the drive and restart the computer.

2. If you are prompted to do so, press any key to boot from the DVD. (If the system fails to prompt and boots from the hard disk instead, you might have to modify your system BIOS settings to use the DVD as the first boot device.) The Install Windows wizard appears.

3. Select the appropriate language and keyboard settings and click Next. The *Install Now* page appears.

4. Click Repair Your Computer. The program scans the computer's drives for Windows 7 installations and displays a *System Recovery Options* dialog box containing the results, as shown in Figure 11-22.

Figure 11-22

The System Recovery Options dialog box

5. Select the instance of the operating system you want to repair, and then click Next. The *Choose a recovery tool* dialog box appears, as shown in Figure 11-23.

6. Click one of the links to launch a recovery tool.

Figure 11-23

The Choose a Recovery Tool dialog box

TAKE NOTE*

If Windows 7 experienced a startup failure immediately before you booted from the DVD, the Startup Repair tool will load automatically.

USING THE SYSTEM RECOVERY TOOLS

When you load Windows RE from the Windows 7 installation DVD, the system provides you with a choice of recovery tools, including the following:

• **Startup Repair:** An automated troubleshooting tool that is capable of diagnosing and repairing a variety of problems that can prevent Windows 7 from starting, including BCD problems and missing startup files. The prompts displayed by the tool vary, depending on the conditions it detects, but all of its activities are logged in a file called SRTTrail.txt, located in the \Windows\System32\LogFiles\SRT folder. When the cause of a startup problem is not immediately apparent, this should be the first tool you use.

- **System Restore:** Enables you to access the restore points on the computer, whether manually or automatically created, and use them to restore the system to an earlier state. This is the same functionality available in the System Restore application, accessible from the System Tools program group in Windows 7 (in normal or safe mode).

- **System Image Recovery:** Enables you to perform a full restoration of your computer, using an image you previously created with the Backup and Restore control panel.

- **Windows Memory Diagnostic:** Tests the computer's memory for hardware errors.

- **Command Prompt:** Displays a command prompt, from which you can run a variety of text-based tools included with Windows RE.

■ Using BranchCache

THE BOTTOM LINE

BranchCache is a new feature in Windows 7 and Windows Server 2008 R2 that enables networks with computers at remote locations to conserve bandwidth by storing frequently accessed files on local drives.

Caching is a process in which computers copy frequently used data to an intermediate storage medium so they can satisfy subsequent requests for the same data more quickly or less expensively. For example, virtually all computers have an area of high-speed memory between the system processor and the main system memory that functions as a cache. Repeated requests for the same data can be satisfied more quickly from the cache memory than the slower main memory. BranchCache works in much the same way, except that it is a disk storage cache that reduces the traffic between branch office computers and a server at another site.

CERTIFICATION READY?
Configure BranchCache.
5.5

Wide area network (WAN) connections between offices are slower and more expensive than the local area network (LAN) connections within an office. When a computer in a branch office requires a file stored on a server at the main office, the server must transmit the file over a WAN connection. If twenty computers at the branch office require that same file, the server must transmit it twenty times, using twenty times the WAN bandwidth.

BranchCache is a feature that can store a copy of the file on a computer at the branch office site, so that the server only has to transmit the files over the WAN connection once. All of the subsequent requests access the file from the cache on the local network.

Understanding Network Infrastructure Requirements

To use BranchCache, you must have a server running Windows Server 2008 R2 at the home office and computers running Windows Server 2008 R2 or Windows 7 at the branch office.

BranchCache is a new feature introduced in Windows Server 2008 R2 and Windows 7 Enterprise and Ultimate editions; only computers running those operating systems can use it. The content server that stores the data initially must be running Windows Server 2008 R2. The workstations at the branch office that access the data must be running Windows 7.

BranchCache is a client/server application that supports two operational modes, as follows:

- *Distributed cache mode:* Each Windows 7 workstation on the branch office network caches data from the content server on its local drive and shares that cached data with other local workstations.

- *Hosted cache mode:* Windows 7 workstations on the branch office network cache data from the content server on a branch office server, enabling other workstations to access the cached data from there.

Obviously, the major difference between the two modes is the need for a second, branch-office server in hosted cache mode, which makes the caching process more efficient, but which adds to the expense of the implementation. In distributed cache mode, each workstation is responsible for maintaining its own cache and processing cache requests from the other workstations on the local network.

Understanding BranchCache Communications

BranchCache clients and servers exchange relatively small messages among themselves to coordinate their caching activities.

BranchCache supports file requests using Server Message Blocks (SMB), the standard Windows file-sharing protocol; Hypertext Transfer Protocol (HTTP), the standard protocol for web communications; and the Background Intelligent Transfer Service (BITS). The BranchCache communications process is as follows:

1. **Client request (BranchCache):** A branch office workstation requests a file from the content server, and identifies itself as a BranchCache client.
2. **Server reply (metadata):** The server replies to the client, not with the requested file, but with a message containing metadata that describes the file. The metadata is much smaller than the requested file, reducing the amount of WAN bandwidth consumed.
3. **Client cache check:** Using the metadata supplied by the server, the client sends messages to the local caching computers, asking if the requested file is available locally.
4. **Caching computer reply:** In hosted cache mode, the local caching server replies to the client, indicating whether the requested file is available in its cache. In distributed cache mode, caching workstations only reply in the positive. If the client workstation receives no replies, it assumes that the requested file is not cached locally.
5. **Client request (non-BranchCache):** The client issues another file request, this time without the BranchCache identifier, and sends it either to a local caching computer or the content server.
6. **Server reply (data):** The computer receiving the request replies by sending the requested file to the client.
7. **Client data cache:** On receiving the requested file, the client caches it for use by other branch office workstations. In hosted cache mode, the client caches the file on the branch office server. In distributed cache mode, the client caches the file on its own local disk.

As a result of this process, the traffic transmitted over the WAN consists primarily of small messages containing client requests and metadata replies, as well as one single copy of every requested file.

It is critical to understand that BranchCache is a read-only caching application. The metadata messages described here occur only when branch office clients are requesting files from the content server, not when they are writing modified files back to the server. BranchCache does not support write caching, which is a far more complicated process, because the systems must account for the possibility of conflicts between multiple versions of the same file.

Configuring BranchCache Settings

To implement BranchCache on your network, you must install the appropriate modules on your server(s) and configure Group Policy settings on both servers and clients.

BranchCache requires a minimum of one content server and one or more branch office workstations. You can install additional content servers at any location that serves files to branch offices.

At the branch office, BranchCache in distributed cache mode can typically support up to 50 workstations. To use hosted cache mode, you must have a branch office server at each location where there are branch office workstations.

CONFIGURING A CONTENT SERVER

To use BranchCache on your network, your files must be stored on a content server running Windows Server 2008 R2. To support SMB requests, the server must have the BranchCache for Network Files role service installed in the File Services role. To support HTTP and BITS requests, you must install the BranchCache feature.

Once you have installed the required BranchCache modules, you must configure a Group Policy setting called Hash Publication for BranchCache. This setting is located in the Computer Configuration\Policies\Administrative Templates\Network\Lanman Server node of a Group Policy object (GPO) or in Local Computer Policy.

The Hash Publication for BranchCache setting, shown in Figure 11-24, enables the server to respond to file requests from BranchCache clients with metadata instead of the files themselves. In this setting, you can stipulate that the server publish hash metadata for all of its shared files or for only the shares you select.

Figure 11-24

The Hash Publication for BranchCache setting in Group Policy

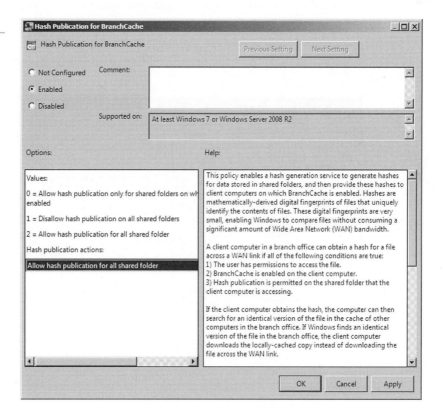

If you select the *Allow hash publication only for shared folders on which BranchCache is enabled* option, you must configure each share for which you want to enable BranchCache by opening the share's Properties sheet in the Share and Storage Management console, clicking Advanced, and selecting an appropriate option on the Caching tab of the Advanced dialog box, as shown in Figure 11-25.

Figure 11-25

The Caching tab of the
Advanced dialog box

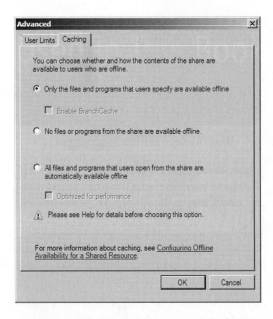

CONFIGURING BRANCHCACHE CLIENTS

BranchCache client computers must be running Windows 7 or Windows Server 2008 R2.
BranchCache is enabled by default in Windows 7. To use a computer running Windows
Server 2008 R2 as a BranchCache client, you must install the BranchCache feature.

To configure BranchCache clients, you must configure the appropriate Group Policy settings found in the Computer Configuration\Policies\Administrative Templates\Network\
BranchCache node of a GPO or in Local Computer Policy, as shown in Figure 11-26.

Figure 11-26

The BranchCache settings in
Group Policy

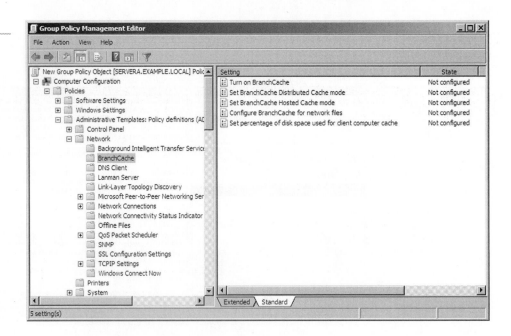

The BranchCache Group Policy settings are as follows:

- **Turn on BranchCache:** Enables BranchCache on the client computer. Enabling this
  setting along with either *Set BranchCache Distributed Cache mode* or *Set BranchCache
  Hosted Cache mode* configures the client to use one of those operational modes. Enabling
  this setting without either one of the mode settings configures the client to cache server
  data on its local drive only, without accessing caches on other computers.

- **Set BranchCache Distributed Cache mode:** When enabled along with the *Turn on BranchCache* setting, configures the client to function in distributed cache mode.
- **Set BranchCache Hosted Cache mode:** When enabled along with the *Turn on BranchCache* setting, configures the client to function in a hosted cache mode. In the *Enter the location of the hosted cache* field, you must specify the address of the computer that will function as the hosted cache server on the branch office network.
- **Configure BranchCache for network files:** When enabled, this setting controls the round trip network latency value that BranchCache uses to differentiate local from remote servers. The default setting is 80 ms. When you decrease the value, the client caches more files; increasing the value causes it to cache fewer files.
- **Set percentage of disk space used for client computer cache:** When enabled, this setting specifies the maximum amount of total disk space that the computer should devote to the BranchCache cache. The default value is 5 percent.

CONFIGURING A HOSTED CACHE MODE SERVER

To use hosted cache mode on your branch office network, you must have a server running Windows Server 2008 R2 with the BranchCache feature installed. You must also configure the *Turn on BranchCache* and *Set BranchCache Hosted Cache mode* Group Policy settings.

The hosted cache mode server must also have a digital certificate issued by a certification authority (CA) that the BranchCache clients trust. You can install an internal CA on the network and use it to issue the certificate, or obtain a certificate from a commercial, third-party CA.

Once you have obtained the certificate, you must use the Certificates snap-in on the hosted cache server to import it. Finally, you must link the certificate to the BranchCache service by opening an elevated command prompt and typing the following command, replacing the thumbprint variable with the thumbprint value from the certificate you imported:

```
netsh http add sslcert ipport=0.0.0.0:443 certhash=thumbprint
appid={d673f5ee-a714-454d-8de2-492e4c1bd8f8}
```

■ Configuring Data Protection

THE BOTTOM LINE

Protecting data from unauthorized access is important, but it is equally critical to protect it from accidental loss or deliberate destruction. To do this, you must create system backups at regular intervals.

Larger, and even some medium-sized, organizations have network-based backup systems that enable multiple workstations to transmit their data to a backup device on the network, such as a magnetic tape drive. Depending on the amount of data involved and the type of storage device, these network backup solutions can easily cost tens of thousands of dollars.

For stand-alone systems or small networks, Windows 7 includes backup tools that you can use to protect your data by copying it to a network drive, another hard disk drive, a USB flash drive, or a series of writable CDs or DVDs. Windows 7 also includes a variety of other tools that you can use to recover from data loss or other system disasters.

Using Backup and Restore

The Windows 7 Backup and Restore control panel enables users to easily set up a repeating regimen of backup jobs using a wizard-based interface.

The backup program included with Windows seems to change significantly with every version of the operating system. The backup program included with Windows XP was capable of getting the job done, but suffered from some serious drawbacks. The software was limited in the types of backup devices it could use, and scheduling repeated backup jobs was difficult.

In Windows Vista, creating a repeating backup job is a simple matter of running the wizard, selecting the files to back up, and selecting the medium you want to use to store the backups. However, the backup program in Vista backs up only document files, not application or operating system files, and there is no way to avoid the wizard and manually create a backup job. To perform a full backup of the entire system, you must use Complete PC, a separate utility.

CREATING A BACKUP JOB

The Windows 7 Backup and Restore control panel integrates the wizard-based file and folder backup and the system image backup capabilities into one program. To create a backup job with the Backup and Restore control panel, use the following procedure.

CREATE A BACKUP JOB

GET READY. Log on to Windows 7 using an account with administrative privileges.

1. Click Start, and then click Control Panel > System and Security > Backup and Restore. The Backup and Restore control panel appears, as shown in Figure 11-27.

Figure 11-27

The Backup and Restore control panel

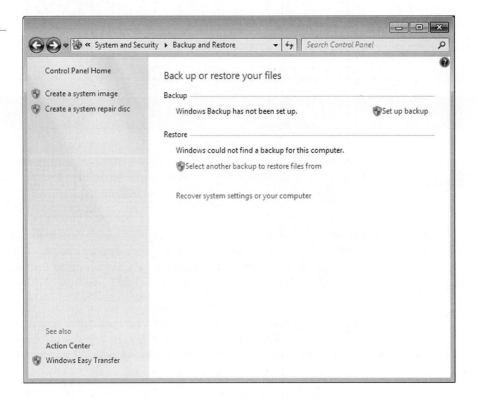

2. Click Set up backup. The *Select where you want to save your backup* page appears, as shown in Figure 11-28.

Figure 11-28

The Select where you want to save your backup page

3. Select one of the destinations in the *Save backup on* list and click Next. Windows Backup supports internal and external hard disks, USB flash drives, writable DVD-ROM and CD-ROM drives, and network locations, subject to the limitations shown in Table 11-3. The *What do you want to back up?* page appears.

Table 11-3

Windows 7 Backup Devices

DEVICE	WINDOWS 7 EDITIONS SUPPORTED	BACKUPS SUPPORTED
Internal hard disks	All editions	Files/folders and system images
External hard disks	All editions	Files/folders and system images
DVD-ROMs	All editions	Files/folders and unscheduled system images
CD-ROMs	All editions	Files/folders and unscheduled system images
USB flash drives	All editions	Files/folders only
Network locations	Windows 7 Professional, Enterprise, and Ultimate only	Files/folders and system images

4. Select one of the following options and click Next. The *Review your backup settings* page appears.

   • **Let Windows choose (recommended):** Backs up files in libraries and in the default windows folders. This setting also creates a system image backup.

   • **Let me choose:** Displays a second *What do you want to back up?* page, as shown in Figure 11-29, on which you can select the files and folders you want to back up. You can also opt to perform a system image backup as well.

Figure 11-29

The second What do you want to back up? page

TAKE NOTE*

The file and folder backup capability in Windows Backup cannot back up system and application files. To protect the entire system drive, you must perform a system image backup.

5. To change the default (weekly) job schedule, click Change schedule. The *How often do you want to back up?* page appears, as shown in Figure 11-30.

Figure 11-30

The How often do you want to back up? page

6. In the *How often* drop-down list, specify whether you want the job to run daily, weekly, or monthly. In the *What day* drop-down list, specify the day of the week or the monthly date that you want the job to run. In the *What time* drop-down list, specify the time of day that you want the job to run. To perform a one-time job, clear the Run backup on a schedule (recommended) check box. Then click OK.

7. Click Save settings and run backup. The program creates the backup job, executes it for the first time, and schedules it to repeat at the interval you selected. The Backup and Restore control panel now displays the status of the backup job, as shown in Figure 11-31.

Figure 11-31

The Backup and Restore control panel, displaying the backup job status

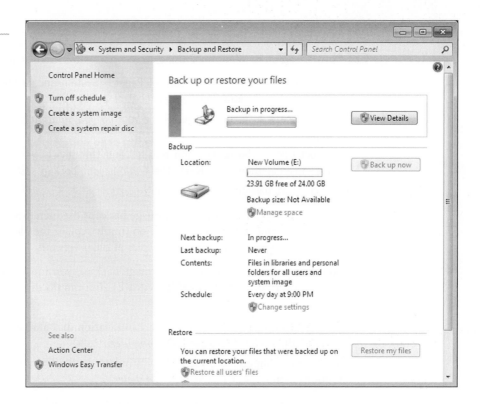

The file and folder backup process stores the selected files in compressed archives with a .zip extension, minimizing the amount of storage space consumed on the backup medium. Windows Backup also conserves space, as well as time, by performing incremental backups automatically.

An *incremental backup* is a type of job that backs up only the files that have changed since the last backup was performed. Windows Backup saves multiple versions of each file that changes, but it does not back up multiple copies of unchanged files. It is possible to restore previous versions of modified files; the program only deletes older versions when the backup medium runs out of space.

Because Windows Backup is designed for use with random access storage devices, it always provides the latest version of every file when performing a restore, unless you specifically select an older version.

CREATING A SYSTEM IMAGE BACKUP

As mentioned earlier, you cannot use the file and folder backup capability in the Backup and Restore control panel to protect the entire system. Even when you use the *Let me choose* option and select the files you want to back up, you cannot select operating system files, such as those in the Windows folder.

To back up the entire system disk, you must perform a *system image backup*, which is a separate backup of the computer's system disk and the reserved partition that Windows 7 creates on the disk during installation. Unlike the file and folder backup, which simply copies files to a compressed archive, a system image backup saves each block of the selected targets to a virtual hard disk (VHD) file on the backup device.

You can create a system image backup as part of your regular scheduled backup job, or you can create one separately on demand, but you cannot schedule a system image backup through the Backup and Restore control panel. You can, however, schedule a job from the command prompt, using the Wbadmin.exe utility.

To perform a system image backup, use the following procedure.

CREATE A SYSTEM IMAGE BACKUP

GET READY. Log on to Windows 7 using an account with administrative privileges.

1. Click Start, and then click Control Panel > System and Security > Backup and Restore. The Backup and Restore control panel appears.

2. Click Create a system image. The *Where do you want to save the backup?* page appears.

3. Select one of the destination options and the device where you want to save the backup, and then click Next. The *Confirm your backup settings* page appears.

4. Click Start backup. The backup job starts.

As with file and folder backups, system image backups use incremental jobs by default. However, the incrementals in this type of job simply replace the older versions of files with new ones. The program does not retain copies of older versions.

To restore the computer from a system image backup, you must boot the system into the Windows Recovery Environment (Windows RE). You can do this in either of the following ways:

- Start the computer using a Windows 7 installation disk and, after selecting your language settings, choose *Repair Your Computer*.
- Restart the computer and press F8 as Windows loads. Then, from the Advanced Boot Options menu, select *Repair Your Computer*.

In either case, you will have to specify the location of the backup, and then you will be able to restore the system to the computer.

CREATING A SYSTEM REPAIR DISK

In addition to performing backups and restores, the Backup and Restore control panel can also create a system repair disk, which enables you to access system recovery options if you do not have a Windows 7 installation disk or a recovery partition.

To create a system repair disk, use the following procedure.

 CREATE A SYSTEM REPAIR DISK

GET READY. Log on to Windows 7 using an account with administrative privileges.

1. Click Start, and then click Control Panel > System and Security > Backup and Restore. The Backup and Restore control panel appears.

2. Click Create a system repair disc. The *Create a system repair disc* dialog box appears, as shown in Figure 11-32.

Figure 11-32

The Create a system repair disc dialog box

Create a system repair disc

Select a CD/DVD drive and insert a blank disc into the drive

A system repair disc can be used to boot your computer. It also contains Windows system recovery tools that can help you recover Windows from a serious error or restore your computer from a system image.

Drive:

Create disc | Cancel

3. Insert a blank DVD-ROM disk into your DVD burner.

4. In the *Drive* drop-down list, select the drive letter corresponding to your DVD burner and click Create disc. The system creates the system repair disk and displays a *Using the system repair disc* page.

5. Click Close.

Store the system repair disk in a safe place, in case you experience a system failure. To use the disk, you simply insert the disk in the drive and boot the system. Windows 7 then displays system recovery options.

CERTIFICATION READY?
Configure file recovery options.

8.3

RESTORING FILES

Once you have completed a file and folder backup job, you can restore specific files from that job at any time. To perform a restore, use the following procedure.

RESTORE FILES

GET READY. Log on to Windows 7 using an account with administrative privileges.

1. Click Start, and then click Control Panel > System and Security > Backup and Restore. The Backup and Restore control panel appears.

2. Click Restore my files. The *Browse or search your backup for files and folders to restore* page appears, as shown in Figure 11-33.

Figure 11-33

The Browse or search your backup for files and folders to restore page

3. Click Browse for files. The *Browse the backup for files* combo box appears, as shown in Figure 11-34.

Figure 11-34

The Browse the backup for files combo box

4. Browse to and select the files you want to restore and click Add files. The files appear on the *Browse or search your backup for files and folders to restore* page.

5. Click Next. The *Where do you want to restore your files?* page appears, as shown in Figure 11-35.

Figure 11-35

The Where do you want to restore your files? page

6. Leave the default In the original location option selected or select In the following location and type or browse to the destination for the restore.

7. Click Restore. The program restores the selected files. If files of the same name exist at the destination, the Copy File dialog box appears, as shown in Figure 11-36.

8. Select one of the file copy options to continue. A *Your files have been restored* page appears.

9. Click Finish.

Figure 11-36

The Copy File dialog box

PERFORMING A SYSTEM RESTORE

Windows 7 automatically creates system restore points on a regular basis, including whenever a backup job runs and whenever Windows Update installs operating system updates. A *system restore point* is a copy of various operating system configuration settings and registry information from a specific point in time. If you experience a problem related to a particular change in the system configuration, you can use the Backup and Restore control panel to restore the computer to the system settings of a time of your choosing.

CERTIFICATION READY?
Configure system recovery options.
8.2

TAKE NOTE*

Performing a system restore is not the same thing as performing a system image restore. A system restore sets the operating system back to a previous state while it's running. A system image restore completely replaces the operating system with an offline copy, and therefore requires that you boot the computer to the Windows RE environment, using a Windows 7 installation disk or its equivalent. For more information, see "Using Recovery Tools," earlier in this lesson.

The primary interface for creating and configuring system protection behavior is the System Protection tab of the System Properties sheet, as shown in Figure 11-37. You can open the System Properties sheet by clicking *Advanced system settings* on the System control panel.

Figure 11-37

The System Protection tab of the System Properties sheet

From the System Protection tab, you can create system restore points at will, as well as configure the protection settings for each volume on the computer. By default, the system volume (usually C:) has system protection turned on, as shown in Figure 11-38. All other volumes have system protection turned off until you turn it on.

Figure 11-38

The System Protection for Local Disk (C:) dialog box

To perform a system restore, use the following procedure.

 PERFORM A SYSTEM RESTORE

GET READY. Log on to Windows 7 using an account with administrative privileges.

1. Click Start, and then click Control Panel > System and Security > Backup and Restore. The Backup and Restore control panel appears.

2. Click Recover system settings or your computer. The *Restore this computer to an earlier point in time* page appears, as shown in Figure 11-39.

Figure 11-39

The Restore this computer to an earlier point in time page

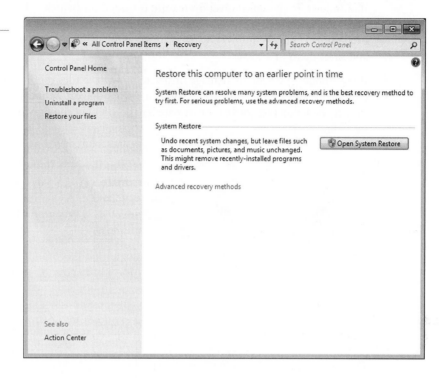

3. Click Open System Restore. The System Restore Wizard appears, displaying the *Restore system files and settings* page.

4. Click Next to continue. The *Restore your computer to the state it was in before the selected event* page appears, as shown in Figure 11-40.

Figure 11-40

The Restore your computer to the state it was in before the selected event page

5. Select one of the listed restore points and click Next. The *Confirm your restore point* page appears.

6. Click Finish. A warning message, indicating that once the system restore process begins, it cannot be interrupted.

7. Click Yes. The wizard restores the system to the selected point and restarts.

RESTORING PREVIOUS VERSIONS

Volume shadow copies are duplicates of files that Windows creates as part of a restore point. If Windows 7's System Protection feature is turned on (which it is by default for the system disk), the system automatically creates restore points at periodic intervals. During the creation of a restore point, Windows creates shadow copies of files that have been added or modified and saves them in a cache.

If you should accidentally damage or delete one of the files that has been protected with either a backup or a shadow copy, you can restore one of the previous versions by opening its Properties dialog box (or that of its parent) and clicking the Previous Versions tab, as shown in Figure 11-41.

Figure 11-41

The Previous Versions tab of a Properties sheet

SKILL SUMMARY

IN THIS LESSON YOU LEARNED:

- When troubleshooting a problem in a professional environment, whether it's a corporate enterprise network, a help desk in a retail store, or a freelance consultancy, it is important to have a set troubleshooting procedure.

- The troubleshooting procedure should include the following: Establish the symptoms. Identify the affected area. Establish what has changed. Select the most probable cause. Implement a solution. Test the result. Document the solution.

- Remote Assistance is a Windows 7 feature that enables an administrator, trainer, or desktop technician at one location to connect to a distant user's computer, chat with the user, and either view all the user's activities or take complete control of the system.

- Remote Desktop is an administrative feature that enables users to access computers from remote locations, with no interaction required at the remote site.

- To troubleshoot a Windows 7 computer that fails to start, you must have an understanding of the startup procedure, and knowledge of the tools that are available.

- Windows RE is a stripped-down operating system that supports the same drivers used in a complete Windows 7 installation, as well as a subset of the Win32 application programming interface (API).

- BranchCache is a new feature in Windows 7 and Windows Server 2008 R2 that enables networks with computers at remote locations to conserve bandwidth by storing frequently accessed files on local drives.

- The Backup and Restore control panel protects users' document files and enables them to restore single files as needed.

- System image backups protect the entire system, enabling you to restore the computer in the event of a catastrophic failure.

- Volume shadow copies are duplicates of files that Windows creates as part of a restore point. If a user should accidentally damage or delete one of the files, they can restore one of the previous versions.

■ Knowledge Assessment

Matching

Complete the following exercise by matching the terms with their corresponding definitions.

    a. conserves WAN bandwidth
    b. files cached on each client
    c. files cached on a central server
    d. files changed since the last backup job
    e. based on the former Terminal Services
    f. configuration settings and registry information
    g. executes PowerShell commands on remote computers
    h. previous versions
    i. accessible from a Window 7 installation disk
    j. saves data to a VHD file

_____ **1.** Remote Desktop

_____ **2.** system image backup

_____ **3.** BranchCache

_____ **4.** distributed cache mode

_____ **5.** volume shadow copies

_____ **6.** incremental backup

_____ **7.** Windows RE

_____ **8.** hosted cache mode

_____ **9.** Windows Remote Management

_____ **10.** system restore point

Multiple Choice

Select one or more correct answers for each of the following questions.

1. Which of the following service priority guidelines are not accurate?
   a. Network-wide problems take precedence over workgroup or departmental problems.
   b. System-wide problems take precedence over application problems.
   c. Shared resources take precedence over individual resources.
   d. You should rate departmental issues according to how the issues affect senior management.

2. Place these troubleshooting steps in the correct order, using the procedure described in this lesson as your guide:
   a. Document the solution
   b. Establish the symptoms
   c. Test the result
   d. Select the most probable cause

3. Which of the following Windows 7 tools does not aid in the network troubleshooting process?
   a. User Accounts control panel
   b. Network Diagnostics
   c. Ipconfig.exe
   d. Tracert.exe

4. Which of the following Windows 7 tools does not aid in the hardware troubleshooting process?
   a. Device Manager
   b. Upgrade Advisor
   c. Nslookup.exe
   d. Performance Monitor

5. Which of the following operating systems cannot use BranchCache? (Choose all that are correct.)
   a. Windows Vista
   b. Windows Server 2008
   c. Windows Server 2008 R2
   d. Windows 7

6. When you load Windows RE from the Windows 7 installation DVD, the system provides you with a choice of recovery tools; which of the following is not included?
   a. System Restore
   b. System Image Recovery
   c. Windows Easy Transfer
   d. Command Prompt

7. Place the following steps of the Windows 7 startup process in their proper order:
   a. Windows Boot Manager phase
   b. Windows Boot Loader phase
   c. Power-on self-test (POST) phase
   d. Initial startup phase

8. Which Windows XP Startup component is no longer needed in Windows 7?
   a. Recovery Console
   b. Ntdetect.com
   c. Boot.ini
   d. NTLDR

9. BranchCache is a client/server application that supports which of the following two operational modes?
   a. Content Server cache mode
   b. Workstation cache mode
   c. Distributed cache mode
   d. Hosted cache mode

10. For stand-alone systems or small networks, Windows 7 includes backup tools that you can use to protect your data. Which of the following devices do the Windows 7 backup tools not permit for backup storage?
    a. An online backup service
    b. Another hard disk drive
    c. A USB flash drive
    d. A series of writable CDs or DVDs

Review Questions

1. Give three reasons why the Remote Assistance tool is safe to use, despite the fact that it can provide a remote user with control over a computer.

2. Place the following phases of the Windows 7 startup sequence in the correct order:

   Logon phase

   Windows Boot Loader phase

   Initial startup phase

   Power-on self-test (POST) phase

   Windows Boot Manager phase

   Kernel loading phase

Case Scenarios

Scenario 11-1: Assigning Troubleshooting Priorities

During a busy shift at the help desk at Litware, Inc., a call comes in at 9:05 a.m. from an angry user whose mouse is not working. At 9:07 a.m., the vice president of the Marketing department calls to report that the hard drive in the file server where the company's ad campaigns are stored has failed. At 9:15 a.m., the manager of the Order Entry department calls to report that the email server that delivers the product orders generated through the company's Web site is down. Between 9:25 and 9:45 a.m., four users on the LAN in the Sales department call to report that they cannot access the company intranet server containing the health insurance forms they need. As the help desk manager, which of these four problems should you address first? Explain your answer, and why you did not choose the other three.

Scenario 11-2: Isolating the Problem

You are a freelance computer consultant providing desktop support to a client, Ralph, with a small business network that you designed and installed. The network consists of five Windows 7 computers connected to a single switch, which is in turn connected to a DSL router, providing Internet access to all of the computers. Ralph calls to report that Internet Explorer is unable to connect to any site on the Internet.

Following are three tasks that you will ask Ralph to perform. Explain how each of the tasks can help you to isolate the component that is causing the problem:

1. Ask Ralph to open a Command Prompt window and try to ping a server on the Internet.
2. Ask Ralph to try to connect to a share on another one of the network's computers.
3. Ask Ralph to log on to one of the other computers on the network and try to access the Internet using Internet Explorer.

Windows 7 Configuration: Exam 70-680

OBJECTIVE DOMAIN	SKILL NUMBER	LESSON NUMBER
Installing, Upgrading, and Migrating to Windows 7		
Perform a clean installation.	1.1	1, 2
Upgrade to Windows 7 from previous versions of Windows.	1.2	1, 2
Migrate user profiles.	1.3	2
Deploying Windows 7		
Capture a system image.	2.1	3
Prepare a system image for deployment.	2.2	3
Deploy a system image.	2.3	3
Configure a VHD.	2.4	4
Configuring Hardware and Applications		
Configure devices.	3.1	4
Configure application compatibility.	3.2	7
Configure application restrictions.	3.3	7
Configure Internet Explorer.	3.4	7
Configuring Network Connectivity		
Configure IPv4 network settings.	4.1	5
Configure IPv6 network settings.	4.2	5
Configure networking settings.	4.3	5, 12
Configure Windows Firewall.	4.4	10
Configure remote management.	4.5	11
Configuring Access to Resources		
Configure shared resources.	5.1	6
Configure file and folder access.	5.2	6, 10
Configure user account control (UAC).	5.3	9

(*continued*)

OBJECTIVE DOMAIN	SKILL NUMBER	LESSON NUMBER
Configure authentication and authorization.	5.4	10
Configure BranchCache.	5.5	11
Configuring Mobile Computing		
Configure BitLocker and BitLocker To Go.	6.1	12
Configure DirectAccess.	6.2	12
Configure mobility options.	6.3	12
Configure remote connections.	6.4	12
Monitoring and Maintaining Systems that Run Windows 7		
Configure updates to Windows 7.	7.1	8
Manage disks.	7.2	4
Monitor systems.	7.3	8
Configure performance settings.	7.4	8
Configuring Backup and Recovery		
Configure backup.	8.1	11
Configure system recovery options.	8.2	11
Configure file recovery options.	8.3	11

Windows 7 Configuration, Exam 70-680: Lab to Textbook Mapping

LAB	TEXTBOOK LESSON	EXAM OBJECTIVE COVERED
1. Upgrading to Windows 7	2	1.2
2. Migrating User Profiles	2	1.3
3. Installing Windows 7	1 & 2	1.1
4. Capturing a Reference Image	3	2.1, 2.2
5. Deploying a Captured Image	3	2.3
6. Working with Disks	4	2.4, 7.2
7. Configuring Network Connections	5	4.1, 4.2, 4.3
8. Working with Shares	6	5.1, 5.2
9. Working with Printers	6	3.1, 5.1
10. Configuring Applications	7	3.2, 3.3, 3.4
11. Managing and Monitoring Performance	8	7.1, 7.3, 7.4
12. Working with Workgroups and Domains	9	5.3
13. Configuring Security Settings	10	4.4, 5.4
14. Remote Windows 7 Administration	11	4.5
15. Administering Windows 7	11	5.5, 8.1, 8.2, 8.3
16. Configuring Mobile Options	12	6.1, 6.3
17. Configuring Mobile Connectivity	12	4.3, 6.2
18. Troubleshooting Windows 7	11	N/A

Index